SEAL TARGET GERONIMO

ALSO BY CHUCK PFARRER

Warrior Soul: The Memoir of a Navy SEAL

Killing Che: A Novel

SEAL TARGET GERONIMO

THE INSIDE STORY OF THE MISSION TO KILL OSAMA BIN LADEN

CHUCK PFARRER

ST. MARTIN'S GRIFFIN
NEW YORK

Printed in the United States of America. For information, address St. Martin's Press, 175 Fifth Avenue, New York, N.Y. 10010.

www.stmartins.com

Library of Congress Cataloging-in-Publication Data Available Upon Request

ISBN 978-1-250-01471-9 (trade paperback)
ISBN 978-1-4299-6025-0 (e-book)

10 9 8 7 6 5 4 3 2

FOR THE RED MEN.

NOW THE WORLD KNOWS WHO YOU ARE.

CONTENTS

THE SEAL ROAD TO ABBOTTABAD

BIN LADEN'S ROAD TO ABBOTTABAD

NEPTUNE'S SPEAR

By knowing things that exist
you can know what does not exist.

MIYAMOTO MUSASHI
The Book of Five Rings

PREFACE TO THE PAPERBACK EDITION: AN INCONVENIENT BIT OF HISTORY

Operation Neptune's Spear, planned by SEAL admiral Bill McRaven, was one of America's most brilliant special operations successes. Thirty-eight minutes on target, zero American casualties, and the terrorist mastermind of 9/11 sent to meet his maker. One for the history books . . . well, not quite.

In the year that had passed since the mission, history, it seems, has been up for grabs. In the days and weeks after the raid, the U.S. government floundered through a series of stories, corrections, and walk backs regarding the operation. In the absence of definitive facts from the government, the story began to morph into an ugly tale of murder.

Five months after the raid, in August 2011, the *New Yorker* magazine published a version of the raid that depicted the SEALs as hit men who blasted their way into the compound, firing indiscriminately, until they got to the third floor—where they shot one of Bin Laden's wives, and then murdered Osama bin Laden in cold blood. It is little wonder that the words "Kill Mission" tripped off the tongues of media pundits.

In order to write history, one needs access to the facts and the accounts of eyewitnesses, or, at the very least, access to people who know what actually happened. *SEAL Target Geronimo* goes to original sources, and I have no doubt that the operators and intelligence professionals who conducted this mission told me the truth.

But before I tell you what happened, let me tell you what did not. There was not a "45-minute firefight," or even a twenty-minute one. There weren't enough bullet holes or broken glass to support this story—and neither the SEAL Team nor civilian casualties supported a tale of urban combat. Zero SEALs were killed or wounded, and only five civilians died, one slightly wounded. My research showed that only twelve bullets were fired during the entire mission.

The downed helicopter story was also suspect. Eyewitnesses told me that the helicopter did not crash on insertion, but only after it had successfully landed assaulters on Bin Laden's roof. This version was also supported by Pakistani eyewitnesses interviewed by an independent investigator. The "crashed on insertion" story never made tactical sense. If the lead helicopter went down approaching the target, why would its backup then divert *outside* the compound and deposit its load of shooters on the wrong side of a twenty-foot concrete wall? In addition, a close-up inspection of the walls of the compound revealed no main rotor strike damage, and the tail rotor left behind was largely intact and its blades undamaged, suggesting that it was not turning when it was thrown outside the walls.

Overhead video imagery confirms that assaulters were delivered successfully to the roof of the main building, and that the crash of the insertion helicopter came twelve to eighteen minutes into the raid—not at the outset. This live video feed was beamed into the White House. As the president and his entourage watched in horror, the helicopter was seen to lift off from the roof, turn tail, and settle into the livestock pen next to the main residence. The cause of the crash is unknown, but may have to do with the catastrophic failure of two flight control systems. The stealth helicopter, now unflyable, was abandoned and blown up in place. Despite this accident, Admiral McRaven's SEALs completed their mission and returned to base without loss or injury. Bin Laden's corpse was flown to the carrier USS *Carl Vinson,* where he was buried at sea.

The administration's pushback started even before *SEAL Target Geronimo* hit its publication date. For the first time in history, the U.S. Special Operations Command (USSOCOM) singled out a military history book for criticism—calling *SEAL Target Geronimo* "a fabrication," and branding me, its author, "a liar." Those are serious accusations to a third-generation naval officer, and I take exception to them. But lost in the government denunciation was a statement that may provide an explanation of why the book was such an annoyance, at least to politicians. An AP article quoted a SOCCOM spokesman as saying that Admiral Bill McRaven ". . . was concerned that the book would lead Americans to doubt the administration's version of the story."

You may count me as a doubter, and an early one.

When politics is mixed with military history, the result is not often pretty. One need only recall the press stories involving Specialist Jessica

Lynch, Ranger Pat Tillman, or "Mission Accomplished" to know what happens when politicians put their spin on battlefield facts.

Indeed, the administration's handling of the narrative could not have been worse: a premature, politically driven announcement, followed by a contradictory story, crowned by a highly negative magazine account and a television dramatization that depicted the raid as a cold-blooded hit. What might have been an important success for the United States in the "information space" was turned into an unmitigated disaster. Reaction to the *New Yorker* article was immediate—flags started burning all over the Middle East, and U.S. Special Operations Forces were seen as a gang of murderers and thugs.

But worse, much worse, by almost immediately confirming that the United States had conducted the operation, President Obama rendered worthless hundreds of items of actionable intelligence—enough to put Al Qaeda out of business forever. As news of the raid spread around the world, Al Qaeda operatives, including Ayman Zawahiri, bolted for cover. The intelligence gathered by the SEALs was squandered in an instant—bartered for a bump in the polls.

When the administration and the military failed to disavow the troubling *New Yorker* article, I was appalled. The brave SEALs who pulled off this mission deserved better, and history deserved the truth. I wrote *SEAL Target Geronimo* to correct the record, and I stand by every word. I've found that the most strident attacks against the book (and me) have been made either anonymously, or by people who did not witness the raid. The mission was filmed, in its entirety, by an RQ-170 Sentinel drone. The people who watched the mission live included: President Barack Obama, VP Joe Biden, Secretary of State Hillary Clinton, Leon Panetta, Brigadier General Brad Webb, Deputy National Security Advisor Denis McDonough, Secretary of Defense Robert Gates, Admiral Mike Mullen, chairman of the Joint Chiefs of Staff; Tom Donilon, national security advisor; White House Chief of Staff William M. Daley; Tony Blinken, national security advisor to the vice president; Audrey Tomason, director for counterterrorism for the National Security Council; John O. Brennan, deputy national security advisor for homeland security and counterterrorism; and James R. Clapper, the director of national intelligence. These people saw the mission, and I believe they saw it happen as I described it in the book.

Not one of these eyewitnesses has come forward to refute or even question what I have written.

I am certain that one, several, or perhaps all of these people will eventually write their memoirs, and it will be interesting to see what they say not only about the raid that killed Osama bin Laden, but why they felt it wasn't necessary to come to the defense of an honest man who wrote the facts.

I have learned long ago never to be disappointed by people—especially politicians.

The Navy SEALs who struck Bin Laden's compound did so with the stealth and precision that has been the hallmark of Naval Special Warfare for more than fifty years. The facts of this operation are a vital part of our nation's history. The events at Abbottabad exemplify the professionalism and fighting spirit of the United States Navy. I have been honored to tell their story.

NEPTUNE'S SPEAR

THE BIGGER PICTURE

The operation that killed Osama bin Laden was a joint, multiservice effort, carried out by the Joint Special Operations Command, SEAL Team Six, and the Central Intelligence Agency. Code-named Neptune's Spear, it was the quintessential information-age mission, conceived by a Navy admiral who wrote the book on special operations and watched on an Internet link by a president with a Twitter account.

The men who entered Osama bin Laden's compound and brought him to justice were members of the smallest and most elite special operations force in the United States military, the Navy SEALs. The exact number of SEALs deployed worldwide is a closely held secret. It can be told, however, that since World War II, fewer than ten thousand men have earned the right to wear the trident: an eagle, anchor, and flintlock badge that marks a sailor as a fully qualified Navy SEAL.

It takes more than two years of intense, nonstop training to earn the basic SEAL qualification of 5326, combat swimmer. From that point on, a rookie SEAL enters one of the most rigorous meritocracies conceived by man. A SEAL is judged not only by the missions he has undertaken but also by his courage, skill, physical ability, and character. Within this small fraternity a man's reputation is earned solely by his standing as an operator. To rise in the ranks, every SEAL, both officer and enlisted, must demonstrate that he can lead physically in combat, and intellectually in the planning cycle. There is no shortcut to command.

This is the history of the operation that killed Osama bin Laden. It is also the story of the SEAL operators themselves, the daunting challenges they faced, and the ever-evolving and dangerous menace posed by Osama bin Laden and his hell-spawned creation, Al Qaeda.

Osama bin Laden declared war on the United States of America, and for fifteen years terrorists working in his pay killed as many people as they possibly could. Surprisingly, for an organization that declared itself to be at war with "Crusaders and Jews," most of Osama bin Laden's victims were Muslims.

In writing this book, certain accommodations have been made to protect operational security and the identity of SEAL Team operators. This is necessary to protect both them and their families. Obscured also are some of the locations of bases and mission elements.

When the government revealed Operation Neptune's Spear, some of the men involved became public figures. I have used their correct names. The names of operational SEALs, past and present, have been changed, as have the names of the intelligence professionals who supported them. I have tried to draw the personalities involved in this mission as accurately as possible. Some of my portraits are frank. In addition, it has been necessary to omit some details of the operation at Bin Laden's compound—so as not to contribute to the tactical understanding of our enemies. The SEALs I have left in shadow, and those serving elsewhere, have the respect and thanks of a grateful nation. I am proud to count myself as a brother.

Every mission the SEALs undertake adds to the "corporate knowledge" of the team. Neptune's Spear was certainly no exception. In order to comprehend the events at Abbottabad, one has to understand the men who conducted the mission. That includes an appreciation for what it takes to become a SEAL—a grueling two-and-half-year process—and the further, decades-long journey a SEAL operator must make before he can be selected for duty at SEAL Team Six: So difficult is the training process, and so skilled are the operators, that the men of SEAL Team Six are called Jedis. This nickname is hardly an exaggeration.

Several key missions were undertaken by SEAL Team Six before the Bin Laden operation; these included an operation to free the captain of the *Maersk Alabama,* Richard Phillips, who had been captured by Somali pirates. Another mission was the pursuit and interdiction of Musab al-Zarqawi, Osama bin Laden's handpicked operational commander in Iraq. Both of these operations contributed to the tactical acumen the SEALs brought to Osama's compound. They are recounted here so the reader may judge the men and the organization that accomplished a nearly impossible operation.

This book will also briefly examine the historical currents and intellectual climate that shaped the character of a man who decided to overthrow the world. The reader will forgive a brief diversion into both the history of Islam and the politics of the Middle East.

These subjects were studied intently by the SEAL operators who descended on Bin Laden's compound. For almost ten years, they read his pronouncements and fatwas, researched his operations and plans, listened in on his phone conversations, and traced the flow of his money. They knew their enemy well.

And on the night of May 1, 2011, they came calling.

ABBOTTABAD: MAY 1, 2011—
LATE THAT NIGHT

ON THE NIGHT THAT OSAMA BIN LADEN was killed, Sohaib Athar could not sleep. The thirty-three-year-old IT consultant had moved his young family to Abbottabad almost six months earlier. He'd come to this quiet city after his wife and son were hit by a car on the teeming streets of Lahore. A physics grad of Forman Christian University, Sohaib also held a master of science from the University of the Punjab. He liked to say that in his previous life he was a "start-up specialist"—he'd come to Abbottabad to open a coffee shop and Internet café. Business was good. His Web site said proudly that his was the first coffee shop in Abbottabad to brew fresh espresso. Sohaib Athar was a quiet man and he wanted a quiet life.

That night, the windows were open in his apartment on the Jadoon Plaza. The heat of the day was slow in breaking, and by midnight, scented wind blew down from the Shimala Hills above the city. Spring was coming to the foothills of the Hindu Kush, and as the days had grown hotter, people were shifting their activity to the evening, when it was cooler. Past midnight, a handful of shops were still open, and now and again a truck would rumble past the dusty strip mall sprawling on either side of Sohaib's balcony. The city of Abbottabad was falling asleep.

Just before one in the morning on May 2, Sohaib heard a buzzing sound; it grew in volume and faded, came in with the wind and left with it. Finally, he could tell it was the noise of a helicopter—or maybe a couple of them.

Sohaib looked out the window toward the echoing hills. The night was hazy, and above the glare of the streetlights he could see nothing. The sound came again and then it was gone, like someone had thrown a switch.

He crossed from the balcony to his laptop and logged on to his Twitter account: "Helicopter hovering above Abbottabad at 1AM (is a rare event)."

Sohaib could have no idea of what was unfolding three miles to the east of his balcony. It was 12:58 a.m., and at a place called Yaba Yar, a team of

United States Navy SEALs were jumping from helicopters into the high-walled compound of Osama bin Laden.

A top secret Stealth Hawk helicopter had lost power and crashed after inserting an assault element on the roof of the main building. Later, a Pentagon spokesman would claim that there had been a "rough landing" but the men who witnessed it, and the others watching overhead monitors knew better.

It was there, hovering above the main building, and then it fell out of the sky. Enveloped in an opaque cloud of dust, 32,000 pounds of top secret American technology slammed into the ground and beat itself to pieces. It took fifteen agonizing seconds for the engines to flame out and for the rotors to stop. During that eternity, broken pieces of aircraft, communications equipment, and flight components were tossed in all directions. The transmission blew itself apart and one of the forty-two-foot-long Kevlar rotors was launched a hundred yards, landing in a field of beans.

It was a flat miracle that no one was killed.

When the dust cleared, SEALs and pilots in the other aircraft could see men moving in the wreckage. Incredibly, the five-member flight crew had survived.

A little more than a mile away, Sohaib stood on his balcony, listening.

He had not heard the helicopter go down—and he was unlikely to have noticed the sound, for the death throes of a real helicopter are nothing like the crashes in the movies. The doomed helicopter's engines had screamed and the disintegrating rotors had made a sound like a stick being pulled across a picket fence. Sohaib listened; another helicopter, this one an MH-47 Chinook, flew nearby and lumbered off to the east. He heard the Chinook, but did not see it. Like the other helicopters used in the assault, this aircraft flew without lights and was painted the exact color of the dusky night.

Sohaib went to his keyboard and tweeted again: "Go away helicopter—before I take out my giant swatter ;-/".

At four minutes past one in the morning, an enormous boom shook the city—a thunder blast out of a cloudless sky. Far away in the darkness, the SEALs had used plastic explosive charges to blow in the front gate of Bin Laden's compound. People who heard the explosion said it sounded like a car bomb.

Sohaib watched the tweets of his friends scroll across his laptop's screen: @m0chin tweeted: "All silent after the blast, but a friend heard it 6 km away too . . . the helicopter is gone . . ."

Then one from han3yy: "OMG: S Bomb Blasts in Abbottabad. I hope everyone is fine ☺".

Traffic on the street below Sohaib's window had now stopped completely. The entire city of Abbottabad seemed to hold its breath. There were two or three more explosions, smaller, muffled, but Sohaib thought they might be just as deadly. Maybe he had been foolish to think that this was a safe place. He walked back into his living room, sat down at his laptop and tweeted again:

"Funny, moving to Abbottabad was part of the 'being safe' strategy."

Sohaib Attar and Osama bin Laden had both come to Abbottabad for the same reasons . . . to put themselves, and their families, beyond danger.

Both of them thought that Abbottabad was a safe place.

One of them had been wrong.

THE SEAL ROAD TO ABBOTTABAD

MEN WITH GREEN FACES

JUNE 2006: JOHNNY COFFEE AND DREW HOLLAND spent all of the sweltering day crowded into a hole slightly more than three feet wide and two feet deep. Camouflaged from head to toe, covered by fallen date fronds and bits of garbage, they were hiding almost in plain sight. They had inserted the night before by helicopter, patrolled along the fringes of a darkened Baghdad neighborhood, through a graveyard, over its crumbling walls and into a grove of date palms. They were dug in with their weapons facing slightly west, three hundred yards from a group of houses in the northwest corner of Baghdad. To an unpracticed eye, there was no place to hide under the palms. There were no bushes, no scrub, no terrain features that looked large enough to hide even a dog, let alone two men loaded down with weapons and communications equipment. But they were in, they were set up, and they were waiting.

Johnny and Drew were a "shooting pair," a sniper and spotter from Joint Task Force 20, a hunter-killer element of the Joint Special Operations Command, JSOC. Pronounced "jay-sock," it is an umbrella organization that oversees America's premier counterterrorism operators, including SEAL Team Six and the Army's Special Forces Operational Detachment-Delta, (SFOD-D), aka Delta Force. Both men hidden in the date grove were members of the smallest and most elite special operations unit in the world: SEAL Team Six.

Johnny Coffee was the designated shooter; he was thirty-four years old and had been a Navy SEAL and a sniper for more than a decade. This was his second tour in Iraq, and his fifth combat deployment. His spotter and boss on this mission, Drew, was six months older than Johnny, but already a master chief petty officer, and the OIC (officer in charge) of the sniper cell of SEAL Team Six. They were operating using the call sign Stingray Zero Two.

Johnny and Drew had been in many hides together, in many places, and knew to trust both their camouflage and each other. In their line of work, this sort of a hiding place was called a "spider hole"—and for good reason. Early after sunup, Johnny had to endure the attentions of a six-inch-long camel spider as it leisurely made its way up his arm, across his shoulder, and over the back of his neck. Even if they didn't care for the neighbors, it was a good layup. They were well hidden, and if things should go wrong, there was hard cover just behind them: a section of mud brick wall and a stretch of canal where they could make a stand if it came to a gunfight.

Both of the men hidden under the trees were masters of their craft. In their lifetimes, they had been on hundreds of missions and in dozens of hides. This operation was important, perhaps even the most important one they would ever perform, but minute to minute and hour to hour, they could be forgiven for thinking that this op was like every other SLJ they'd ever been sent on. "LJ" stands for "little job," and the "S" can stand for a couple of things.

They waited, and they sweated. The building they were watching was an Al Qaeda safe house. In it, intel told them, was Musab al-Zarqawi, Osama bin Laden's operational commander in Iraq. But intel was sometimes wrong.

In front of them, where the date grove ended, was a dusty playing field and the corner of a sprawling dump. Johnny put his rifle scope on the last house on the end, a two-story place where the dirt road turned off to the north. All day, no one came in or out. Women, children, and old men walked by the house but no one seemed to visit. That was reason enough to keep watching.

Johnny and Drew had chosen their layup well—that had been proven shortly after noon, when a group of children and their mother walked into the grove and gathered some of the fallen fronds to cook their lunch. For ten agonizing minutes, the children trotted back and forth in front of their hiding place, gathering scraps of wood and breaking stems of date palms. Finally, mother and kids wandered back to their village and the SEALs could exhale.

The afternoon passed like a slow, hazy, and not-so-pleasant daydream.

Johnny and Drew had operated together so long that they half joked that they could read each other's minds. When snipers are in a hide, they do not speak to each other, even in whispers. They make themselves understood using hand signals—a simple language sufficient to communicate range, direction, weapon status, and the presence of an enemy. When on an operation, there is no need to communicate abstract ideas or idle chat. All of their attention, and all of their beings, are projected downrange. Such concentration is necessary if one is to take a one-thousand-yard head shot.

At two o'clock a white Toyota truck stopped in front of the house, but drove off after a few seconds. There was no sign of Zarqawi, and Johnny began to wonder, *Maybe there's no HVI at all.* "HVI" is SEALspeak for a "high-value individual." Johnny and Drew were prepared to wait all night, and the next night, if necessary. If there was a shot to take—they would make it.

A little after three o'clock, a dump truck arrived and tipped a stinking bin full of glutinous trash. It landed close enough for Johnny to count the plops it made hitting the ground. First came the stink, and then came the flies. The afternoon seemed to stretch into an infinity of small annoyances and gnawing frustration.

At 1600 hours, 4:00 p.m., Drew texted "no joy" on the burst transmitter. They'd been watching the house now for a little over twelve hours, and had seen no one. They could not ID the man they had been sent after. Drew received a two-word answer from the Joint Operations Center: "Wait. Out."

When it was full dark, Johnny pointed a thermal imaging scope at the house. In reds and blues, he could see a plume of heat coming from the chimney; dinner was being prepared, and now and again someone would move past the gate and the head-high mud wall that enclosed the front yard. Whoever lived in the house slept during the day.

Two nights earlier, the SEALs had captured one of Zarqawi's couriers, a nineteen-year-old Jordanian who had volunteered as a *shaheed*—a martyr. When captured, the would-be martyr had a change of heart. Soon after processing, he asked about the bounty that coalition forces had offered for information concerning Zarqawi's whereabouts.

The defector was told that if he wanted cash he had to provide something valuable. He did. He gave up both his boss's location and a cell phone number. Drew and Johnny were inserted even before the man had finished talking.

Nothing had happened for twelve hours, and now, as usual, everything was happening at once. An hour after dark, a car arrived and two men got out. Another two arrived on foot and went inside. Two more pickup trucks arrived, delivering about a dozen more men into the house. Johnny had seen AK-47s and RPG launchers, and heavy backpacks that might contain explosives—or things that were even more dangerous.

Now there were at least fourteen armed men inside the house . . . maybe more. It occurred to both of the SEALs that they might have been lured into a trap. Johnny and Drew had infiltrated as stealthily as possible; they had a plan to defend themselves, and another plan to break contact, but both knew they were very far from help if things should *really* go south.

Drew sent an update on his burst transmitter: "14 MAM, small arms Location Fisher Cat No Joy on HVI." Fourteen military-aged males, with AKs and RPGs at the target—and still no sign of Musab al-Zarqawi.

Drew was careful to keep the light from the screen covered as an answer scrolled back from the Joint Operations Center at Task Force 20: "Ears on."

Drew tapped his partner on the shoulder. He placed two fingers of his right hand under his eyes, the SEAL hand signal meaning "enemy in sight." Drew touched his headphone and Johnny nodded—they had their man on the cell phone, and he was talking.

At 10:10 p.m., Musab al-Zarqawi finally made a call, and Task Force 20 was listening. Zarqawi's words were beamed around the world, compared to previously intercepted communications, and his voiceprint was analyzed. Technicians in Langley, Virginia, confirmed the identification, and a second text message was flashed by satellite.

"Stingray Zero Two is cleared hot."

For the past eighteen months, Zarqawi had recruited truck bombers, killed journalists and politicians, and staged videotaped beheadings—all to force the nation of Iraq to adopt a government based on Islamic law. Now he was presiding over a meeting of armed men. No one had any idea what Zarqawi had planned for the night—a kidnapping, a bombing, or maybe both.

Zarqawi was in the building, and the SEALs had authorization to engage the target. The fact remained that Johnny and Drew were outnumbered, but being invisible had its advantages. The two SEALs had the element of surprise, and they had technology. Drew's thumb depressed a switch on a rectangular box fixed to the receiver of his rifle. From an AN/PEQ-2 laser illuminator, an invisible, infrared beam streamed toward the second floor of the building.

Johnny typed out another text: "Laser hot."

The answer scrolled back: "Reaper Copies."

Abu Musab al-Zarqawi had less than ninety seconds to live.

Six miles above the date grove, unseen and unheard, a Predator drone, call sign Reaper Three Zero, banked at the edge of the stratosphere. Its sensors rolled over the city below. Streetlights, car headlights, the lights of houses spread in a rolling blanket, like a mosaic of stars. The lights marked progress and peace, businesses and places where families lived. In the dark places there was poverty, frustration, and anger. The dark places were where men like Zarqawi preached hatred and planned murder.

One hundred miles away from Baghdad, in an air-conditioned van parked off the runway at a secret air base, a pair of CIA pilots sat in front of a wall filled with computer monitors. Some of their screens showed maps, others flight paths, some showed the status of communication links and satellites, and some of them were digital representations of flight instruments that controlled a forty-six-foot-long, turbo-powered messenger of death.

The pilot pulled back a small joystick and placed a Predator drone into a lazy figure-eight turn, while the copilot armed up a pair of AGM 114 Hellfire missiles. Cameras zoomed: the pilots could see the Euphrates River snaking through the center of Baghdad; the north part of the city; Sadr City, gloomy and sprawling; and the sharp edge of the Army Canal. The cameras that panned in the feed went to infrared. The lens drifted over Bilal al Habashi Street, where the fields started to open up. Then the dump, the playing field, and the date palms, all rendered in shades of green.

Tucked into the edge of the date grove was Stingray Zero Two. Drew and Johnny showed up as hot, oblong blips, betrayed by body temperature.

As the pilots watched, Drew's laser beam glittered and pointed across the open spaces, illuminating the second floor of the mud-walled house where the road turned into the fields. In the Predator's control van, the pilot pressed a button. A pair of missiles dropped from the drone's outboard pylons and silently fell away into the dark sky. Their rocket engines ignited, and the missiles started to spiral toward their target.

The Hellfires quickly went transonic, then supersonic, traveling faster than the roar made by their rocket engines. The warheads homed unerringly on the laser beam. In the date grove, Drew and Johnny waited for the sound of the rocket motors' ignition, a sort of muffled thud from the clouds above. They heard it, ten seconds after it happened, a sound like someone beating dust from a rug, *whump*, *whump*.

It meant the missiles were on their way.

Even if Musab al-Zarqawi looked up and saw them coming, there was no place he could run. Johnny made sure that the laser was locked on the building. If Zarqawi jumped into a car, Johnny would put the laser on him.

It was over.

Zarqawi didn't show his face, but it didn't matter. The missiles found him.

Moving too fast to see, the first Hellfire ripped through the roof of the house and detonated in a splash of orange-white light. The initial explosion seemed to widen the walls and lift the roof. The second missile struck the courtyard just in front of the building, cratering it and destroying the three vehicles parked on the road. But then another blast tore through the building. It was what the SEALs called a secondary; the missiles had set off a cache of explosives—bomb-making materials Zarqawi had planned to use in his campaign of terror. This last explosion obliterated the structure, turning it upside down and inside out.

The explosions echoed back from the riverbanks, and as they faded away, there came the sound of whizzing bits of concrete, the fluttering descent of shattered doors and roof tiles, the thuds made by bits of furniture, the clank of car parts, pots and pans, ammo crates and bits of glass. Also falling to earth were pieces of men.

Drew remembered that after the blast, the night seemed impossibly still and quiet. For five minutes, not even the crickets sang.

The two SEALs collected their equipment, checked their weapons and slipped back into the dump, over the crumbling wall toward their extract point. The mission was over, and now all they had to do was get out.

Musab al-Zarqawi, Osama bin Laden's handpicked deputy in Iraq, had killed thousands of people in an attempt to send the world back to the sixth century. In a fitting bit of irony, two operators from SEAL Team Six had killed him with an invisible laser beam and a flying robot.

The United States military has a long on-again and off-again love affair with special operations forces. Throughout its history, the United States has created special purpose units, battalions of sharpshooters, rangers and pathfinders, parachutists, and various sorts of frogmen and commandos, only to disband the units after their wars had been won.

As the Cold War wound through the fifties and sixties, the Pentagon faced a series of low-intensity conflicts with Soviet proxies, but still had to worry about fighting "the Big One," a global war with the Warsaw Pact. While it was correctly seen that brush wars did not require the deployment of Normandy-style invasions, the Pentagon was not allowed the luxury of creating purpose-built special operations forces to fight boutique wars. The threat posed by the Soviet Union meant that the U.S. had to keep a large, standing force in being.

The Green Berets and the SEALs were both created by President John F. Kennedy in 1962. The U.S. Army's special forces were originally envisioned as trainers. In the event that the Soviet Union invaded Western Europe, the Green Berets were to be left behind to organize resistance movements within the occupied countries. Each Green Beret A-Team was designed to form a nucleus about which guerrilla forces could grow. Of course, in order to teach the black arts, it is first necessary to master them, and the Green Berets were superbly trained. Each member of a Green Beret A-Team had both language training and an operational specialty. Some were communicators, some demolition experts; some were air operations specialists and some were scuba trained. All Green Berets were parachute qualified and schooled in intelligence collection, covert communication, tradecraft, and operational planning.

The Navy created its special warfare program from the famed Underwater Demolition Teams who served in World War II and Korea. This new force would be called the SEAL Teams— "SEAL" being short for the elements in which they would be trained to operate—sea, air, and land.

The operational element of the Green Berets is an A-Team, a unit roughly analogous to a SEAL platoon, that is, two officers and twelve enlisted men. A-Teams tend to specialize: one might be trained demolitionists, another arctic warfare specialists, and still another equipped to carry out high-altitude parachute operations. The Army set out to create the skeleton around which it could grow partisan armies to harass the flanks and rear of the Soviet juggernaut.

The SEAL Teams were created with another mission in mind—direct action against the enemy. SEALs retain the ability to serve as special operations trainers, and have the capability to organize indigenous forces, but their primary mission, their raison d'être, is hurting the enemy. And in that mission, they are the best in the world.

It is one thing to announce the formation of a handpicked unit. It is quite another thing to bring one into existence. When President Kennedy authorized the formation of the Green Berets and the SEAL Teams, the Pentagon had to answer two questions: Whom do you pick? And how do you train them?

The Army split the difference between quantity and quality. The Navy set out from the beginning to make Cadillacs. The SEAL Teams started with slightly over fifty men on two coasts. SEAL Teams One and Two were so top secret that volunteers from the Underwater Demolition Teams were initially not told the name of the unit or its mission. They had to volunteer blind.

The men chosen for the first SEAL Teams underwent a whirlwind of training. It was decided from the beginning that every SEAL operator would be trained in every skill. There would be no specialist subunits. Every SEAL was to be proficient in all aspects of special ops. Each trained to jump, dive, do underwater demolition, navigate small boats, and operate in all environments— jungle, swamp, and glacier. From the outset, SEALs took on missions that were beyond the Army's capability—maritime sabotage and submarine-based reconnaissance. Because their training is so much more expensive, the SEALs have always been a considerably smaller outfit. By 1964, there were thousands of Green Berets. In 1965, the Navy had fewer than one hundred SEALs.

In Vietnam, SEALs appeared where no enemy thought possible and struck with a ferocity far out of proportion to their number. The Vietcong called them "the men with green faces," and put bounties on their heads.

Basic Underwater Demolition SEAL (BUD/S) training takes place on the Naval Amphibious Base in Coronado, California. A mile or so down from the picturesque Hotel del Coronado, and nestled among the whispering dunes of California's Silver Strand State Park, it's ironic that one of the most beautiful places in the state of California is the epicenter of so much misery. BUD/S is considered to be the toughest school in the United States military. The course of training is so difficult that there have been classes where no one graduated—everyone quit. It is especially daunting for SEAL students when they remember that BUD/S is not the end of their selection and training as Naval special warfare operators—it is only the beginning.

Of a thousand volunteers who want to become SEALs, only about two hundred will actually be placed into a class. Before the first day of training, a would-be frogman is subjected to medical, psychological, and academic testing. Immediately disqualified are applicants with police or juvenile records, domestic violence convictions, substance abuse problems, bankruptcies or excessive debt—even being a *suspect* of a crime is enough to disqualify a candidate. Students selected for a BUD/S class must have perfect hearing and meet stringent vision requirements. They must pass the Navy's comprehensive aviation and diving physicals. Trainees are poked, prodded, X-rayed, CAT scanned, interviewed by shrinks, and then examined again. All of this is done, not to keep people out of SEAL training, but to make sure that the students admitted to the program are highly qualified and therefore most likely to succeed.

The Navy has spent millions of dollars on testing and psychological profiles to identify what type of man is most likely to hold up under the stress. But the truth is, they don't know. Olympic athletes, NFL players, survivalists, and fitness gurus have all numbered among the dropouts. And among the graduates the Navy can count surfer dudes, carpenters, computer geeks, and farm boys from Iowa who'd never before seen the ocean. No one can tell if a man has what it takes to become a Navy SEAL. There is no way to quantify desire.

To be selected for SEAL training, one must already be in the Navy. A small handful of students might come directly from Navy boot camp, but most are petty officers and officers who have undergone at least a year or so of training. All, of course, are volunteers.

The youngest sailor in a BUD/S class might be seventeen and a half, a rare occurrence, as this would assume that his mother signed a document allowing him to join the service. The oldest student in a SEAL class would be age thirty-three, positively ancient. Such a candidate would likely be a chief petty officer or a Navy lieutenant with as much as eight or ten years of sea time. Older students are expected to emerge as class leaders—if not physically, then morally. This double burden makes it even harder for an old dog to be taught new tricks. It is possible to receive a waiver to attempt training after age thirty-four, but that sort of paper is about as worthless as Confederate money.

BUD/S is a six-month-long ordeal that is blithely described by the Navy as being "physically and mentally demanding." That might be one of the understatements of all time. After being classed up, students begin a two-week regime of "pretraining." During long days and nights, trainees learn the ropes. If they somehow graduated boot camp without a grasp of marching and polishing shoes and brass, they are reintroduced to the practices. Their beachfront rooms are inspected, found to be filled with sand, torn apart, and inspected again. They are introduced to a program of extreme calisthenics called "BUD/S PT." This muscle-racking set of exercises was designed by kinesiologists to stress and flex literally every muscle in the human body. For the next six months the students will perform this ninety-minute set of exercises daily.

They will run, they will run, and they will run. The students are led on an ever-lengthening series of "conditioning hikes." At least that's what it says on the schedule. Prodded together into platoon-sized groups, the classes are led on beach runs by SEAL instructors who never seem to break a sweat. As weaker runners fall back into the pack, the fastest assume the first ranks behind the instructor. To fall back into the pack is to stumble among the pounding feet of thirty other men who are breathing the dust of fifty more in front of them.

Nor is the SEAL at the front of the pack the only one the students have to worry about. During pretraining no run leaves the compound without a half-dozen instructors following close behind. Like wolves picking off migrating Bambis, the instructors dart in and out of those trailing behind. Slower students are encouraged to run harder by being given push-ups, sit-ups, and jumping jacks to do while their classmates trudge ever farther toward the horizon. Soon, the instructors have achieved their aim—to cut off the slowest 20 percent of the class.

These men are harried and circled into a separate group called the Goon Squad. The Goon Squad gets its name because the slowest people on any run tend also to be the largest. Members of the Goon Squad are frequently over six feet tall. A significant percentage of students who were football players or bodybuilders wind up as denizens of the Goon Squad.

There, they find themselves in the tender care of instructors who earnestly entreat them to run faster. And to do it quickly. The instructor's orders are hard to comply with, because members of the Goon Squad are frequently given numerous opportunities to rest—in push-up position, with generous helpings of California surf smashing down over their backs. For good measure, members of the Goon Squad can always enjoy a sugar cookie—which means rolling on the beach until every square inch of their skin and every orifice of their body is filled with sand. Thus fortified, they can return to their run.

Every day, the slowest students are badgered in this manner. Instructors continually tell the class that "it pays to be a winner," and "the only easy day was yesterday." No matter how bad training gets, a student can always tell himself, "At least I'm not on the Goon Squad." Almost every trainee will wind up being gooned at least once. It's an experience no one wants to repeat. But for some students, the Goon Squad is an everyday occurrence.

After a couple of weeks, a certain mystique begins to form around the survivors. The other students watch as the Goon Squad guys get hammered, morning, noon, and night. Often these are some of the most determined men in the class. The men of the Goon Squad have what it takes to become a SEAL in every respect—except for being able to run like a gazelle, swim like a dolphin, or negotiate the obstacle course like a chimpanzee. Some Goon Squadders will go on to become the SEAL Teams' strongest and best operators. But mostly, cut off from the pack, alone and overwhelmed, they will just quit.

"You have to really want it back there," said one Goon Squad veteran. "The instructors make you pay for it every day."

Finishing "up front" on a beach run means a couple of cold sips of water from the fountain, or maybe a few minutes where the instructors aren't on your back. As the members of the Goon Squad stagger back into the compound, it doesn't take long for the students to realize that it pays to be a winner. This mantra will be beaten into them over the next months. Another SEAL maxim is that "winners never quit, and quitters never win."

Slowly, the trainees make the transition to "Team Time"—meaning eighteen-hour days and often workdays of twenty hours or more. Sleep is a precious commodity to be had only after one's room is clean, one's floor is brushed and buffed, and one's uniform and equipment are made shipshape. Teamwork is taught by the simple technique of making roommates share the fate of individual failures. If one man's locker is not put in order, all the adjoining lockers get turned upside down. If one man's uniform is unsatisfactory, his roommates will join him in hitting the surf, which means sprinting over the sand dunes behind the barracks, enjoying a bracing dip in the Pacific, and returning back to the inspection line where another instructor is even more likely to find fault with a dripping, sand-clotted uniform. No one gets through BUD/S alone. The SEAL Teams are not looking for loners. The instructors watch carefully to see that each man is pulling his own weight and functioning as a member of the team.

In the movies, drill instructors are portrayed as people with bulging eyeballs and anger-management problems. It is not necessary for a SEAL instructor to yell. If he has to give the command a second time, there will quickly be hell to pay.

The first phase of BUD/S focuses primarily on physical conditioning. It's often said that BUD/S will break you and then rebuild you. It is an excruciating process. Each day begins at 5:00 a.m. with ninety minutes of calisthenics. These exercises are performed together, in unison, as a class. Each repetition is counted out loud by the instructor and echoed by the class. Students failing to show the appropriate level of enthusiasm or class spirit will find themselves invited to hit the surf, roll in the sand, and continue exercising in a wet uniform.

After morning PT, the class forms up and runs a mile to the base chow hall. BUD/S students do not walk, they *run* everywhere they go. Students are given only an hour to put on a presentable uniform, cover the distance to the chow hall, wolf their food, run the mile back to the training area, gear up and report, as a class, precisely on time for the next scheduled event. The streets of the Naval Amphibious Base are often spattered with food that the students "rented" rather than bought.

Every day they will run timed distances, negotiate the obstacle course, paddle inflatable boats, and swim in timed events called "evolutions." All of the students' runs are conducted in fatigue pants and combat boots. Pounding out the miles in combat boots frequently leads to stress fractures of the legs and ankles. Lengthy swims in the cold Pacific can bring on hypothermia and even pneumonia. It is literally possible for a BUD/S student to go from heat stroke to chilblains in the course of one afternoon. And the medical attention is not particularly fawning. If a student is not dead or exhibiting a compound bone fracture, the docs in sick bay invariably prescribe an aspirin and a nice, long run.

Every time a physical evolution is performed, a student is expected to improve. Once a week the students will run a six-mile course against the clock. They will also complete a two-mile swim, and a trip through the obstacle course. If the student turns in a time that is higher than his previous attempt, he will come in for some extra attention. A first offense is likely to earn a trip to the surf zone, a roll in the sand, and the opportunity to run again. Running six miles on the beach is hard enough; it's a lot tougher in wet trousers that are filled with sand. And the Goon Squad waits for those who are unable to "get with the program" and turn in faster times.

During the first phase of training, students take academic classes, including communication, first aid, lifesaving, and the history of Naval Special Warfare. Students who fall asleep in class are splashed awake with waste baskets full of seawater. Class members quickly learn that class time should not be confused with nap time—the coursework only gets more involved in the second and third phases, and many would-be SEALs have found themselves dismissed for poor academic performance.

Since staying in BUD/S is so hard, the instructors make quitting very, very easy. A student can quit, any time he wants, twenty-four hours a day, seven days a week. In the courtyard outside the instructors' office is a bell. To quit, all a student has to do is ring it three times. He doesn't need a reason, and he won't be asked to fill out a form. No one will try to talk him out of it. No prejudicial remarks will be placed in his record; he can leave Coronado Island that afternoon, and may resume his previous Naval occupation. Students who drop from the program place their helmets in an ever-lengthening line under the bell. The helmets are the way the instructors count coup.

Every morning, there are two or three more helmets under the bell.

Some mornings there are a dozen. Four weeks into first phase, and six weeks after students come to Coronado, training culminates in a six-day ordeal called "Hell Week." In the era before the Discovery Channel, SEAL students entered this black hole with no idea of what it entailed, or what it would take for them to survive. Now, any American with a television set can watch Hell Week in convenient, one-hour episodes.

Living through Hell Week is another thing entirely.

During first phase, students are lined up by height, tallest to smallest. Based on this criterion they are assigned to boat crews. Groups of men are assigned to an IBS, inflatable boat small. It's inflatable, but at ten feet, it isn't that small. And it weighs almost two hundred pounds, empty.

For the next six weeks students will live, breathe, eat, and sleep with their boat. It will become an object that they love and hate in equal measure. During Hell Week, students will take their IBS with them everywhere, running with it balanced on their heads. They will carry it to the chow hall and back. They will swim towing it. They will drag it through the obstacle course. They will place guards to watch over it when they use the bathroom. Occasionally, they will even use it in the way it was intended and paddle it from Coronado, California, to Tijuana, Mexico, and back. Their IBS will be taken into the biggest surf the instructors can find, and in a legendary evolution called "Rock Portage," the students will heave out into the surf, turn around, and deliberately land their boats on the ten-foot granite boulders of the breakwater in front of the Hotel del Coronado.

During Rock Portage, it's not unusual for students to break arms or legs or simply quit—because it's just too damn scary.

Hell Week begins with a simulated firefight called "Breakout." Machine guns are fired over the students' heads, and they are sprayed with fire hoses as artillery simulators, flash-crashes, and smoke grenades are tossed into their ranks. A series of contradictory orders are shouted by instructors over bullhorns. The object of Breakout is to frighten and disorient—and it works.

Instructors tell the astonished students that the whole week is going to be like this—and that the worst is yet to come. It's not unusual for ten or fifteen students to quit during the first hour.

Those who survive Breakout are assigned new boat crews. Blinking in the light of parachute flares, deafened by machine-gun fire and the explosions of quarter-pound blocks of TNT, class officers and petty officers are told to muster their men and account for the missing. It is as close to real combat as the instructors can make it.

Hell Week has just gotten started.

During this six-day ordeal, students are permitted not more than four hours of sleep. The evolutions go on twenty-four hours a day, and are conducted by three shifts of instructors who are rotated in fresh day and night.

Every evolution students undertake is a race against the other boat crews. Every time someone quits, the remainder of their boat crew has to carry the departed man's load. A boat that loses one man has lost 16 percent of its muscle. Two people quit, and the boat has lost 30 percent of its strength. Hell Week becomes an object lesson in teamwork.

Class officers and petty officers are expected to lead—from the front. Officers who find themselves wanting in leadership have the matter brought to their attention by the instructors. BUD/S is one of the only schools in the United States military where officers and enlisted men are trained together. The course and curriculum is exactly the same for enlisted man and officer alike. At BUD/S, there is an officer assigned to oversee each phase of training, but the principal instruction is given by enlisted men. The case can be made that in the SEALs, enlisted men select the officers who will eventually lead them. In BUD/S, it's not just the weak officers who are culled from training. The imperious, the impulsive, and the reckless will also find it impossible to graduate.

As always, it pays to be a winner. In a series of races, long-distance paddles, and problem-solving exercises, boat crews who finish last are hammered, and made to do the evolution all over again. Those who come in first place might be allowed an extra cup of coffee with their chow, or the chance to doze in their boat for ten minutes while the other crews try to catch up.

During Hell Week, students are fed four times a day—breakfast, lunch, dinner, and a midnight snack called "midrats." Of course, this means they have to get to and from the chow hall—which means that their daily excursion is now eight miles round trip instead of six. And they will carry their two-hundred-pound inflatable boat on their heads everywhere they go.

A constant game of psychological warfare plays out between instructors and students. Often, instructors will offer a cup of hot coffee and a doughnut to the first person to quit. For students who have been awake for five days, and just spent hours bobbing around the Pacific Ocean, the temptation represented by a cup of hot coffee is overwhelming. When a man is faltering, there is always an instructor to remind him that it's perfectly okay to quit for medical reasons. "This stuff is crazy," a smooth-talking instructor will tell a member of the Goon Squad. "There's no reason to put yourself through this. You've got nothing to prove. We'll give you a ride back to the barracks, you can take a hot shower, and we'll get your orders out tomorrow morning. No one will even know."

By the time Hell Week is over, a class will be reduced as much as 90 percent.

Hell Week starts with a bang, and it ends with a whimper. Sometime on Saturday morning, six days after they started, instructors quietly tell the students to secure their boats and return to the barracks. No SEAL will ever forget the moment that his boat crew was told that Hell Week was over. The survivors look like shipwreck victims. Their uniforms are torn and their feet are so blistered and ulcerated that a class can be tracked by the bloody footprints left by its members. By Saturday morning, some men can no longer walk without support. Some have hands and feet that are swollen like balloons, and others are sunburned beyond recognition, the skin on their faces peeling off in sheets.

But all of them have one thing in common—they did not, and would not, quit.

After Hell Week, students are allowed for the first time to wear olive-drab T-shirts under their camouflage utilities. This is the only acknowledgment instructors will give them, but it marks a fundamental change in the relationship between teacher and trainee. From this day forward, the students are treated as if they are worth teaching.

In the second phase of BUD/S, students are taught the science of combat swimming. They are introduced first to basic open circuit scuba and then to the more exotic world of oxygen rebreathers and mixed gas breathing rigs. They are taught to swim long distances underwater, precisely navigating from point to point. Students will dive two to three times a day, and in between dives carry out physical evolutions such as timed runs, obstacle courses, and, of course, more swimming.

The academics get harder as well. Not only will the students learn diving physics and the mechanical and electronic characteristics of their diving rigs, they will also learn how to operate submarine escape trunks and study the physiology of diving casualties, such as gas embolism, nitrogen narcosis, and the bends. They will learn the principles of hyperbaric medicine, and how to operate diving rescue chambers. Students who don't make it academically will be out just as quickly as those who don't cut it on the runs.

The third phase of training is land warfare. It begins with marksmanship training and an introduction to the venerable M-16 assault rifle. Students also learn to assemble and disassemble every weapon in the U.S. arsenal, including pistols, machine guns, submachine guns, assault and sniper rifles, as well as antitank weapons and grenade launchers. Stopwatches will click as blindfolded students disassemble and reassemble these weapons for time. Trainees will also learn to operate the principal weapons used by the enemies of the United States, including the AK-47 and its variants the RPK, AKM, and AK-74.

The last six weeks of third phase are spent on a Navy-owned island off the Pacific coast called San Clemente. There, students will undergo accelerated classes in land navigation, small-unit tactics, communications, combat marksmanship, advanced first aid, and demolitions.

They will learn the art of hydrographic reconnaissance, and how to slip ashore at night to reconnoiter a target, use infrared cameras, and draw maps. Training on the island culminates in a seven-day "war," where students recon a section of the island, locate and blow up underwater obstacles, and conduct demolition raids.

All of those exercises are conducted with live ammunition and real explosives. The margin for error and the tolerance for mistakes is zero. There are SEALs who will tell you that the last six weeks on San Clemente were harder than Hell Week. Maybe they are. The strain is certainly higher on the class officers who have to plan and brief attacks and demolition raids under the watchful eye of their instructors—all of whom are combat veterans who have done these operations for real.

Twenty-six weeks after the beginning of BUD/S, students will find themselves standing once again on the asphalt in the courtyard of the Naval Special Warfare Training Group. The graduation ceremonies at BUD/S are low-key. Unlike the Green Berets' Q Course, where students graduate and are handed the headgear of their dreams, sailors graduating from BUD/S are not yet considered SEALs. Ahead of them is an additional year and a half of advanced training, to include military freefall parachuting and advanced courses in everything from counterterrorism operations to the rudiments of chemical, biological, and nuclear weapons.

It's been said that SEAL training is not so much a battle of wills, but a struggle against oneself. No amount of physical conditioning is enough to prepare a student to meet the challenge. Students are made to come to grips with misery. The test is always against oneself.

But as difficult as it is to get through BUD/S, life is tougher in the operational SEAL Teams. What happens on Coronado is practice. SEAL operations in the real world are combat. BUD/S has to be difficult. It is imperative that the men who come into the Teams are individuals who can be counted on, men who think, and adapt, and never quit.

SEALs operate at the pinnacle of the military's hierarchy. In the Teams officers are frequently addressed by their first names, and the spit and polish is kept to a minimum. Every SEAL who mounts out for a mission has earned the right to be there. And every SEAL knows that one screwup, one malfunction, one misstep in planning or execution could cost the life of a brother.

This is a world so far removed from the typical civilian workplace that it is almost incomprehensible. Imagine the politics in your own office or shop. Think of some difficult, incompetent, or vindictive coworker. Now imagine that you are in a swirling firefight in a back alley in a remote corner of Maz-i-Sharif. When your office adversary stumbles, you will move without thinking and without hesitation. You will break cover, expose yourself to enemy fire, and drag this person to safety. Anything less than your full commitment, any hesitation whatsoever, any unwillingness, any fear or backtalk will disqualify you instantly and forever from continuing with the Teams.

It is almost impossible for civilians to conceive how much these men care for and trust each other. In the career of a typical SEAL operator, his life will be saved a dozen times by teammates who will variously drag him from burning wreckage, kick sizzling hand grenades out of range, keep firing while he is pinned down, or pull him half drowned back into a submarine. In the Teams, these are not seen as heroic acts—far from it—they are the actions expected in everyday work.

SEALs themselves will tell you, "It ain't for everybody."

Team members are hardwired with an aversion to publicity. With the exception of spokespersons specifically authorized by the secretary of defense, no active-duty SEAL has ever granted an interview. Though the Navy has allowed some parts of SEAL training to be filmed, it has done so reluctantly. The goal was to get more civilians to volunteer. If the decision had been left to the Teams, nothing at all would've been revealed. There are still a few old frogmen who remember the days when the Navy denied even the existence of the SEAL Teams. As far as they were concerned, if a young man wants to become a SEAL, the first test is to figure out how to get in.

The secrecy under which SEALs live is a double-edged sword. On the positive side, it contributes to an incredible sense of esprit de corps. Airtight operational security also cuts Team members off from what they call "the regular world." These men train together, operate together, and deploy together. In their free time, they run marathons, skydive, climb mountains, surf, dive, kayak, and ride dirt bikes with friends who are almost always other SEALs. The world may be their operational area, but their personal lives would fit into the palm of your hand.

If, unsuspectingly, you were to meet a Navy SEAL you would find him to be confident, personable, and perhaps even glib. Though he would seem outgoing, you would find it curiously impossible to know him well. SEALs are wary of strangers, and it takes a long time, a very long time, for a civilian, male or female, to gain their trust or confidence.

SEAL operations depend upon stealth and technical innovation. SEALs keep their own secrets, and have done so for more than fifty years. They are bound together not only by sworn oaths, but also by the obligations of their brotherhood.

AN INVISIBLE EMPIRE

The Birth of the Joint Special Operations Command

THE FIRST MULTISERVICE SPECIAL OPERATION in American military history was carried out in November 1970. At the height of the Vietnam War, U.S. intelligence identified a prisoner of war camp twenty miles north of Hanoi. Reconnaissance flights by top secret "Buffalo Hunter" drones and SR-71 Blackbirds confirmed that a walled compound outside the North Vietnamese village of Son Tay was being used to hold American prisoners of war. The major prisons in Hanoi, Ly Nam, and the infamous Hanoi Hilton had been pinpointed, but were judged to be too heavily defended to raid. Decades before Saddam Hussein made "human shields" famous, the North Vietnamese stashed dozens of American prisoners of war into its largest power plant, to prevent it from being bombed. Hanoi's prisons were ringed with fighter bases, surface-to-air missiles, and radar-controlled antiaircraft artillery. But Son Tay was another matter. It was isolated, it had no major air defense units around it, and it was ripe for the picking.

An operation was quickly planned to strike the camp, neutralize the guard force, liberate the prisoners, and fly them to safety.

Placed in command of the rescue was a gruff, cigar-chomping Special Forces colonel named Arthur D. "Bull" Simons. Simons was Army all the way, and insisted that his assault force be comprised of Green Berets. He got his wish, and training started at once.

Code-named Barbara, a full-size replica of the compound was built in a remote area of Eglin Air Force Base in Florida. Working in stringent secrecy, Simons trained his men, and drove his planners crazy by insisting they provide for dozens of contingencies. In early November, the force was airlifted to a CIA base in Thailand and waited for a go.

At approximately 1:00 a.m. on the twenty-first of November, four Air Force HH-53 "Jolly Green Giant" helicopters delivered the assault force to Son Tay prison.

The North Vietnamese had no idea what hit them.

The first helicopter over the target, call sign Apple 3, popped over the tree line and opened fire with a quartet of Vulcan miniguns. What had been a quiet night exploded in a torrent of tracer fire. High above the prison, a C-130 E Combat Talon pumped out a series of "night sun" magnesium flares that lit the surrounding country as bright as day. A second Jolly Green, call sign Apple 2, also took the buildings under fire, raking them with deadly, concentrated firepower. In fifteen seconds, the two aircraft expended more than five thousand rounds that cut down the watch towers and raked the guards' headquarters, reducing parts of the building to kindling. The guard force ran for their lives or shot blindly at each other. The assaulters had achieved near total surprise.

But then things started to go wrong.

The helicopter carrying the first group of rescuers, call sign Blue Boy 1, plowed directly into a pair of one-hundred-foot pine trees. These trees had been marked on the Americans' maps, but the photo reconnaissance guys had estimated their height at twenty feet. They were almost eighty feet taller.

Survivors say that when Blue Boy 1 hit the ground it looked like a tornado tearing through a trailer park. The helicopter's giant rotors hacked through the tree trunks, blasting bark and branches into a violent cyclone. The helicopter pitched down and slammed into the dirt just outside the prison walls. The impact broke the aircraft in three pieces. Miraculously, it did not catch fire, and only one person was injured, an Air Force gunner whose leg was broken when one of the rotors ripped through the fuselage.

Aboard the crashed helo, Special Forces captain Richard Meadows calmly unfastened his safety harness, stood up, and ordered his assault team out of the wreckage.

As his men swarmed into the prison, Meadows's calm voice came over a bullhorn, saying, "We're Americans. Keep your heads down. Get on the floor. We'll be in your cells in a minute."

Meadows and his team quickly fanned out, cutting power and communications lines to the camp. As one of his assault elements battled the guards, Meadows sent another group to lay an ambush along the road, a hundred yards from the front gate.

Gunfire crackled overhead. Some of the guards fanatically defended every inch of the camp. Meadows found cover and returned fire. He looked up into the sky, now hung with dozens of flares. His own helicopter was a smoldering wreck. He was now fighting it out with a guard force of undetermined size and he had no idea where the rest of the rescue party had gone. Bull Simons, the mission commander, and a second helicopter full of assaulters was nowhere in sight.

Where was the rest of the mission? Where was his backup?

It turns out that they were lost. And worse, they were now in a firefight of their own.

Simons and his team, call sign Greenleaf, had been inserted almost five hundred yards south of the prison, at a stone-walled, tile-roofed compound known as the "secondary school." Simons and his team sprinted down the tail ramp of the helicopter and spread out. As his insertion platform lifted off, Simons realized at once that he had been put down south of his objective.

To his horror, Simons discovered that not only had he been put down in the *wrong* place—it was a very *bad* place, too. The secondary school was swarming with North Vietnamese soldiers—hundreds of them. More than three companies of Chinese military advisers and North Vietnamese engineers had been billeted at the school, and Simons and his team had landed right on top of them.

Simons's tactical options were limited. He could run away, or strike the enemy hard before the NVA figured out that they outnumbered the Green Berets ten to one. Simons did what any good officer would do—he attacked.

In a swirling, close-quarters battle, Simons's team waded into the barracks, throwing grenades and sweeping the rooms with automatic fire. Within five minutes, more than a hundred Chinese soldiers were killed. The rest fled in confusion. Simons quickly radioed for extraction, reembarked his assault group, and landed at the main prison compound.

By the time that Greenleaf arrived at the main camp, the prison guards had scattered and the firing had died down. Meadows ran to the helicopter and found his boss.

"Bad news," he said. "There's nobody here. They moved them. They're all gone."

There had been American POWs at the camp, but they had been moved sixteen weeks earlier. Alerted by the two firefights and the blazing galaxy of flares, the entire countryside was now swarming with North Vietnamese troops. Simons ordered the damaged helicopter to be blown up, withdrew his forces, and flew back to Thailand.

The entire raid had taken twenty-eight minutes.

The following morning, when the North Vietnamese returned to the prison at Son Tay, they found the wreckage of an HH-53. Its broken tail unit jutted up like a monument in the front yard of the commandant's office.

When and why the American prisoners were moved from Son Tay remains a mystery. After the war it was learned that the prisoners had been moved four months previously to a satellite camp called Dong Hoi. No American prisoners had been freed by the Son Tay raid, but it sent a message. The North Vietnamese moved all American POWs to Hanoi, and their treatment began to improve. Morale among the prisoners sky-rocketed when the news spread that a special operation had been launched to free them.

The Son Tay raid was a watershed in U.S. special operations planning. It was to become one of the most often studied missions in spec ops, and would teach valuable lessons that would be used decades later in Neptune's Spear. The assault team had been inserted deep into North Vietnam, struck their target, and extracted without loss—even though one of the helicopters crashed during insert. It's a monument to both the skill of the planners and the steadfast valor of the operators that not a single American lost his life in a raid that killed or wounded more than five hundred of the enemy.

The operational plan for the Son Tay raid was worked on by Green Berets, Air Force Special Operations officers, and a cadre of Navy SEALs led by a blunt, outspoken, sandy-haired former linebacker named Marvin Krupinsky.

Krupinsky's oft-stated opinions had made him some enemies within the SEAL community, but his genius as both a planner and a tactician were quickly recognized. Krupinsky was to have an important effect on the training of SEAL Team operators, especially junior officers. After graduation from BUD/S, SEAL officers were put through an intense six-month special warfare operations and planning course. Graduates have said it was every bit the academic equivalent of BUD/S. Krupinsky's salient points were these: 1) One is none—always have a backup, whether it's a gun, a helicopter, or a plan. 2) Everything that can go wrong will go wrong, and at the worst possible moment. Prepare for the unexpected. 3) The men must not only survive the plan, the plan must survive the blunders of men.

These maxims would pay dividends in a series of meticulously planned SEAL Team operations carried out in the eighties, nineties, and the first decade of the twenty-first century.

The concept of a joint, multiservice special operations force would seem like a no-brainer. But it took almost twenty years after the success of Son Tay for the Joint Special Operations Command to come into being. And it took a military disaster to get the admirals and generals to finally work together.

On November 4, 1979, a mob surged over the fence of the American embassy in Tehran. On October 23 of that year, the United States had granted refugee status to the deposed shah of Iran, admitting him to California for the treatment of terminal cancer. Outraged, the government of Ayatollah Khomeini organized a massive demonstration targeting the American embassy. Using the demonstration as cover, armed members of the Pasdaran, the Revolutionary Guard Corps, broke into the embassy's safe rooms and took fifty-two diplomats, embassy workers, and U.S. Marines prisoner. Negotiations for the return of the hostages dragged on for months.

Frustrated with Iranian intransigence, and fearing for the safety of the hostages, President Jimmy Carter ordered Operation Eagle Claw, one of the first deployments of the Army's newly formed Special Forces Operational Detachment-Delta.

The operation was complex, and its lines of authority, command, and control were vague. The operation ended in disaster when a Marine Corps CH-53 helicopter collided with an Air Force C-130 tanker aircraft at a desert refueling site deep inside Iran. The fiery crash killed eight service members, burned four others, and led to the destruction of two aircraft and the abandonment of five intact helicopters as well as their communications and cryptological equipment and a dozen copies of the rescue plan.

The debacle contributed to the electoral defeat of President Jimmy Carter. The Iranians kept the American hostages for a total of 444 days, releasing them only after the election of Ronald Reagan. With the failure of the Iranian rescue mission in mind, the Joint Special Operations Command was formed in December 1980.

Until JSOC's creation, the special forces of every service had to carve their budgets out of regular service dollars. Within the special operations community, operators tended to triumph over politicians. While this created good working conditions at the unit level, it left the special forces, especially the SEAL Teams, open to attack from above.

The SEALs suffered under another handicap: they were not particularly loved by the Navy. For many years it was nearly impossible for a Naval Academy graduate to become a SEAL Team officer. It was somehow seen as beneath the dignity of an Annapolis man to become a snake eater. The SEALs may have recruited from their own, but it made them vulnerable in places where they couldn't fight, like Washington, D.C. This meant that the community was underrepresented among the Navy's flag officers, the admirals who made the decisions and cut the checks.

Not many SEALs wanted to serve at the Pentagon, so they tended to retire before they were too senior to be sent into the field. On more than one occasion after Vietnam, the United States Navy considered disbanding the SEAL community completely. At least one training class graduated from BUD/S but was sent back to the fleet—there was no room in the Teams for new operators.

JSOC quickly moved to coordinate the special mission units of the U.S. military. Funding was increased for Delta Force, the Navy's SEAL Team Six, and Task Force 160—the aviation component of America's premier counterterrorism operators. These outfits, all black programs, were manned by handpicked volunteers. JSOC's budget, manning, command structure, and even the location of its bases and headquarters remain classified. JSOC's mission and mandate are global; it is the United States' principal weapon against terrorism. One of its unofficial mottos is "Anywhere, anytime."

Screening for SEAL Team Six, Delta, and 160th SOAR is competitive and by invitation only. Only the best SEAL operators, soldiers, and combat aircrew are allowed to even *inquire* about the program. After a lengthy interview process, the most experienced and highly regarded operators are allowed to undergo rigorous "selection courses"—punishing training regimes that winnow out all but the most proficient, accomplished, and dedicated.

The military had a name for the operators at SEAL Team Six and Delta. They were called "Jedis."

TEAM JEDI

IN 1980, SEAL TEAM SIX WAS FORMED by Dick Marcinko, then the operations officer of SEAL Team Two. America's premier counterterrorism unit started as a single platoon from SEAL Team Two. Volunteers were told they were being trained as a "maritime intercept" unit. On the organizational charts, Marcinko's outfit was first called "Sixth Platoon." The name was changed in a couple of months to "Mobility Six." This was soon shortened to Mob Six—"Mob" being short for "mobility" and a not-so-subtle acknowledgment of the power Marcinko was accumulating. His methods owed a lot to *The Godfather,* and Dick Marcinko was nothing if not an empire builder. In a short time he parlayed seventeen guys into a global counterterrorism conglomerate.

Marcinko was in the right place at the right time. Delta Force had just fallen on its sword. The debacle at Desert One forced military planners to rethink the idea of placing all their counterterrorism eggs in a single, Army basket. The SEAL Teams had an unparalleled reputation as counterinsurgency operators in Vietnam. Marcinko had completed a tour at the Pentagon as the Navy's counterterrorism action officer. There, he had worked the E ring, buttonholing admirals and lining up support. He sold the chief of naval operations, Admiral Thomas B. Hayward, on creating a mission-specific Navy counterterrorism team, handpicked from the best SEALs in the business. Marcinko was given the go-ahead and a thick checkbook.

When Marcinko returned to the operational teams at Little Creek, Virginia, he was a lieutenant commander—too junior to skipper a SEAL Team, and too senior to command a mere platoon. So he wrote his own job description, expanded his mandate, and started stepping on toes. Officially assigned as the operations officer at SEAL Two, Marcinko managed to fob off this job and take over the day-to-day operation of Mob Six. He built SEAL Team Six from the ground up, picking the best operators from the other teams, and laying his hands on the best weapons and equipment, regardless of where they were made. Marcinko was a master at working the margins of the Pentagon's growing "black" counterterrorism budget. He made sure that every dime spent on Delta Force was matched by money sent to Mob Six. He soon had the cash, and a working team, but then came the delicate question of who, exactly, was giving him orders.

Marcinko pulled every string he could find to get his nascent command attached to JSOC, and not the Naval Special Warfare Group at Little Creek. This was a textbook example of insubordination, but somehow, Marcinko got away with it. With breathtaking audacity, he had not only short-circuited his own commanding officer at SEAL Team Two, but also the commodore of Naval Special Warfare Group Two and a pair of do-nothing SEAL Team admirals who could only blink and sputter in fury.

JSOC was a creation of the U.S. Army. Its commanders and most of its senior officers were Army. There were a few Air Force guys around, but they were almost irrelevant, as the new outfit also created a stand-alone, Army-based aviation component called Task Force 160. Marcinko, at times charming, always opportunistic, and occasionally ruthless, managed to wheedle his way into the graces of the JSOC commander, Major General Richard Scholtes. Selling the Navy had been easy—pretty much a matter of Go Navy, Beat Army. To the generals in his path, Marcinko played down Six's land-based mandate, concentrating on operations at sea and across the beach. Marcinko told the general that if he wanted an organization with global reach, he needed SEALs. Seventy-one percent of the world's surface was ocean. Delta Force could take the land and SEAL Team Six could handle the water. It seemed like a fairly rational idea. Marcinko had his swim fin in the door. The rest is history.

Within the Teams, there were whispers that Marcinko had sold out and gone Army. Mostly, this assessment was to be heard from officers whom Marcinko did not invite into the new unit. Mob Six was officially commissioned as a SEAL Team in 1981. It was Marcinko himself who picked the number six to confuse the enemy. At the time there were only two SEAL Teams, SEAL One in Coronado, and SEAL Two at Little Creek. Six is also the number given in Navy radio traffic for the leader of a squadron. Marcinko was staking a claim that his would be the best Team in Naval Special Warfare.

He had driven a political wedge between himself and Naval Special Warfare Group Two, the command staff in charge of the East Coast SEAL Teams. Seeing how there was no love lost, Marcinko now added a little physical distance as well. Since World War II, East Coast Naval Special Warfare units had been based on the Naval Amphibious Base in Little Creek, a sleepy suburb of Virginia Beach. Marcinko picked out a stretch of forest at a disused Naval communication station close to the North Carolina border and wrote a check for a new building. "Hell," he said, "make it a couple of buildings."

Marcinko built an iron curtain around his new kingdom. Sequestering himself on the new base, he went so far as to tell the operators of SEAL Team Six not to associate with their brethren across town. The "find new playmates" rule didn't make him many friends among his former colleagues, and "the secret mission" of Six was the worst kept secret in the SEALs. But that's just the way Marcinko wanted it—he was building brand recognition.

The mission of Six was easily guessed at—maritime and coastal targets all over the world—but not much else about the command was general knowledge. SEAL Team Six, like Delta, was on a constant war footing. Within a very short period the entire Team would be ready to deploy and fight anywhere in the world. SEAL Team Six was, and is, on the highest alert level of any unit in the U.S. military.

In creating SEAL Team Six, Marcinko made enemies on all sides. Other teams resented Six's unlimited budget and the brain drain of their best operators. Not that Six had to spend much on recruitment. Marcinko made sure, however, to keep his bread buttered with Admiral Hayward, chief of Naval Operations, and for a while that made him, and Team Six, untouchable.

On June 2, 1982, Admiral Hayward did as all four-star admirals and chiefs of Naval Operations must do: he retired. Marcinko had lost his top cover, and the knives came out.

With no allies left in the SEAL community, Marcinko was rotated out of command and replaced by Captain Bob Gormly, an experienced, capable officer. In taking over SEAL Six, Gormly faced an uphill battle. Marcinko had thrown a tantrum when his two-year command slot was not extended. In an act that endeared him to no one, Marcinko split for Europe on the day Bob Gormly assumed command. Skipping the change of command ceremony was an unforgivable breach of Naval etiquette and put the final nail in the coffin of Dick Marcinko's reputation. Even his die-hard stalwarts were put off. SEAL Team Six, like its creator, was acquiring a reputation as the cantankerous diva of Naval Special Warfare.

There were whispers at the other Teams that Six was "All show, no go." Single-handedly, Bob Gormly set out to make Six live up to its operational mandate. Tall, taciturn Bob Gormly had grown up in Virginia Beach. His first association with the Teams was with a couple of surfers he met riding the waves at Rudee Inlet. Gormly thought they might be military. They didn't seem to work normal hours. They were pretty good on their boards, they obviously loved the ocean, and eventually Gormly asked one of them what they did.

"We're in the Navy," came back the standard reply.

"What part of the Navy?" he asked.

"The Atlantic part . . ."

This went on for a couple of weeks, until, at last, someone gave the kid the right answer. They were members of the UDT, the Underwater Demolition Teams. When Bob asked what they did, one of the surfers said, "We're the guys who jump into the water to rescue space capsules."

Gormly was hooked.

After college, he tried out for BUD/S and made it. Before transferring to Six, Gormly had a long and storied career in Naval Special Warfare. He had conducted beach recons during the Cuban Missile Crisis, and led a team of swimmer scouts during America's brief invasion of the Dominican Republic. He made several tours in Vietnam, earned a chest full of medals and a reputation as a no-nonsense professional.

In a lot of ways, Bob Gormly was the antithesis of Dick Marcinko. It was Bob Gormly more than any other officer who made Team Six what it is today. Team Six under Marcinko had been a faux meritocracy married to a sycophantic sort of personality cult. Marcinko had come up through the ranks, a Mustang, and although he was the captain of the team, he had scant respect for other commissioned officers. Starting in the days of Mob Six, Marcinko had kept alive a spirit of devotion to himself—but he did so by deliberately undercutting the other officers in the Team. He was in the habit of replacing his assault group commanders without warning, and firing them immediately if they conflicted with his senior chief petty officers or himself. Although this system prided itself on collegiality, it brokered no dissent. There was one tactical opinion, and that was Marcinko's. This "you're the boss" arrangement prompted devotion, but it also brought out the worst of deadly "group think," a sort of collective megalomania, where a Team begins to think that they are too good to fail.

It is one of the fundamental strengths of the SEAL Teams that individual operators contribute to the execution of the mission, and to the planning cycle as well. People are in the SEAL Teams because they're good at what they do. Gormly brought the Team back together, welding both officers and enlisted operators into a cohesive combat-ready unit. It was Bob Gormly who led SEAL Team Six into the command's baptism of fire.

SEAL Team Six was originally set up with three operational entities, two operational teams, and a training cadre. In theory, one team would be deployed, one team would be in training, and one team would be on stand down, or what came to be called "schools/deployment." By the time of the Grenada Operation, the terrorism business was booming. It was soon found necessary to expand the assault teams to three (and later four) operational units, and a full-time training unit, called Green Team.

Though they were trained, manned, and equipped identically, each assault element at SEAL Team Six has a unique and distinct character and ethos. For purposes of command and control, the assault elements are color coded, but are most often referred to by their nicknames. One crew is the Pirates, the Bones Men, and wear a patch featuring the Jolly Roger. A second crew is nicknamed after the trident-tailed lion they wear as a recognition patch. The third operational team has gone by the call sign Apache, or Arapahoe, and are subsequently known as the Red Men.

SEAL Team Six has the jack, and it shows. The gear issued to its operators is the top of the line, and the best of everything. Every operator has a cage, his own personal space, warehouse, and dominion. There are few pieces of equipment held in common—everything is issued to, and signed for, by individual operators. Each operator's cage looks like an Aladdin's cave of spec ops gear, an astonishing amount of stuff: Scuba gear, parachutes, climbing harnesses, crampons and ropes, carabiners, lock picks, survival kits, Nomex flight suits, custom wetsuits, and dozens of different combat uniforms. Each operator maintains his own personal arsenal.

For special operations, most shooters prefer some variant of the M-4 carbine, though SCAR rifles and customized M-14 sniping variants are not unknown. The M-4 is the workhorse of the SEALs. It is a modular system that allows operators to "dial in" their weapon for mission-specific tasks. An ingenious rail system allows shooters to place laser illuminators, rifle scopes, flashlights, and holographic sights as necessary for long-range desert patrol or close-quarters combat. A deadly 40 mm grenade launcher can be snapped onto the weapon—making it a piece of pocket artillery firing lethal and sublethal munitions out to eight hundred yards.

Most SEALs also keep at least one tricked-out Kalashnikov AK-47. Favored for its go-anywhere ruggedness and jam-proof reliability, the AK is also the weapon used most often by terrorists. SEALs will often "one up" the bad guys, fitting the venerable AK with modular rails, so that it may carry the high-tech lasers and holographic sites that the SEALs prefer. These are placed in low-profile mounts so the AK retains its characteristic "bad guy" shape. The surprise comes when the SEALs open fire. The laser designators and holographic weapon sites extend the AK's effective range by several hundred yards—a critical distance in a firefight.

As an "all-star" outfit, individual operators are given a lot of leeway as to the weapons they carry. For close-in, silenced work, the HK-416 is still a favorite. A variant of the M-4 carbine, the HK-416 is the apex design of the venerable M-16 platform. For longer ranges, some prefer the SCAR-H assault rifle, a behemoth of a long gun that fires 7.62 mm ammo out to beyond eight hundred yards. Also common are highly modified M-60 machine guns and SAWs (squad automatic weapons), often carried with feed trays and backpack-mounted ammunition systems that allow an operator to carry as many as one thousand rounds. Pistols are another discretionary item. In the armory one can still find the occasional stainless steel Smith & Wesson model 686 .357 magnum (for water work), and a variety of Glock, Ruger, Beretta, and SIG Sauer pistols. For concealed carry, every operator is issued a blue-steel Walther PPK, just like James Bond.

All of this equipment, and more, is issued to students arriving to try out for Green Team. How long they hold on to it is up to them. Green Team is a year-long ordeal, every bit as physically and mentally demanding as BUD/S. There are SEAL Team Six operators who tell you that they thought it was tougher than BUD/S—much tougher.

"At BUD/S it's a question of survival," one Team Six operator summed up. "You get up in the morning and you try to survive until breakfast. But Green Team isn't just a matter of obeying orders and hanging on. You're competing against the best SEALs in the business. Green Team is a race, and the prize is a slot on the operational team."

A few months after Gormly assumed command, in October 1983, a coup d'état occurred on the Caribbean island of Grenada. Its circumstances were highly suspicious. On Grenada, hundreds of Cuban "construction workers" had been sent to the island to complete work on an international airport. American satellites revealed that the runway had been completed in reasonable time, but the Cubans stayed on, using bulldozers to push dirt back and forth over the pavement. Ominously, the Cubans began receiving ever-increasing shipments of "equipment" that were transferred from the docks, at night, and assembled in closed hangars. The Cuban engineers were in fact

Special Forces soldiers, and the equipment turned out to be armored vehicles, antiaircraft guns, and surface-to-air missiles.

Hudson Austin, a Grenadian army officer with communist leanings, had the island's president, Maurice Bishop, assassinated. He also kidnapped the island governor-general, Sir Peter Schoon. When the Grenadian people started to protest, Austin ordered a twenty-four-hour-a-day, shoot-on-sight curfew. It was then that the Cubans played their hand. The armored vehicles and antiaircraft guns were driven to key places on the island. This was a Cuban show all the way.

There were about a thousand U.S. medical students on Grenada, attending the University of St. George. The Cubans surrounded the university and ordered the Americans into their dorm rooms. Fearing a repeat of the Iranian hostage drama, President Ronald Reagan ordered an invasion.

Operation Urgent Fury was a turning point for Naval Special Warfare.

Team Six had spectacular successes but it also had tragedy; before the opening of hostilities, four SEALs were lost conducting an at-sea rendezvous. The loss was made bitter because of its futility. It was a needless accident caused by complicity.

Once on the ground in Grenada, SEAL Six more than proved its mettle. Led by Bob Gormly, operational elements of SEAL Team Six rescued Governor-General Scoon, and took out the radio transmitter of Radio Free Grenada—two epic special operations that proved to JSOC and to Washington that SEAL Six could deliver.

Postinvasion analysis showed that the intelligence about the island had been woefully inaccurate. CIA officers provided one SEAL assault element with a tourist brochure with a target location circled in ballpoint pen. Assessments of the fighting capabilities of the Cuban engineers, too, had been dangerously underestimated. U.S. ground forces found themselves facing state-of-the-art Soviet-designed, Cuban-manned antiaircraft weapons. Combat-hardened Cuban forces drove armored vehicles that were able to shoot down helicopters and surround inserted SEAL Teams. It was a rude awakening.

On Grenada, the CIA continued to disappoint. When a SEAL element, led by Commander Donald Campbell, took over the studios of Radio Free Grenada, his mission plan stated that a CIA guide would lead a Marine company to the transmitter to secure it by 0900 hours.

The CIA never showed. The Marines were willing, but had no maps—the CIA was supposed to provide those as well. Campbell and his team of

Red Men held the radio station for more than ten hours—beating off repeated attacks by Cuban infantry backed up by armored vehicles. Campbell's SEALs, finally running out of ammunition, set explosive charges, blew up the station, and fled into the jungle.

Campbell and three of his team were wounded, and their satellite radio had been shot to pieces. They went to two prearranged pickup positions, only to find that the CIA, again, had forgotten to show. Disgusted, hunted by Cuban armor and infantry, Donald Campbell played the only card he had left. As night fell, he ordered his men to jump off a cliff into the water. Though wounded himself, Donald Campbell dragged another more seriously wounded member of his team out into the Atlantic, and led his team on a five-mile swim to an American destroyer.

From that moment forward, SEAL Team Six would never again put a mission into the field based on CIA-provided information. Though relations at the top remained cordial, on the operator level, the CIA became a joke.

But the weekend wasn't even over. Across the world, another SEAL Team was about to get a very unpleasant surprise . . . and this, too, because local CIA case officers hadn't seen the ball since kickoff. While the combined task force of SEALs, Delta, U.S. Marines, and Army Rangers were mopping up in Grenada, a new enemy reared its head.

In Beirut.

GOING SOLO

ON THE MORNING OF OCTOBER 23, 1983, a four-ton Mercedes truck passed through a Lebanese Army checkpoint and into the parking lot of the Beirut International Airport. It turned a circle, gathering speed, then crashed through a steel fence. The truck bulldozed its way through the sandbagged bunker at the entrance of the headquarters. Tires squealing on lobby tiles, it plowed on, dragging Marine sentries on its bumper as it rushed into the open center courtyard of the building.

Then it detonated—killing 243 American Marines who had been sent to Lebanon as part of a multinational peacekeeping force. The bomb that took out the Marine Battalion Landing Team headquarters in Beirut was the largest non-nuclear explosion in the history of warfare. Great portions of the building were turned to powder. Across town, twenty-eight seconds later, a second, identical, truck bomb was detonated outside the headquarters of the French Foreign Legion detachment. This bomb killed sixty French paratroopers and wounded fifty more. Until 9/11, the Beirut bombings were the most deadly acts of terrorism ever committed against the United States.

A simple bronze statue in Jacksonville, North Carolina, was erected to honor those killed in the Beirut Marine Barracks bombing. Under the figure of a Marine standing in combat uniform are four words: "They Came in Peace." The statue, like the incident itself, has been mostly forgotten.

In Washington, D.C., the forgetting was much more purposeful. The Beirut station of the CIA had no idea that anyone was planning to bomb the Marines that October. To the SEALs on the ground in Beirut, the CIA in country had proven itself a nonplayer. But there was an American intelligence agency that was gathering information in Lebanon. The only problem was, they weren't sharing.

Early in October 1983, the National Security Agency intercepted radio traffic between Tehran and the Iranian embassy in Damascus. Though not decoded until weeks after the attacks, these messages proved that two massive, sophisticated truck bombs were ordered by the Iranian government. The VBIEDs (vehicle-borne improvised explosive devices) were built by technicians of the Iranian Revolutionary Guard Corps, and transported through the Bekaa Valley with the complicity of the Syrian army.

The date chosen for the attack was a Sunday morning, October 23, 1983—six years to the day since the United States granted political asylum to the shah of Iran. All of this could have been known, in advance, by the NSA—had they translated a backlog of intercepted message traffic. The failure of the National Security Agency to provide actionable intelligence to the Marines in Beirut was the single most negligent and catastrophic failure of U.S. intelligence since Pearl Harbor. The NSA would fail again, even more horrendously, on 9/11. But that was two decades in the future.

After the Beirut bombing, the NSA launched one of the most shameful and cynical cover-ups in American history. Even before the last Marine body had been pulled from the wreckage, the NSA began to stonewall.

As the Marine Corps, and then Congress, conducted hearings on the military disaster, NSA director Lincoln D. Faurer failed to disclose certain NSA intercepts. This cynical move ensured that blame for the attack would fall on the few Marine officers who survived the blast. The NSA, abetted by the CIA, went so far as to create "battle damage assessments" that blamed the two highly sophisticated truck bombs on a Beirut street gang called Amal. The fix was in.

Colonel Tim Geraghty, the Marine commander in Lebanon, then a likely candidate for general, had his career ended by the issuing of a "nonpunitive letter of caution," blaming him, incredibly, for failing to anticipate the bombing. His executive officer, Lieutenant Colonel Jim Gerlicht, had been made a quadriplegic by the blast. He had his career-killing letter handed to him in the Bethesda Naval Hospital.

The CIA and NSA made sure that the Marine officers at the airport took the rap. There's no other example in American military history of more cold-blooded or ruthless interagency politics. Lincoln Faurer lived to see the Marine officers sent into early retirement and disgrace, while he managed to hold on to his job and get promoted to four-star general.

Transcripts of the Tehran–Damascus messages were only released in 2003, after repeated Freedom of Information Act (FOIA) requests filed by Colonel Geraghty, the commander of the Marine forces in Beirut. For the two decades following the Beirut attack, the National Security Agency would continuously fail to issue timely, predictive, or even relevant intelligence to decision-makers and military commanders. JSOC watched all of this and learned.

After Beirut and Grenada, the commanders at JSOC realized that they could not depend on conventional intelligence channels to gather targeting information, or frame predictive actions by the enemy. Privately, JSOC planners began to refer to NSA, CIA, and FBI as "the Three Stooges." A combination of petty politics, technical shortcomings, interagency rivalry, and serial incompetence made it obvious that if JSOC wanted timely, target-specific information they would have to gather it themselves.

As SEAL Team Six expanded, JSOC set about gathering its own specialists in technical and signals intelligence and investigations and research. A fourth operational element would join JSOC and complete the "Invisible Empire." JSOC's intelligence component was the blackest of all black programs. It would go through many names and monikers and frequently change its organizational structure and physical location, making it impossible for anyone outside JSOC to either find it physically or figure out exactly what it did. The name given to this new unit was fitting: It was called "Grey Fox."

As the war on terror went on, JSOC did its own analysis and picked its own targets. Over at CIA there were a few human intelligence types left, but those working counterterrorism were as petty and incestuous as the creative writing department at an Ivy League college. Several former SEALs founded defense contracting firms that provided assessments of terrorist operational techniques and abilities. Even SEALS who weren't SEALs anymore were beating the agency at its own game.

It's one thing to break the enemies' codes—it is another thing to just capture the guy who wrote the message and have him read it to you. NSA's billion-dollar super computers were increasingly irrelevant as JSOC came to grips with terrorist organizations who were smart enough to stay off their satellite phones and rely on trusted couriers to communicate their orders and plans.

In 1985, half a dozen Palestinian hijackers stormed aboard the *Achille Lauro,* an Italian cruise ship in the Mediterranean. Intending originally to head for Syria, they were refused entry. In frustration, they murdered Leon Klinghoffer, a disabled Jewish-American passenger.

SEAL Team Six deployed and prepared to take back the ship. Warned of the coming assault by Russian code breakers in Damascus, the hijackers put the ship around and hightailed into the Egyptian port of Alexandria. They were welcomed as heroes. There, President Hosni Mubarak cut a cash deal with Yasser Arafat and put the hijackers and their boss—master terrorist Abu Abbas—onto an Egypt Air 737. Escorted by a squad of Egyptian secret police, the airliner took off for Tunisia. It didn't get far. Tomcat fighters from the carrier USS *Saratoga* forced the Egyptian airliner to land at the NATO airbase in Sigonella, Sicily.

Waiting for them on the runway was a squadron of Bones Men led by Lieutenant Commander Avril Pikeman. He quickly deployed snipers, blocked the aircraft's wheels, and demanded that the terrorists surrender. Moments later, two C-141s containing assault elements from the Red Men landed behind the Egypt Air passenger liner. The hijackers had been hijacked.

Faced with an ultimatum, the terrorists quickly surrendered.

The surrender deal stipulated that they would be taken into Italian custody. That was a mistake. Italian Prime Minister Bettino Craxi quickly cut a side deal that separated Abu Abbas and two other senior PLO terrorists from the actual trigger pullers. Within hours, Craxi had provided the terrorists with Italian air force uniforms, fresh travel documents, and a police escort onto an Iraqi Air flight departing for Baghdad. Klinghoffer's murderers were eventually brought to trial in Italy, but Craxi made sure that the big fish got away.

In April 1986, Libyan dictator Muammar Gaddafi ordered the bombing of a Berlin disco, killing two U.S. servicemen and four German civilians, and wounding more than two hundred and fifty people. President Ronald Reagan ordered Operation El Dorado Canyon in response.

On the night of April 14, SEAL Six inserted two target-spotting elements across the beach into Tripoli. Call signed Apache and Arapahoe, these elements set up laser-target designators and illuminated Colonel Gaddafi's headquarters at Bab al-Azizia.

Still smarting from the Achille Lauro, Italy did everything it could to thwart the American operation. First, the Italian government refused permission for the strike airplanes to fuel at the NATO airbase in Sigonella. Then Prime Minister Bettino Craxi crossed the line from obstructionism to treason. He placed a phone call to Libya's Colonel Gaddafi and warned him that an American air strike was on its way. Gaddafi fled from his palatial compound moments before the bombs struck. He was lucky he did.

Lit up by Apache and Arapahoe, thirteen out of sixteen laser-guided bombs splashed the compound—the best hit-to-miss ratio of any component of the air raids. Gaddafi would later claim that an adopted stepdaughter had been killed in the attack. That's unlikely, but the colonel realized just how close *he* had come to dying for his country. Gaddafi would spend the rest of the eighties and nineties moving between a dozen different houses scattered throughout the country, seldom sleeping in the same place twice.

Other targets were struck in the El Dorado Canyon Operation, including military airfields and terrorist training camps. In the confusion following the air strikes, the SEALs of Apache and Arapahoe slipped through a girls' military college, crossed the beach, and were extracted at sea.

One member of Arapahoe remembered watching the Libyan antiaircraft gunners splattering tracers up into the dark, empty sky. "It looked like Disneyland," he said. Bab al-Azizia was a fantastic SEAL Team Six accomplishment.

SEAL Team Six carried out numerous supporting roles in the Persian Gulf during Operation Prime Chance in 1987. Assisted by elements of the Army's Night Stalker Special Operations Aviation Regiment (SOAR), SEAL Teams boarded and captured an Iranian warship named *Iran Ajar.* The ship's deck was full of sea mines she had been sowing into the Persian Gulf.

Other SEAL operations ambushed Iranian Boghammar patrol boats that were stalking the sea lanes to attack neutral shipping. SEALs captured oil rigs in the Persian Gulf that were being used as Iranian observation and weapons platforms. All of these successes were carried out with minimal CIA input, and no help from the NSA. The SEALs liked it that way.

SEAL Team Six carried out clandestine missions in the disputed zone between Chad and Libya in Operation Mount Hope III in 1988. In the 1989 U.S. invasion of Panama, Operation Just Cause, SEAL Six hunted for Panamanian strong man and drug boss Manuel Noriega—helping corner him in the Vatican embassy. During operations in Kuwait and Iraq (Operations Desert Shield and Desert Storm) in 1991, SEAL Team Six carried out numerous special reconnaissance operations, penetrating deep behind Iraqi lines. Fast attack vehicles (FAVs) from SEAL Team Six were first into Kuwait City, and liberated both the parliament and the American embassy.

The command carried out operations in Somalia, both overt in Operation Restore Hope, and covert in the chillingly named Operation Gothic Serpent, where SEAL Team Six elements hunted Somali warlords.

After 9/11, SEAL Team Six's deployment cycles doubled, and then tripled. SEAL Six has carried out countless operations against high-value targets in Iraq and Afghanistan. Nor have they neglected their worldwide commitments. In Operation Aztec Silence in 2003, SEAL Team Six broke up an Al Qaeda plan to kidnap drivers in the Paris to Dakar car rally. The command has participated in numerous other still-classified special operations, including High Value Individual (HVI) operations in Chad, Somalia, the Philippines, Syria, and Pakistan.

There is no place on Earth or in the sea that is beyond the reach of Team Six. And on April 8, 2009, when a gang of armed Somali pirates hijacked an American cargo ship in the Gulf of Aden, they would prove it.

MAERSK ALABAMA

MANY OPERATIONS PROVIDED LESSONS used in Operation Neptune's Spear. One of them was a mission that SEAL Team Six called "The Bainbridge Op."

In the Gulf of Aden there is little twilight; at dawn, purple clouds give way to a blazing sun, and at the end of each fierce, blistering day, there are only a few minutes of dusk before the sun sinks toward the African shore, taking with it all the light, like debris pulled down around a foundering ship.

This close to the equator, halfway into the Indian Ocean, there are no seasons—there is only a rolling blue sea and the pitiless sun. On the night of April 8, 2009, the sun went out of the sky almost at once. The moon had yet to rise when four pirates set off from a mother ship two hundred miles off the coast of Somalia. Armed with automatic weapons, they turned a high-speed motor launch north and east toward the Gulf of Aden. Their target: a U.S.-flagged containership carrying relief supplies to Mombasa, Kenya. The vessel's name: *Maersk Alabama*.

Operating from the postapocalyptic port of Eyl, on the Horn of Africa, a flotilla of pirates has attacked almost a hundred merchant ships since 2008. The ransoming of cargo and crews has emerged as a multimillion-dollar business in the failed state of Somalia. It was inevitable that they would eventually attack a U.S.-flagged vessel. Unfortunately for the pirates, SEAL Team Six was ready.

Using grappling hooks, the pirates climbed *Maersk Alabama*'s stern and rushed across her decks. In moments, they were in control of the bridge. At gunpoint, they ordered the navigator to set a course for their base in the harbor at Eyl—where the hostages were to be *sold* to the highest bidder. For the first time since 9/11, Americans had fallen into the hands of hijackers.

But the hijackers' plan had gone badly awry. Though the pirates had captured the ship's captain and one of the officers, the rest of the crew had made it to a secure hiding place. In a secondary control room the ship's engineers, led by Chief Engineer Mike Perry, first cycled the ship's rudder, swamping and sinking the pirates' speedboat. Belowdecks, Perry took control of the ship's systems, rendering the bridge controls useless.

At the risk of their own lives, Perry and his gang were able to disarm and capture one of the pirates—seizing his weapon. After a tense standoff, Perry offered a trade: Give us our captain, and we'll give you back your pirate. The pirates pretended to agree, and then pulled a double cross—as they were being shown how to launch a motor lifeboat, they pushed their captive, Captain Richard Phillips, inside the boat and fled, setting off an epic, globe-spanning special operation.

Within hours the destroyer USS *Bainbridge* and the amphibious assault ship USS *Boxer* surrounded the pirates and their captive. Negotiations started immediately over the lifeboat's radio. The pirates had no idea that SEAL Team Six had parachuted an entire assault element into the shark-infested waters of the Gulf of Aden, and put a team of snipers onto *Bainbridge*.

Beyond USS *Boxer* lurked a pair of SEAL Team Six deadly high-speed assault craft. Invisible to surface radar, armed with chain guns, automatic grenade launchers, and capable of forty knots, these boats were the SEALs' knockout punch. Also parachuted onto the *Bainbridge* was another SEAL Team Six secret weapon, a mobile tactical operations center (TOC), manned by a platoon of non-SEAL überdweebs assigned to Team Six. The Navy called them Support Detachment Alpha, but to the shooters they were "the Twidgets," geeks on steroids. The TOC was their Super Bowl. They quickly established communications with Washington and with a Seawolf-class submarine trailing the lifeboat at a depth of three hundred feet. These same men would prove invaluable during Operation Neptune's Spear.

Battlefield information, however exquisite, does not exist in a vacuum, and flickering on a separate set of fourteen-inch screens was a slice of the real world: the network news feeds from Fox, CNN, the Reuters wire service, and the BBC Web page.

Det Alpha set up shop in the *Bainbridge*'s wardroom, running a parallel and complimentary operation to the Command Information Center. Captain Greg Wilson, the commanding officer of SEAL Team Six, was the on-scene commander, and though he was riding Commander Frank Costello's ship, eating his chow, and borrowing his bunk, Greg Wilson's command wire went straight to Vice Admiral Bill McRaven at the Joint Special Operations Command. From JSOC, by one remove, Wilson's orders came from National Command Authority—the Joint Chiefs of Staff and the president.

The situation was deteriorating. A day into the hostage taking, Captain Phillips had taken a chance and tried to swim away—but was recaptured by the pirates. On the morning of the eleventh, pirates had fired shots at a frigate, the USS *Halyburton*.

As the winds and seas picked up, negotiators aboard *Bainbridge* persuaded the pirates to accept a towline from *Bainbridge*. The SEALs waited. Almost two days passed before a decision came down from President Obama, and when it did it was excruciatingly vague. The SEALs and the crew of *Bainbridge* were authorized to take action if they deemed that the hostage's life was in immediate danger. It was a political shrug. Succeed, and you'll be heroes. Mess up, and we'll disavow that you were given any orders to act.

The SEALs kept the lifeboat under constant twenty-four-hour surveillance with video and thermal imagery. In the intel feed from the boat they were identified as Alpha, Bravo, Charlie, and Delta. Subject Charlie—the pirate named Nadif—did the most talking. Bravo, Erasto, did the least. Subject Delta, Ghadi, had a high-pitched, nasal voice. He bitched about everything.

The pirates agreed to accept a transfer of food and water, and one of them, Subject Alpha, Abduwali Muse, took the opportunity to come aboard *Bainbridge* to "negotiate." As soon as he was aboard the American destroyer Muse surrendered and started talking to an interpreter and a pair of FBI negotiators. His almost casual surrender had reduced the bad guys' firepower by 25 percent.

The SEALs were able to listen to conversations within the boat by pointing a laser beam at the lifeboat's Plexiglas windows. The pirates' conversations were translated in real time and transcribed on typed sheets. Since Abduwali had gone aboard the destroyer, the pirates became increasingly nervous. The plan was to sweat them, stress them, and it was working. Wilson now hoped it wasn't working too well. He thought the pinch would come at dusk, and it had.

Greg Wilson had deployed SEAL snipers into an aft compartment below *Bainbridge*'s flight deck. During the day they draped a piece of mosquito netting over the inside of a pair of portholes that faced aft, a technique that works remarkably well to prevent a distant eye from seeing in an open window. The sniper cell rotated a shooting pair, one trigger and a spotter, on and off in four-hour shifts. The first few rotations the shooters ran pieces of tubular nylon webbing from shackles on the overhead. Looping the cord around the fore grips of their rifles allowed the snipers to keep their weapons constantly trained on the lifeboat. The snipers were in the TACTAS compartment, a room intended to be the underwater eyes of the ship during antisubmarine warfare; now the compartment looked backward as *Bainbridge* towed a boatload of pirates.

The muzzles of the snipers' weapons were a foot back from the openings, allowing them to observe and cover the lifeboat from air-conditioned comfort. No shooters were visible on the fantail or flight deck. During the day the mosquito netting prevented even a glimpse inside. At night, the pairs rotated, the net was lifted and optical scopes were traded for electronic, low-light aim points.

The snipers' craft and equipment was impressive. The SEALs have no "standard" sniper weapon—no single firearm could perform all the jobs the SEALs are required to do—and the Navy gives individual operators considerable leeway. But there are favorites. One is the Heckler & Koch PSG-2. The weapon is essentially a match-grade version of the German G-2 assault rifle. The PSG-2 is an exceptionally accurate and versatile weapon. It can use five-, ten-, or thirty-round magazines, has provision for fast changes of aiming packages, and has the option of fully automatic fire.

The PSG-2 has earned its spurs with the SEALs, and has served in combat as a precision rifle and antisniper weapon in hundreds of deployments. It was the weapon of choice for the primary shooters in the TACTAS perch. The snipers were loaded with M855 green tip "Predator" cartridges. Unlike ball ammunition, or even conventional hollow points, Predator rounds can be counted on to fly straight and true, even after initial impact. The bullet itself is an aerodynamic masterpiece. A case-hardened steel needle is covered with an aluminum "ogive," a shroud designed to allow the bullet to pass through the outer walls of a vehicle, building, or boat and still retain linear flight—that is, until it hits something soft, where the bullet is designed to spall and do maximum damage.

Predator rounds would allow the snipers to engage targets *inside* the boat.

Every SEAL marksman is paired with a spotter, who is himself a trained and designated sniper. The spotter's job is to provide cover for the primary shooter, work communications, and update firing information. In a fixed hide position, or "stoop," the spotter will usually observe the target with a powerful optical spotting scope. In the TACTAS compartment, the snipers were "screwed in," meaning they had established a fixed, customized shooting stage. Settled in, zeroed out, the snipers came to know by face and body movements each of the men on the lifeboat. They knew them all, and kept a running fix on where in the boat they were at any moment. The lifeboat was thirty feet long and nine feet wide. Three pairs of eyes and three trigger fingers were fixed on it twenty-four hours a day.

The sniper cell was run by Master Chief Mel Hoyle, a huge, shambling bear of a man with a slow walk and a West Virginia drawl. Mel is a twenty-five-year veteran of the SEALs; for nineteen of those years he has been an operator at Six, first as a "door kicker" on an assault team, where he helped to capture Abu Abbas. He was then selected for sniper training with the British Special Air Service. Mel is a prickly, exacting man, with a reputation for telling it like it is; he is also very seldom wrong. Since the jump, Mel had supervised the deployment of the sniper team members, those rotating through the TACTAS room, and a pair on five-minute standby with a Seahawk helicopter aboard USS *Boxer.* Mel and his leading petty officer, John Hall, filled in on all the slots, taking their own turns behind rifle scopes, in addition to standing six-hour desk watches in the TOC. Mel was big, but no one ever saw him eat; as far as his teammates could tell, he ran on caffeine and nicotine. He constantly had a cup of coffee in hand and a dip of Copenhagen snuff packed into his lower lip. In the last five days Mel had racked up maybe ten hours of sleep, most of that on the rolling deck in the TACTAS room.

In the Navy it's said that an officer can never do anything that a chief hasn't already figured out, and as Greg Wilson and Frank Costello came out of their meeting in the stateroom, Mel walked into the TOC. He could read the skipper's face. It was now 17:45, on Easter Sunday, daylight was over, and there would be approximately twenty-four minutes of nautical twilight before full dark.

Mel Hoyle reported that since the surrender of Abduwali Muse the bad guys were prairie dogging, sticking their heads up through the forward hatch and peering over the top of the pilothouse. They'd started to transmit on the bridge-to-bridge radio; channel thirteen crackled with the voice of subject Delta, Ghadi. What he said was largely unintelligible, a couple of words of pissed-off, broken English, and Abduwali's name spoken again and again like a tape loop.

"They want their playmate back," Wilson said.

"They aren't going to get him," Mel said calmly.

Overhead on the command set, the lifeboat was projected on half a dozen monitors from as many angles. Someone was standing in the forward hatch, and shapes, human shapes, flitted by the pilothouse windows. The light was fading quickly, and a layer of high clouds covered the stars. The moon was nearly full, for the last four nights it lit the sea like a parking lot—but tonight it would not rise until 8:00 p.m.

That gave the team two hours of near perfect, murky darkness.

Wilson, Costello, and Mel stood and watched the screens. On one roll, they could see directly into the pilothouse. Two men were standing close to each other, gesticulating, obviously arguing. As they watched one of them scooted out and peered through the back hatch. The head in the bow hatch ducked for a moment, then popped back up.

Wilson said, "How's your view back there?"

"We own them, skipper," Mel said. "We own them."

"The sea state is building. It'll be force three by 2200," Costello said. "The swell's already coming up."

The ship was stable, the swell and the wind were not huge, but they all could occasionally feel the deck rise under their feet. It had been calm for several days, but it would not stay calm forever. Nor was their situation open-ended.

Wilson sat on an edge of the wardroom table and crossed his legs. His hands gripped the edges and he looked at the lifeboat and the positions of the other assets. He'd been awake himself for the best part of a week, living like Mel on caffeine but without the speedy benefits of Copenhagen. Wilson made himself think slowly, burning the position of all his teams into his mind, forming a perfect three-dimensional picture of the lifeboat, the assault boats, the destroyer, the carrier, and the submarine. Wilson was a graduate of the Navy War College and the Naval Postgraduate School. He'd studied Mahan, Groshkov, and von Clausewitz; all of them said it is dangerous, but necessary, to try to predict the actions of an enemy. Greg Wilson had five days of behavior to guide him. Five days of what they did. He'd been applying a steady pressure. It sucked in the lifeboat. He knew that. And he knew that the pirates could not be counted on to remain rational. Nothing could be predicted, but several things could be anticipated.

Wilson put himself in the position of the pirates, now one man down, with night falling. They themselves operated at night, and they knew, too, that the moon would not be up for more than two hours. What would they do?

They were pissed.

Were they pissed enough to kill the hostage?

No. That would be death. These guys didn't want to die. They would if they had to. But they would not bring it on. If they shot the hostage, they knew they would be cut to pieces.

Predicting what an opponent will do is more art than science. Now Greg

Wilson thought of Miyamoto Musashi, a sixteenth-century Japanese samurai who wrote a guide to life and the art of Kendo. The maxims in *The Book of Five Rings* had become old saws in Naval Special Warfare. They had even been taken up by bankers and businessmen, but Wilson didn't allow the late fans to spoil the message. He watched the lifeboat heave in the low-light video. He put himself in the boat. He imagined what they could see on a hazy, dark, moonless night . . . almost nothing. In his head ran a principal axiom of *The Book of Five Rings*: "You must watch both sides without moving your eyes."

Wilson knew he could watch both sides.

The pirates could not.

"We're going to open a window," Wilson said.

A "window" was a set time period where the snipers would be authorized to engage; the "green light" heard so often in action movies.

Wilson looked at Mel Hoyle. The master chief and the captain had known each other almost two decades. They were comrades, but not always friends.

"Can you go three for three?"

"It's eighty feet, Skipper."

"Three at once, Mel. I know the range," Wilson said.

The TOC was silent. The ventilators hummed. Behind the workstations and laptops, technicians and watch officers sat still. Frank Costello crossed his arms. Mel Hoyle, master chief badass, king of snipers, was on the spot. He didn't show it. The big man's lip went up under the walrus mustache. It wasn't as much a smile as a sneer.

"We can get them," he said.

Full dark. In the lifeboat there was only a single light—the small digital numbers on the bridge-to-bridge radio showing the number "13." They cast a small puddle of lime color onto the top of the throttle console, but lit nothing else. Bounded by windows, the lifeboat's pilothouse was less dark than it was under the deck forward, but only because the night outside diluted the perfect blackness. Forward, on the starboard benches, the shadow was opaque and complete—like something solid.

The hostage Richard Phillips was awake now, or maybe just less asleep. He had ignored the arguments throughout the day. It was his policy to stay calm and to move as little as possible. He could not comprehend any of the lisping, sputtering things that were said, but he understood perfectly what was wrong. He knew to a perfect pitch what the feelings were.

When the bow hatch was opened, Phillips had taken pleasure in the smallest stirring of the air. The heat was less now, but it was not pleasant in the boat. The lifeboat had never been anything but a torment. The temperature was bearable only in the small hours in the morning, a few minutes before a damp, clammy cold set in, and then the sun came up and hammered the boat, making it ring inside with implacable heat. He'd counted the passage of time from night to night, telling himself if he made it through the day, the nights would be easy. His captors stayed up all night, watching, listening, they were quiet then, and he could curl up, pricking his ears, too, but unlike the others he could drop off to sleep—hoping for what they feared most.

But tonight was different. Abduwali, the English speaker, was gone. There was tension in the boat; it had flooded in all afternoon, as real as waist-deep bilge water. Phillips had opened his eyes and watched Ghadi yammer into the radio. He was surprised that they did not make him speak on it. Not that they could tell him what to say. Not that they would let him aft of the stanchion. He was kept in the forward starboard bench now, always, ever since he'd dived out the back hatch. They made him stay there, and even when he had to piss they made him piss into one of the bailers. Not that he pissed much. Phillips moved slowly onto his side. In the bow, Erasto had his head through the hatch, standing with legs spread, swaying as the boat rose and fell. Phillips watched him for a while, then stared deliberately at the blank wall. His wrists burned and his ankles were rubbed raw. His hips and legs were stiff and painful. He wanted to stand up, but the time to move safely was over. They were all wired up now and Phillips knew it. At dusk they were always on guard, especially right after sundown and just before dawn. That was when the oldest one prodded everyone awake . . . sometimes even insisting that Phillips himself sit up. It was too late to stand and stretch without causing a commotion. He must stay still now that night was on them. And maybe they would calm down after the moon came up and they could see.

Nadif stood against the back hatch, leaning against the wall, his head just touching the top deck. He was behind the wheel and engine console, three or four feet from the windshield. The orange bow moved up and down, and occasionally right and left as it plowed through the water. Nadif could see the stern of the ship, but not at all well. There were moments when Nadif could hardly see it at all, and though he knew it was there, it was as fleeting as a cloud shadow.

He looked through the back hatch into the sky. A few scattered stars flitted behind the clouds. Nadif knew there were airplanes there. And helicopters; twice they had been flown over and once they had pinned the boat in a blinding light. Nadif was certain they were there, but he could not hear them. Even when he put his head outside the pilothouse and held his head in the lee, he could hear only the wind past his ear, and the steady whisper of water down the sides.

Nadif ducked back inside, and was angry again.

"Who has tracers?" he said.

Neither Erasto or Ghadi moved.

"Give me a clip, idiot," he barked at Ghadi.

The shadow standing next to him thumbed a lever by the trigger guard of his AK-47 and handed over the magazine. In the bow, Phillips heard the click, a hard metal sound in the fiberglass cocoon. He knew they could not see his face, but he watched the two shadows framed against the darkness of the back hatch.

Nadif's face dipped into the small green pool of light behind the radio, and Phillips heard the *clink, clink clink* of bullets being thumbed out of the magazine onto the short plastic tray behind the wheel. Ghadi found one green-tipped bullet, then another. He pulled his own magazine from his rifle, stripped out a pair of cartridges, and replaced them with two tracers. He threaded the mag into the receiver and racked home the bolt.

Now Phillips closed his eyes. They were arguing again, but not furiously. Phillips thought it possible that they were going to shoot him, and he remained perfectly still and silent. If a hand grabbed him and jerked him up, he thought it would be the end. He had several long seconds to remember the sound of the bolt going home. Erasto moved, passing close to him in the darkness, and Phillips heard him climb up on the thwart.

No hand jerked him up. No one pressed a muzzle against his ear and Phillips allowed himself to breathe. *Not now. Not yet.*

Ghadi picked up the radio microphone, pushed the squelch button off and on to attract attention, and droned singsong, quick-linked syllables in Somali, a goblin language. Phillips heard Abduwali's name called repeatedly, but the destroyer did not answer. He turned his head slightly, again looking aft and up toward the hatch. Phillips saw Nadif pull himself up, his silhouette dark against the almost opaque night, and he could see the profile of the AK and its crescent-shaped magazine.

There was a small snick as the safety went down and Nadif steadied himself with one hand. He swung out past the port side window, and aimed the weapon up and forward. The gun went off with a loud metallic crash, and the inside of the boat was lit in a quarter flash, like a brief stroke of lightning.

Out of the front hatch Erasto watched as a single green round of tracer arced up into the sky and curved out over the ship. It arched up into the low, black sky and burned out somewhere to the north, a pale green falling star. The bullet had been aimed to pass by *Bainbridge*'s wheelhouse.

"They have to have seen that," Erasto grunted. "They saw it. Tell them to answer us."

Phillips had no idea what the words were, but they were not frantic; they had been matter of fact.

Nadif remained framed in the hatchway, the gun swinging in one hand. His voice was clipped, tight and angry. "Abduwali is a fucker," he said. "An asshole and a faggot."

Phillips saw Nadif duck back through the hatch, he saw him outlined there, a shadow against darkness.

"Fuck him! Fuck him! The turd!"

In the TOC, reports poured in of a single shot fired. The tracer had been seen and reported by Zorro 1 and 2. The sniper observers aboard *Boxer* rogered, and as the gunshot resonated through the hollow fiberglass shell of the lifeboat it was picked up on the submarine's passive sonar and confirmed verbally on an underwater communications circuit.

As the data came in, Greg Wilson stood focused on the command set. He asked that the ScanEagle rerun the footage showing the shot. Within seconds one of the screen windows rewound, looped, and rambled forward. A single subject came out of the back hatch, raised his rifle, and fired one-handed over the top of the destroyer. Wilson watched as the man swayed outside the hatch, watching the glowing bullet fly off into the sky.

"Bravo," said one of the Twidgets.

"What the hell?" Costello grunted.

"They're trying to signal," Wilson said quietly.

"They got two boxes of flares on the boat. And smoke."

Wilson knew that even if Phillips showed them where the flares were, the Somalis wouldn't know how to use them.

"I'm declaring an imminent threat," Wilson said.

Across the wardroom, Frank Costello nodded. "I concur."

Wilson picked up a Motorola 2600 radio from a charger rack and keyed it.

"Stoop Zero Seven," he said. "This is Tango."

Stoop was the sniper cell's call sign—"zero seven" is the number given to the senior-most enlisted member of a unit. Stoop Zero Seven was Mel Hoyle's personal handle.

Hoyle was now back in the TACTAS compartment. He had made room for himself on the bench, wedged between the primary shooting pair and the additional spotter. His eye was pressed to an MO-4 night sight, a compact 4X power digital scope. In it, he had the pilothouse framed. The MO-4 rendered the night into a light green day, the colors muted, but still discernable as reds, blues, and tans. The lifeboat was a dark green-orange, the foam sputtering from under its bow a pale crème de menthe. Mel could see faces through the pilothouse windows and he could see that they were clean-shaven. He could tell that they were holding rifles.

Mel pressed the send button. "Go Tango."

"Send your traffic."

"Two, armed, pilothouse. One, armed, periodic, bow hatch. No cargo."

A terse, emotionless statement of the target. Two bad guys visible through the windows, one popping in and out of the bow hatch. No sign of the hostage.

Wilson's voice came again in his earpiece: "Are you getting flushes?"

All three shooters, visible, were a flush. Two was a deuce, one was a loner.

"Affirmative."

"Stand by. We're going to open a window in approximately zero five mikes."

"Copy, zero five mikes."

In the TACTAS room, there was a communal exhalation. After nearly four days of waiting and watching, now would come a shot. Or maybe not. It was time to turn on the Zen. Behind the primary weapon, Mike Buckwalter twisted the gain switch on his MO-4. He centered the small white cross on the starboard pilothouse windshield. There was no moonlight to reflect off the glass, none at all, and when the bow of the lifeboat was down, he could plainly see the head and shoulders of two men. One wore a T-shirt. One wore a light-colored checked number with a tattered collar. Bravo and Charlie.

Buck looked over at Doug MacQuarrie, his spotter, and across his back to Mel, his boss. The third spotter, Bubba Holland, was opening the bipod on his PS2, folding it down, checking the magazine and chambering a round. When Mel entered the compartment he ordered all three shooters to pick a target. He'd said nothing else, except for them to "make a hole" for him on the platform.

Mel in their mix and the skipper on the tactical net. Everyone knew a shot was likely to come. They'd seen the tracer, and heard the radio traffic. They were on hide, in the stoop, and they didn't ask questions. They would often go the entire four-hour shift without speaking. Their heads were down range, their minds focused on perfection. They listened, and they aimed.

In the darkness, a jade-green circle of light was projected onto Mel's cheek. He wore no expression that anyone could name; it was his shooting face. The platform groaned as the ship rolled. There was almost a half ton of men, sensors, radios, and weapons on it. Buck and Doug were positioned behind the starboard, outboard bung, two muzzles down range, and Bubba behind the port side opening, inboard. Mel was positioned slightly behind Bubba, his weapon was hanging behind them on one of the reels—the match-grade M-14 he shot each year at the nationals. Mel was holding his spotting scope up on his crooked elbow, steadying it with his left hand clutching his right wrist. The shooters pulled their weapons into the hollows of their shoulders, tucking them firmly. They were all still physically, and now they went through the rituals of quieting their breath.

It was not time to go on line. Not yet. They all knew the window might never open. They all knew there might not be a shot at all. Not tonight, or not ever. Dealing with the now is what they had to do. They would not anticipate orders, and they would not be frustrated when orders failed to come. The snipers held their weapons in an easy ready; they watched and they waited at cool zero.

In the greenroom on USS *Boxer,* the standby snipers comprising Stoop Zero Three, Frank Bracken and Sean O'Hallaran, pulled their armor over their heads and quickly fastened the buckles, snaps, and Velcro that held together their kit. Both pushed earpieces into their ears, pulled on their helmets, and snapped down their night vision goggles. They stepped onto the blackness of the flight deck, led by a yellow shirt toward the gray SH-60 helicopter turning up on spot two. It was go time.

For three days, Bracken and O'Hallaran had been on five-minute standby. Geared up, they squatted on a single nylon cot in the ten-by-twenty-foot room adjoining *Boxer*'s flight deck. Their meals were brought up, and their coffee; one of them always on the radio, one always rogering the communications checks, keeping an ear to the tactical frequency and the separate sniper's net. For three days the Scan Eagle Feed came over a black laptop perched on O'Hallaran's pack—every inch of the lifeboat, every curve, every nook, and blind spot was burned into their brains. Now the laptop, the live-action feed, was snapped closed and stuffed into a day pack. They snatched up their rifles and jogged toward the helicopter.

When the call came in for shots fired, Stoop Three "stood up," went on line, and in five minutes they were expected to be in their helo, airborne and covering the approach of the high-speed assault boats. The SEALs called this "going from stupor to trooper." Their job now was to cover the approach of the high-speed boats—provide sniper cover hanging out the doors of a moving helicopter, at night, shooting with night vision goggles.

After the close, airless greenroom, being out on the flight deck was like having the whole world yawn open. They peered around with their night vision goggles; the green steel of the compartment was now replaced by the vast digital green of night.

Bracken, the designated spotter, carried a match-grade M-14 rifle with both an MO-4 and a laser bolted on. O'Hallaran's load was no lighter; he carried a full-stocked PS2 with a heavy sound suppressor, the same MO-4 and a day pack containing ten PS2 and M-14 magazines of 7.62 ammo: tracer, armor piercing, armor piercing incendiary, predator, and depleted uranium rounds. The full load.

The yellow shirt led them all the way to the door. As they crawled into the Seahawk, there was the high whine of turbines and the rotors began to swing round. Bracken snapped his climbing harness and carabiner into a deck ring on the port side, O'Hallaran on the starboard side behind the pilot. From the cockpit, a goggled, insectlike head clicked around. O'Hallaran snapped into the internal communications jack and keyed his mike.

"We're good," he said.

The pilot gave a thumbs-up, the Seahawk roared, and jet exhaust gusted heat and the smell of kerosene through the open door. The helicopter lifted off.

O'Hallaran saw the *Boxer*'s superstructure and deck sink down below, then angle away as the helo turned sharply left. The green-black sea flashed under them. O'Hallaran checked his harness, checked his magazine, and switched on the MO-4. The wind through the open door rippled his flight suit and his legs were pushed back as the helicopter gathered speed.

On the tactical net he heard the beep of the code sinks, then the voice of Mike Geiger, the HSAC commander.

"Sea Fox six and eight, inbound on pattern three."

Pattern three was a racetrack course that would bring the high-speed assault boats in a wide loop a mile astern of the lifeboat. The Sea Foxes were moving, and the whole big contraption was springing to life. O'Hallaran knew where to look, and he knew what to look for, but he could not see the HSACs. Painted in long gray stripes, low and deadly, they were designed *not* to be seen, their sloped sides and reversed bows made them look like waves, not boats. O'Hallaran pointed his lenses into the dense night behind the carrier and stared. He was supposed to shadow the high-speed boats toward the targets and now he couldn't even see them. *Jesus,* he thought, *what's the use of having invisible boats?* The sea and sky were merged at the horizon like a smudge. Down there somewhere were twelve SEAL assaulters in two HSACs doing forty knots.

Where?

Finally, a flicker of gray lunged across the *Boxer*'s broad, pale wake. It was followed by another, the shadow of a shadow, deadly things as narrow as ghosts.

O'Hallaran keyed his microphone: "Stoop Zero three is inbound with Sea Fox package."

The TOC answered, calm and serene, like they could see everything: "All units, Tango actual, window will open at 1905. Standby to go hot."

Wilson was opening a window for action. Aboard *Bainbridge,* Mel's sniper cell would engage the targets and take out the bad guys. The high-speed assault craft, covered by the helo-borne snipers, would assault the lifeboat, engage any surviving bad guys and liberate the hostage. The outcome depended on a thousand things going right and nothing going wrong.

In the TOC, Greg Wilson could see everything; everything except what he needed to see most—inside the lifeboat. The *Bainbridge*'s own flight deck cameras were low-light capable and pointed aft. They covered the boat perfectly, but they could not see through the decks. *Bainbridge*'s cameras were one of half a dozen video-feed windows on the command display. Launched from the USS *Boxer,* a ScanEagle drone churned out a circular flight plan covering the entire area. Its low-light cameras pinned the lifeboat from the west, and directly overhead at 20,000 feet, a PC-3 Orion patrol plane did a ten-mile-wide orbit over the ships.

On the command screens, the lifeboat was towing eighty feet behind *Bainbridge,* their plot symbols touching. To the right, the east, *Boxer* ghosted along on a parallel course, three miles to starboard. The Sea Fox package, two stealth boats with the wave-skimming Seahawk close behind, were making a broad, clockwise turn to come in perpendicular to the lifeboat.

The job of the Sea Foxes was to intercept the lifeboat without crossing behind it and fouling Mel's fields of fire.

Mel's shots would have to be magic, and the Sea Fox package would have to work some sorcery of their own. They had to make their approach unseen, timing it based on a guess. They couldn't get closer than a quarter of a mile until Mel's guys shot. And once the snipers went hot, the assault teams of Sea Fox had to instantly assault and board the lifeboat to prevent any surviving pirates from shooting Phillips in cold blood.

Wilson watched a trio of blips heading obliquely away from the *Boxer*; the helicopter and the HSACs. Invisible even to *Bainbridge*'s radar, the assault boats' position was revealed only because they transmitted an identification code on the Naval Tactical Data System. The only platform that could actually detect the boats was the submarine, which could track the high-speed scream of their titanium propellers. The blips came on, the helicopter trailing.

At one of the stations in the TOC, Greg Wilson rolled a trackball across the data display, triggering a time/speed/distance logarithm. At forty knots, forty-six miles an hour, on pattern three, it was three minutes and fifty seconds until the HSACs intersected the target. Moore saw the trackball wipe over the screen, and he heard the voice of the operations officer.

"Three minutes out."

"Notify *Bainbridge*."

One of the Twidgets contacted *Bainbridge*'s combat information center, "Be advised, Sea Fox package is three minutes out."

It was Frank Costello's voice that answered back from the destroyer, "*Bainbridge* copies."

There were maybe thirty seconds of tense silence.

The blips representing the boats were two circles, the symbol for the trailing helicopter was a half rectangle overlaid with a "T." The symbols blinked slowly, overlapping as they moved forward. Now they were two and half miles from the boat.

In the TACTAS room, Mel and his shooters were ready. In the TOC, Wilson stared at the command screens, making sure he saw everything correctly. The boats and helicopters were converging.

In an opaque night, three bad guys and a hostage heaved up and down in a closed lifeboat. Would they hear the helicopter? Would they see the HSACs coming?

"Alert Stoop Zero Seven, window is open," Wilson said. "Sea Fox package continue to phase line Alpha."

The orders were passed.

Wilson had authorized Mel to fire when he had the shot. All three at once, or nothing at all.

Now it was a roll of the dice.

In the TACTAS compartment, the earphones all hissed together. On the shooting platform, Mel put his legs apart, lifting them up and over the calves of the shooters to his right and left. The four men sprawled together, looking out of the two ports, their legs locked like teenagers watching a horror movie on TV.

Mel acknowledged the open window on the tactical net, and then said quietly to the men next to him, "Hold and track, I will initiate."

"Check."

"Check."

"Check."

Mel then keyed the sniper's net. "Stoop Zero Three, track and hold. You are red-light."

O'Hallaran's voice came over the radio, buffeted by the wind through the open helicopter door. "Stop Zero Three, track and hold. We are red-light."

Mel stared at the boat through his MO-4. He wasn't going to shoot, he was going to call the shots. Green on green—he could see a pair of heads in the pilothouse. T-shirt and collared shirt. Mel pressed his shins down on the calves to his right and left.

"Who has?" Mel intoned.

"Bravo has," Buckwalter said.

"Charlie has," whispered MacQuarrie.

There was a pause, a deliberate, purposed interval of silence and Bubba Holland said, "No joy."

It was the ritual language of surveillance and snipers. Their plaint and plainsong, part update, part incantation. Each of the shooters had a target. Each a specific kill. Subjects Bravo and Charlie were in the pilothouse, one on the starboard side, the other on the port. They were Buck's and Doug's. No matter where they went on the boat, no matter what hole they popped out of. They were tagged. They were visible head and shoulders through the windshield. They were *had.*

Bubba strained his eye against the green disk of his sight. There was nothing in the bow hatch. He could not see Delta.

Seconds passed like days.

Mel kept his eye on the spotting scope. The bow hatch was open, but there was no silhouette in it. Delta was not to be seen.

He watched, they all watched. Seconds ticked. The lifeboat heaved up and down as it breasted the swells. Mel knew, they all knew, that the Sea Fox package was coming, and with it, a great clamoring, jet-powered helicopter. The bad guys were jacked up and had been shooting off rounds. They wanted their friend back. If they heard a helicopter, or saw the boats . . .

Mel pressed his legs apart, renewing contact, touch, with his shooters.

"Who has?"

"Bravo has."

"Charlie has."

Then Bubba Holland said firmly, "Delta has."

Mel saw them all, locked them all in his eyes, and as he opened his mouth the lifeboat lurched over the top of a cross swell and wallowed sharply. The towline jerked taught and above them it gave an audible twang.

The heads in the pilothouse disappeared.

The words strangled off in Mel's throat.

"No joy!"

"Nada."

The bow of the lifeboat went deep and then bobbed up nearly vertically. Still square in the hatch, Delta pitched forward, bent at his waist. Holding his rifle in one hand, the other sprawled out, fingers clutching at the bow cleat, Erasto managed barely to keep upright. Now he was visible, objective Delta, but in the pilothouse the other heads vanished.

Half a minute passed, an eternity.

"Who has?"

"_______"

"_______"

Only Bubba whispered: "Delta has."

A vile string of blasphemy unspooled in Mel's head. No one on the planet can string obscenity like a master chief petty officer in the United States Navy. But nothing came out of his mouth, not a sound.

Mel glanced to the left, outside of the light of his scope. He looked east, to the place in which the moon would eventually rise. It was gray-black darkness. Mel saw nothing, but he knew two HSACs were ripping toward them. He knew they were trailed by a Seahawk helicopter flying not higher than six feet off the water. He prayed a sinner's prayer: *Don't let them be seen,* and then, *Please God, please, don't let me fuck this up.*

The lifeboat wallowed and then lifted its bow like a horse that had stumbled. Out of the bow hatch Erasto was still fully visible. He turned around, back turned toward the ship, looking back at the pilothouse windows. Behind the lifeboat's windscreen, one head came up. Then another.

Mel had his scope zoomed on the bow. He could see Delta's face so clearly he could see that his pupils were dilated. Erasto was staring into the night, gawking after shadows, his eyes cranked open to maximum. Two silhouettes in the pilothouse. Just two.

Then, Mel saw Delta jerk to his right. He saw Erasto lift his hand and point off to the east, point away from the destroyer's starboard quarter. Mel tried to force away the thought that they had seen the HSACs, or that they had heard or seen the helicopter.

There was no time anymore, no seconds or minutes, everything was slow, moving as it does when the slack is taken out of a trigger, when the weapon is against your shoulder and you've done everything to stalk and aim and it comes down to an even, straight pull.

Delta was lifting his AK-47. He had a hand on the pistol grip and his fingers were closing over the forestock. Delta was aiming at something off the right side of the lifeboat. Behind the windshield the two shadows moved together, both of them now on the starboard side, one slightly in front of the other.

Mel kept his voice dead flat and even; his breath automatically controlled. Delta was aiming his rifle, but it did not matter, Mel and his boys were at cool zero.

"Who has?"

"Bravo has."

"Charlie has."

"Delta has."

They were flush. Mel keyed the microphone and said over the tactical net: "Fire."

Three bullets. Three kills. It was over. The pirates who had taken *Maersk Alabama* were dead, and Captain Richard Phillips was free.

BIN LADEN'S ROAD TO ABBOTTABAD

THE DAY THE WORLD CHANGED

SEPTEMBER 11, 2001

AT 8:46 A.M., ON THE MORNING OF September 11, 2001, American Airlines Flight 11 tore through the ninety-third floor of the World Trade Center's building number one. There was not a cloud in the sky, and not one person in America's counterterrorism apparatus, no one from the FBI director to the newest field agent, no one from the CIA director to the first tour case officer, analyst, or technician, *no one* thought it could be an accident.

From the first terrible instant of the 9/11 attacks American intelligence agencies knew that they had been had.

In the weeks and months prior to 9/11, the FBI and CIA had received and processed dozens of explicit warnings—these included both raw reports from officers and assets in the field, as well as polished memoranda and white papers from foreign intelligence services. Some warned of a general attack, others stated specifically that Osama bin Laden and Al Qaeda intended to crash hijacked airliners into American targets.

But all these reports, both foreign and domestic, were ignored.

The information had filtered up through the ossified bureaucracies of two equally dysfunctional organizations. This intelligence crossed the same gray, government-issued desks at both the CIA and FBI. At both places, officers and analysts had their workspaces arranged into cubicle plantations where one anonymous, vindictive, or lazy person could derail an investigation, kill a lead, or spike a report. At the CIA, especially, such lethal office politics had been raised to an art form. And things were nearly as bad at the FBI, where a newly appointed director had surrounded himself with careerist survivors marking time until retirement.

No one who lived through 9/11 will ever forget where they were, what they were doing, or what they felt when they heard the news. The entire country ground to a halt under a staggering series of blows. It was an epoch-changing moment—one of the darkest in American history. The bloody hijackings, the crashes, the fires, the senseless deaths, the constant dread that even worse was to come, made the events all seem like a blur. Even now, America struggles with a sort of posttraumatic shock about 9/11.

There was chaos on the streets of Manhattan, and fear in the power corridors of Washington, D.C.

But America's day of heroism and sorrow was only beginning.

At 9:37 a.m., a third set of hijackers flew American Airlines Flight 77 into the Pentagon, killing all aboard and 137 people on the ground, most of them civilians.

Five minutes before 10:00 a.m., passengers aboard the fourth hijacked airliner, United Airlines Flight 93, rose against the men who intended to murder them. After a protracted and bloody struggle, passengers used a drink cart to batter their way into the cockpit. As these brave men and women fought terrorists for control of the aircraft, the 767 rolled onto its back, went into a dive, and crashed into a field outside of Shanksville, Pennsylvania.

The fifty-one passengers and crew aboard Flight 93 had proven that they, like New York's brave firemen and police officers, were willing to sacrifice themselves for people that they had never met. The selfless bravery of these average Americans saved the lives of hundreds, if not thousands of additional victims. It is believed that Flight 93's intended target was the Capitol building in Washington, D.C.

In Florida, President Bush returned by motorcade to Air Force One, then parked on a secured taxiway at the Sarasota airport. Using wartime emergency departure protocols, Air Force One rocketed quickly to 45,000 feet and began a meandering cross-country trip that would take the commander in chief across fourteen states and parts of the Gulf of Mexico, only returning to Washington eight hours after every other aircraft flying over the United States had been forced to land.

September 11 was the most catastrophic intelligence failure in America's history. For both the CIA and FBI, a series of small, almost inconsequential mistakes in analysis, investigation, and intelligence collection melded together. The systems were broken. But the major malfunctions were at the top.

On the morning of September 11, 2001, CIA director George Tenet stood at the windows of his seventh-floor office and watched the cloud of smoke rising from the wreckage of the Pentagon, a mere ten miles away. Tenet had come to the directorship of the CIA after the abrupt resignation of John Deutch in December 1996. Tenet, a political appointee, had zero field experience; he had drifted into intelligence by working as a senator's assistant. After serving on President Bill Clinton's National Security Transition Team, Tenet found himself appointed first to the National Security Council, and then, after two years as deputy director of the CIA, he became DCI, director of Central Intelligence. His career at the CIA was marked by miscalculations, mistakes, and staggering screwups.

In 1998, Tenet's CIA had failed to prevent twin truck bomb attacks on the American embassies in Tanzania and Kenya. On May 7, 1999, during the Kosovo war, CIA-provided targeting data put five precision-guided JDAM bombs through the roof of the Chinese embassy in Belgrade, Yugoslavia. Three Chinese diplomats were killed and more than a dozen people were wounded. On January 3, 2003, CIA officers in Yemen were clueless about a suicide bomb attempt against the American destroyer USS *The Sullivans.* In a farcical comedy of errors, Al Qaeda's first plot failed when their speedboat, overloaded with explosives, sank in the harbor. CIA's boots on the ground in Yemen were so oblivious that Osama bin Laden's operatives were able to salvage the explosives and use them nine months later in a successful attack against the USS *Cole.*

But Tenet's CIA had even more breathtaking acts of incompetence left in it.

Twenty-four months after the African embassy bombings, Tenet had presided over another catastrophic failure of intelligence, his sixth. Manhattan was in flames, the Pentagon was burning, American airliners were falling out of the sky—but whatever else he did that morning, George Tenet managed to cover his backside and hang on to his job.

He was nothing if not a survivor.

Across town, at FBI headquarters on Pennsylvania Avenue, Director Robert Mueller watched on CNN as the south tower fell. Like his archrival across the Potomac, Mueller was shocked to discover that his agency, too, had presided over an intelligence disaster of the first order.

If Tenet was a creature of Democratic party politics, Robert Mueller proved that incompetence was a bipartisan thing. Mueller shared with Tenet a résumé that was long on political connections and spotty on basic skill. Mueller was a Republican Beltway insider with no prior experience in either counterintelligence or basic law enforcement. Mueller had been at his job for less than a week when 9/11 struck, and it might be argued that he was less culpable for the failure of his agency to predict or prevent the attacks.

One could try to make that point, but the FBI, too, had ignored a litany of detailed warnings.

When Mueller called a meeting of FBI deputy directors that morning, he was sickened to discover that for the last year and a half, FBI headquarters had disregarded repeated entreaties from field agents warning, *specifically,* that airborne terror attacks were being planned.

Within a half hour of the first impact, the CIA and FBI began dueling exercises in damage control. Incredibly, both Mueller and Tenet would manage to burrow deep into the carpet and hold on to their jobs. But there was plenty of blame to go around.

Following the attacks, Condoleezza Rice said, "I don't think anybody could have predicted that . . . they would try to use an airplane as a missile, a hijacked airplane as a missile."

She knew, or should have known, that the threat was real. Warnings that Al Qaeda might use passenger airliners to attack ground targets came as early as 1999. These were written predictions, and they were unambiguous. A report prepared by the National Intelligence Council stated explicitly: "Suicide bombers belonging to al-Qaida's Martyrdom Battalion [sic] could crash-land an aircraft packed with high explosives into the Pentagon, the headquarters of the Central Intelligence Agency or the White House."

Intelligence doesn't usually get much more specific than that.

Five months before 9/11, the National Intelligence Council had named the attackers, and also listed the targets and means of attack.

The inability of the American government to predict or prevent the attacks of 9/11 was not a failure of intelligence collection, but was the result of egregious failures in leadership and analysis.

The events of 9/11 revealed that the upper echelons of the FBI and CIA were paralyzed by cronyism, political correctness, and staggering incompetence. On the seventh floor, it didn't matter what you knew, or even if you knew what you were doing—what mattered was whom you knew in elected office. Senior positions in both agencies were passed out as political plums. Added to this "close to the boss" attitude was a poisonous culture of middle management. Both organizations had surrendered daily operations to a cadre of bureaucrats, who waged intramural combat with memos, performance reviews, and budget documents. New ideas were promptly stepped on. Innovations were referred to committee and quietly smothered. Special agents and intelligence officers who did not knuckle under were reassigned or transferred out.

Before 9/11, the FBI and CIA seemed to exist in some kind of parallel universe. Some of their gaffes—both at the top and in the middle—were so grotesquely unprofessional that it is hard to understand how such people ever managed to find employment in the first place—much less earn and maintain a security clearance.

In the period between 1999 and 2001, the FBI and CIA picked up literally hundreds of detailed, specific warnings that Al Qaeda was planning an airborne attack. In 1999, the FBI learned that Ihab Mohammed Ali Nawawi, a participant in the 1998 embassy bombings in Africa, had been sent for pilot training in Oklahoma. In September 2000, federal prosecutors revealed to a grand jury that an associate of Ali's had attended a meeting as early as 1993 where Al Qaeda members discussed Western air traffic control procedures, with the intent of obscuring the movements of hijacked passenger planes. On July 10, 2001, eight weeks before the 9/11 attack, Special Agent Kenneth Williams cabled FBI headquarters from the Phoenix field office. He did not mince his words: "The purpose of this communication is to advise the bureau and New York of the possibility of a coordinated effort by Osama bin Laden to send students to the United States to attend civil aviation universities and colleges."

Williams's message continues, and recommends a half-dozen courses of action that would have put the 9/11 hijackers out of business. It landed on a desk at FBI headquarters and was ignored.

Almost by accident, FBI agents did arrest one of Al Qaeda's 9/11 hijackers. Zacarias Moussaoui was picked up on an immigration violation after he had told an incredulous flight instructor that he was interested in piloting only large passenger aircraft, and that he didn't need to learn how to take off or land—only to fly.

Moussaoui was taken into custody, but FBI headquarters refused seventy requests from field agents to authorize examination of his laptop computer or search his apartment. The FBI agent in charge of the investigation, Colleen Rowley, correctly named Zacarias Moussaoui as a handpicked member of an Al Qaeda hijacking team. In her repeated memos, Rowley stated that Moussaoui was in contact with people targeting buildings in New York City.

Her messages, too, were ignored by FBI headquarters.

For her efforts, Ms. Rowley was booted out of the FBI thirty-six months after 9/11. Hounded by her former organization, she was forced to invoke federal whistleblower protection status to shield both herself and her family.

But it wasn't necessary to read top secret message traffic to predict an airborne terrorist attack against the United States. All anyone had to do was open a newspaper. On the night of September 11, 1994, Frank Eugene Corder stole a Cessna 150 from Aldino Airport in Maryland. Though monitored by radars at Andrews Air Force Base and D.C.'s National Airport, Corder managed to penetrate controlled airspace and fly around the Washington Monument. Over Pennsylvania Avenue, Corder switched off his engine, conducted a "dead stick" approach, and smashed his airplane into the front of the White House. The burning wreckage came to rest two stories below President Clinton's bathroom window.

The first family was not in the White House at the time, and Corder's light plane did little damage, but he had succeeded. Seven years to the day before the 9/11 attacks, the civilian airplane was validated as a weapons system.

If conclusions might not have been drawn from the suicide attack on the White House or the National Intelligence Council report, warning might have been gleaned from classified exercises conducted by the U.S. military. Throughout the eighties and nineties SEAL Team Six demonstrated that airliners could be commandeered in flight and their autopilots used to program crashes into specific targets. After setting the flight controls SEALs parachuted from the aircraft. Besides proving that this threat was real, these operations confirmed that even non-martyrdom hijackers could use airliners as a weapon.

Following 9/11, two myths have persisted: the first is that the airline suicide attacks were an Al Qaeda innovation. This is patently false. The controlled flight of civilian aircraft into an important target had already succeeded, and that target had been the White House.

The second fiction perpetuated after 9/11 was that suicide hijacking could not have been prevented, because no one perceived that such a threat existed. This, too, is nonsense.

There was no failure to anticipate the 9/11 attacks. A blue-ribbon intelligence committee had stated specifically that Osama bin Laden and Al Qaeda were likely to carry out an attack using hijacked airplanes as weapons. That global transportation systems and airline passengers remained open to terrorist exploitation was a failure of policy makers and elected officials who ignored, disregarded, or failed to grasp the deadly serious nature of the threat.

The only people who weren't paying attention were the ones at the top.

RICH KID

MARCH 1957–DECEMBER 1979

OSAMA BIN LADEN WAS BORN on March 10, 1957, the son of Saudi millionaire Mohammed bin Laden and Hamida Ghanem, a woman who was in bonded service to the Bin Laden family. When Sauda Arabia finally outlawed all forms of slavery in 1962, Osama became a full-fledged Bin Laden son. In 1967, when he was just ten years old, two events occurred that would shape the terrorist leader. The first was personal: His father was killed in an airplane crash. This brought Osama and his mother closer to the bosom of the Bin Laden family in Jeddah, where his eldest brother, Salem bin Laden, enrolled Osama in the al Thagher Model School, where a core component of the curriculum was compulsory Islamic studies. The other event that was to shape him irrevocably was the 1967 Arab-Israeli War.

The 1967 Arab-Israeli war had been an unmitigated disaster for the Egyptian and Syrian people, and the war in 1973 was hardly an unalloyed success. Though Arab military dictators managed to hold on to power and muzzle dissent, the Arab people seethed.

The military defeats handed out by Israel in 1967 loomed on the Arab world's geographical and intellectual horizons. In addition to the loss of tens of thousands of troops and hundreds of millions of dollars in military hardware, the Arab countries of the region were swamped with refugees. Wherever the Israelis advanced, Palestinian civilians ran away. More than a million noncombatants fled the rampaging Israeli army and crowded into squalid camps in Syria, Jordan, and Lebanon. There, they strained resources to the breaking point.

As Osama entered puberty, hatred for Israel and fear of its military might were pervasive. When the smoke cleared, Arab politicians, students, and religious scholars were left to ponder: How could this have happened? Following the Arab defeats in 1967, voices were heard in the mosques saying that the root cause of the disaster was not military buffoonery, but the will of God. The Arab nations had been defeated because they had turned their back on Islam. This message began to gain intellectual traction—even as Syria, Iraq, and Egypt cracked down on religious dissenters.

Members of the Muslim Brotherhood preached that the Arabs had been beaten because of the treachery of Israel and the military support of the United States. They believed that the Muslim people were being chastised by God, because they had turned away from the one true faith. They believed the only way to destroy the nation of Israel was for the Arab people to unite under a Muslim government. These fundamentalists asserted, like the godless Marxists before them, that violence was the only legitimate means of social change. Their creed was absolutist. The only way to bring peace and justice to the world was for mankind to accept Islam, both as a religion and as a unifying world government. To those young Muslim men who wanted payback for years of Arab humiliation, this call to holy war was irresistible.

At al Thagher, Osama came in contact with Jihadi philosophy through one of his teachers, a religious refugee from Syria. Osama bin Laden was an unlikely revolutionary. He'd lost his father as a young boy, but had grown up without ever tasting want or recognizing the injustices that made his family's wealth possible. He was a child of privilege who could buy whatever he wanted, live the way he wished, and use the family airplane whenever he felt like it. He was religious, but not a fanatic. He had a pretty good life.

Neither Osama bin Laden's stepfather nor his mother were overtly pious. It is not likely that he heard either hatred or bigotry at home. Friends and family members have both stated that in the course of his studies at al Thagher, Osama became increasingly religious. By age fourteen, Osama had set a goal for himself to become a *hafiz,* a person who has memorized the entire Koran. It's doubtful if he ever finished. But he became part of a small clique of students who were zealous in prayer and talked about the Koran late into the night.

Osama often wore wrinkled clothing, in imitation, he thought, of the Prophet Muhammad. He grew a wispy beard and quit wearing shorts to soccer practice because he considered short pants to be un-Islamic. Across the globe, in the United States, certain groups of college students just as firmly embraced Christianity. They witnessed on street corners and also affected the laid-back manner of their own prophet, Jesus Christ. In America, these students were fondly referred to as "Jesus freaks." Religious students in Saudi Arabia didn't have a nickname. Saudi Arabia is a profoundly religious country, and to find that some of its students were fervently devoted to Islam was a surprise to no one. Osama bin Laden was a long way from wishing harm on anyone and even further from espousing violence.

When Osama was sixteen, he married his first cousin, Najwa Ghanem. He was still in high school; she was fourteen. They had known each other all of their lives. The young couple settled into a small apartment in his mother's home just off the Jeddah highway and started to build a life together. That they were teenagers was unremarkable. It was not unusual for upper-class Saudis to marry young. Osama's own mother had given birth to him when she was just fifteen.

Unlike many of his brothers and sisters, Osama chose not to attend university abroad. Though he had been a mediocre student, his wealth would have bought admission at any university he chose—several Bin Ladens have attended first-rate American universities, including Harvard. Osama's decision to attend King Abdul Aziz University in Jeddah was based not so much on a loathing of the West, but on a desire to remain close to his family.

At university, Osama studied business administration. When he did go to class, he was driven in a chauffeured Mercedes-Benz. He traveled frequently to visit his mother's village in Syria, and also occasionally to Beirut. Accompanied by other young Saudi millionaires, Osama would hunt big game in Africa, keep an aerie of expensive falcons, and find time to climb mountains in Turkey. Although his Islamic beliefs were firm, Osama was not didactic. He had yet to show the almost masochistic avoidance of luxury that he would exhibit in his thirties and forties. He spent money on himself and others. He was an excellent horseman and owned a ranch south of Jeddah.

While at al Thagher, Osama continued his fascination with the ideas of Islamic fundamentalists, notably those of the Muslim Brotherhood, and a curious scholar-poet turned revolutionary, Sayyid Qutb.

So powerful were these ideas that they would change Osama bin Laden from the underachieving son of a Saudi millionaire, to the most feared terrorist on Earth.

LEARNING TO HATE

IN 1977, OSAMA BECAME A FATHER. His wife, Najwa, was fifteen years old and the birth of their son, Abdulla, was a source of joy to them both. Osama attended classes at Abdul Aziz University, played with his son, and lived on a stipend from his family.

Oil money continued to pour into Saudi Arabia. The price of Saudi crude oil leapt sixfold after the Arab oil embargo in the early seventies. Petroleum revenues for the kingdom were $4.5 billion in 1973; in 1981 they totaled almost $102 billion. With the petro-dollars came big-ticket construction projects, and the Saudi Bin Laden Group continued to expand.

Inundated with cash, the Saudi monarchy jetted around the world, dropping millions in casinos and living a stratospheric high life. The boozy hijinks of Saudi princes became legendary. King Faisal made known his displeasure, commenting that, "In one generation we went from riding camels to driving Cadillacs." His majesty did his best to curb the worst excesses of the Saudi princes, but he had little effect on the jet-setting royal progeny.

Faisal bin Musaid was a nephew of the king who had been sent abroad to study political science. At the University of Colorado, he lived a beatnik life, drinking and womanizing. In Boulder, Colorado, Musaid was arrested for drug possession, and pleaded guilty to conspiring to sell LSD. He dropped out of the University of Colorado, turned up briefly at UC Berkeley, flunked out, and wafted back to Saudi Arabia and a frosty royal reception.

In 1965, Musaid's brother was shot and killed by Saudi riot police during a protest against a television studio in Riyadh. The protesters were religious fundamentalists who feared that television was undermining the faith of Islam. For ten years, Faisal bin Musaid held a smoldering grudge for his brother's death.

In 1970, he added religion to a deadly mix of alcohol and pills, and on March 25, 1975, Musaid decided to strike a blow to both avenge his brother and cleanse the Islamic faith. Musaid slipped into a royal reception, produced a .38 caliber pistol, and fired three shots at King Faisal. The King's bodyguard pounced on Musaid and the mortally wounded King was rushed to Central Hospital in Riyadh. He died hours later of his wounds.

The kingdom was in shock. The Bin Laden family had built its wealth and its construction empire on the patronage of King Faisal. In a country where construction projects were awarded on the basis of royal favor, it was left to Salem bin Laden to forge a new relationship with Crown Prince Fahd, who would soon assume duties as the monarch of Saudi Arabia.

By the time King Faisal was assassinated, Osama bin Laden was a fully admitted member of the Muslim Brotherhood. He was neither a well-read Islamic scholar nor a keen student of politics, but he accepted the political line of the Muslim Brotherhood, which held that the only legitimate governments were those based firmly on Islamic precepts. Members of the Muslim Brotherhood were Salafists, meaning that they closely adhered to the manners and customs of the prophet Muhammad's earliest companions.

Salafi Muslims seek also to reestablish the caliphate—that is, Islamic domination of all the lands from Spain to China occupied at the high point of the Muslim conquest. Osama embraced the concept of the new caliphate, but was ambiguous about who should rule the Muslim world. The fortunes of the Bin Laden family, and Osama's monthly stipend, were inextricably tied to the fortunes of the Saudi monarchy. Muslim Brother or not, Osama saw the assassination, as did the world, as the act of a lunatic. Osama did not condone regicide, or the overthrow of the Saudi monarchy. That would come later.

It was while he was a student at Abdul Aziz University that Osama was introduced to the works of the Islamist radical Sayyid Qutb. Executed by Anwar Sadat in 1966, Sayyid Qutb was the guiding light of the Egyptian Muslim Brotherhood. Qutb's works were published widely in the Muslim world and became the intellectual foundation of the philosophy of Jihad. Upon his death, Qutb became the Muslim Brotherhood's principal martyr.

Qutb had traveled to the United States in the 1950s and was badly shaken by the experience. He found life in the United States "spiritually primitive" and was appalled by what he called "the loose sexual openness" of American women. Qutb wrote contemptuously of America's then burgeoning jazz culture, calling it "the music that Negroes invented to satisfy their primitive inclinations, as well as their desire to be noisy on the one hand and excite their bestial tendencies on the other."

Strangely, despite his racial bigotry, Qutb was capable of writing spiritual meditations on God and man. But democracy, he claimed, was a failed system. It was corrupt because mankind had been corrupted. Qutb's writings enjoined Muslims that Jihad against unbelievers was a holy obligation.

For Qutb, Jihad meant not just the defense of Muslim lands, but a worldwide revolution, "to safeguard the mission of spreading Islam." Qutb maintained that the entire world was in a state of *jahiliyah*—a condition of subhuman stupidity and chaos where ignorance clouded mankind's understanding of God. Since chaos and the will of God cannot coexist, offensive Jihad was necessary to destroy corrupt societies and bring the world to Islam.

Qutb wrote and preached that Islam offered a perfect system of justice and morality. For Qutb and the Muslim Brotherhood armed struggle was the necessary means to bring about paradise on Earth. He believed Islam was surrounded by enemies. Whether democratically elected, monarchical, or rooted in military dictatorship, any regime that did not practice sharia law was apostate, and therefore a legitimate target. An Islamic revolution, in Qutb's view, was necessary to bring about a change in both government and the hearts of men.

Qutb's acolytes designated what they called "near enemies"; these included Israel and every secular government in the Arab world. They named also a group of "far enemies"—including the United States—whose unpardonable crime was moral corruption and military support for the nation of Israel.

Sayyid Qutb was both a warrior and a poet who believed that the souls of martyrs would be carried to heaven in the bellies of green birds. His writings were woven through with mysticism, misogyny, and relentless bigotry. But Qutb and the Muslim Brotherhood did not spill out their venom on the great Satan alone. The far enemies also included the European powers that had once held dominion over colonies in the Middle East: Great Britain, France, and Italy.

It's doubtful that Osama read very deeply into Sayyid Qutb's thirty volumes of Koranic commentary. But he got the gist. Like millions of other young Muslim men, Osama, through his readings, came to believe that the Jihadis had the answer to the world's problems.

And that answer was bloodshed.

How did the concept of Jihad hijack the soul of Islam? What made the prospect of bloody sectarian war so attractive to generations of young Arab men? To answer that question, to find out what animated Osama bin Laden's personal concept of Jihad, it's necessary to make a brief trip through the history of the Middle East, as seen through *Arab* and not occidental eyes.

An old SEAL adage says, "See it like your enemy." That means in order to understand a tactical problem, or to try to guess an opponent's next move, a SEAL needs to think like his opposite number. One way to do that is to learn what the enemy has learned—assemble his "fact set" and look at the problem from his side of the fence. This doesn't mean you have to agree, but you will be in a much better position to anticipate his actions. To that end, let's consider it from the *Arab point of view*: The conflict at hand is called the Global Salafist Jihad. Those who wage it call themselves Jihadis, and they are attacking the West for religious reasons. But the mainspring of their grievances is not a religious disagreement, but a geopolitical inequity. The central issue, for the Arabs, is the question of Palestine.

It is one of the ironies of history that the most emblematic weapon of Islamic terrorism, the truck bomb, was invented not by a Muslim fundamentalist, but by a radical Jew. Menachem Begin, the son of a Russian timber merchant, came to Palestine as a member of the Polish army. Born in the city of Brest-Litovsk in Belarus, Menachem Begin had earned a law degree by the age of twenty-seven, and served two years in Stalin's gulag for political agitation. Starvation and torture left a mark on him.

In 1942, Begin talked his way out of a concentration camp by volunteering for military service under a Soviet puppet named Wladyslaw Anders. He was made an officer and sent with an expeditionary unit to Palestine. There, he quickly threw off his uniform, deserted, and joined the Zionist terrorist organization called Irgun. The group had formed earlier, in 1931, and was an offshoot of Haganah, another Zionist insurgent group. A brilliant orator and organizer, Begin rose rapidly within its ranks.

In 1948, the nation of Israel came into being after a prolonged campaign staged by Haganah. Both organizations waged armed struggle for a Jewish homeland, but the Irgun, led by Begin, was willing to use terror as a weapon. Under a policy called "Active Defense," Irgun members in Palestine assassinated British military officers and Arab policemen, bombed marketplaces and movie theaters, and carried out a sustained series of attacks against Arab-owned businesses. A favorite Irgun tactic was to place a small explosive in a corner of a crowded market, detonate it, and then hit the rescuers with a second, even larger explosive.

SEAL trainees take on the Pacific Ocean. During Basic Underwater Demolition SEAL training in Coronado, California, teamwork is taught by putting students into the biggest surf the instructors can find. (Courtesy of U.S. Navy)

(Above left) Members of the Goon Squad are reminded that it pays to be a winner. (Courtesy of U.S. Navy) *(Right)* During Hell Week, instructors make it easy for students to quit. Here, the bell has been moved from the instructors' offices to the beach. All a student needs to do to quit is to ring the bell three times, and he's out—no questions asked. (Courtesy of U.S. Navy)

SEAL instructors lead students on a "conditioning hike" during Hell Week. Basic Underwater Demolition SEAL training is a grueling six-month ordeal that is regarded by many as the toughest military training in the world. As much as 70 percent of a typical class will quit before the end of the first phase of training. (Courtesy of U.S. Navy)

Members of the SEAL platoon insert into a desert landing zone. Helicopter-borne operations are just one of the ways SEALs can infiltrate a target. (Courtesy of U.S. Navy)

SEALs practice maritime intercept operations in the Caribbean Sea. SEAL Teams can parachute RIBEX raiding craft like this one anywhere in the world within a matter of hours. This capability allowed the SEAL Teams to respond immediately when the U.S.-flagged *Maersk Alabama* was hijacked off the coast of Somalia. (Courtesy of U.S. Navy)

A SEAL delivery vehicle leaves a specially modified nuclear submarine on a recon operation. SEAL Teams can operate from submarines to infiltrate coastal targets. It's a frequent joke among SEALs that they are just as good as the U.S. Army's Delta Force except, "We can do everything they do, upside down, underwater, and in the dark." (Courtesy of U.S. Navy)

The Hippodrome in West Beirut. This horse-racing track was an alleged PLO training facility and was hit by thousands of Israeli artillery rounds and aerial bombs. The neighborhoods around the track were laid to waste. (Courtesy of U.S. Navy)

The American position at Green Beach, Beirut, Lebanon, 1983. A platoon from SEAL Team Four was based here in a series of underground bunkers. By August, even the heavily armed SEALs could leave their positions only after dark. The sailors and the marines at Green Beach were for all intents cut off from the marines at the airport visible in the distance. (Courtesy of U.S. Navy)

(Below) Before and after: the Marine Battalion Landing Team headquarters at the Beirut airport. Congressional interference prevented the U.S. Marine forces commander from placing cement obstacles in the parking lot. The Iranian-built truck bomb drove straight down the driveway and into the lobby. (Courtesy of U.S. Navy)

The 1982 massacre of Palestinian civilians at the Sabra and Shatila refugee camps in Lebanon took the lives of more than five thousand men, women, and children. The murderers were Lebanese Christians, and they were abetted by Israeli forces. This event would radicalize tens of thousands of Muslim men, including a Saudi college dropout named Osama bin Laden. (Courtesy of Helios Global, Inc.) *(Inset)* *Time* magazine cover: the events at Sabra and Shatila were quickly forgotten by the United States, though within months 243 U.S. servicemen would be killed in a retaliatory bombing orchestrated by Iranian intelligence. (Courtesy of Helios Global, Inc.)

(Above left) On July 22, 1946, Menachem Begin, head of the Zionist terrorist organization the Irgun, is credited with the first truck bombing in history. His target was the offices of the British military and diplomatic authority in Palestine located in the King David Hotel. (Courtesy of Helios Global, Inc.) *(Above right)* President Jimmy Carter congratulates the president of Egypt, Anwar Sadat, and the prime minister of Israel, Menachem Begin, after the signing of the Camp David Accords in 1979. Sadat and Begin would share the Nobel Peace Prize. Three years later, Anwar Sadat would be assassinated by the Muslim Brotherhood for "selling out Palestine." In 1982, Menachem Begin would launch an invasion of Lebanon—Israel would continue to occupy parts of Lebanon until the present day. (Courtesy of Helios Global, Inc.)

April 25, 1980: Iranian troops examine the wreckage of a U.S. helicopter after a failed attempt to rescue American hostages held by Iran. A C-130 tanker and an MH-53 helicopter had collided during refueling operations on a remote Iranian airstrip code-named Desert One. The debacle at Desert One killed eight American pilots and commandos. The mission's failure would bring down the Carter presidency. (Courtesy of Helios Global, Inc.)

(Above left) Capitalizing on the failure at Desert One, commander Richard Marcinko established SEAL Team Six as a maritime counterterrorism force. Team Six would soon become America's most elite special-operations organization. (Courtesy of U.S. Navy) *(Above right)* SEAL Team Six conducts a shipped intercept operation. Note the MP5 machine pistols—dating the operation to the late 1980s. (Courtesy of U.S. Navy)

SEAL Team Six operators pose in front of an American Trans Air 727–200 airliner after a successful parachute operation. During the 1980s and 90s, the Joint Special Operations Command demonstrated that even nonmartyrdom hijackers could commandeer passenger aircraft and set the planes autopilot to crash into ground targets. The author is fifth from the left standing. (Author's Collection)

December 1994: French GSGN commandos storm the cockpit of Air France flight 8969. The hijackers were killed during the rescue operation, but subsequent information revealed that the original intent had been to crash the aircraft into downtown Paris. Still, 9/11 came as "a terrible surprise." (Courtesy of Helios Global, Inc.)

(Above left) The faces of terror in Iraq. Jordanian-born Abu Musab al-Zarqawi was chief of Al Qaeda's operations in Iraq. His bombs and assassins also targeted Jordanian hotels and Shiite Muslims. (Courtesy of Helios Global, Inc.) *(Above right)* Al Qaeda in Iraq reads a video statement before beheading an American hostage. (Courtesy of Helios Global, Inc.)

Intelligence analysts sift the rubble of Zarqawi's hideout in north Baghdad. Zarqawi's corpse was eventually recovered, but the difficulties posed by identifying his scattered human remains were one of the factors that dictated a "direct action" raid against Osama bin Laden. (Courtesy of Helios Global, Inc.) *(Inset)* Zarqawi at autopsy. (Courtesy of Helios Global, Inc.)

Osama bin Laden and his Svengali, Ayman al-Zawahiri. Zawahiri was arrested in Egypt for complicity in the assassination of Anwar Sadat in 1981. He was released from prison after informing on other conspirators and fled first to Saudi Arabia and then to Pakistan. He eventually met and befriended Osama bin Laden. Zawahiri is credited with urging Bin Laden to expand his funding to include worldwide terror operations against both the "near enemy," Israel and secular Arab governments, and the "far enemy," the United States of America. (Courtesy of Helios Global, Inc.)

The unctuous Dr. Zawahiri used Bin Laden's money and influence to pursue his own terror agenda. In 1989, Zawahiri orchestrated the murder of the Palestinian Islamic scholar Abdullah Yusuf Azzam, Osama bin Laden's mentor and cofounder of the Afghan Services Bureau. After Azzam's murder, Zawahiri infiltrated Bin Laden's organization with Egyptian hard-liners. Zawahiri attempted to assassinate Egyptian president Hosni Mubarak during a visit to Ethiopia in 1995. The botched attack forced Sudan to kick out Bin Laden and his followers. By 2001, SEAL Team intelligence analysts had started to refer to Zawahiri and Bin Laden as "Bert and Ernie" after the Sesame Street characters. Eventually, Zawahiri would turn on Bin Laden by deliberately exposing a courier to CIA surveillance. (Courtesy of Helios Global, Inc.)

(Above left) Osama bin Laden's headquarters outside Khartoum in 1996. It was here that the 9/11 attacks were conceived and planned. (Courtesy of Helios Global, Inc.) *(Above right)* Clinton national security advisor Sandy Berger refused repeated entreaties from the government of Sudan offering to extradite Bin Laden in exchange for the easing of U.S. sanctions. Sudan later allowed the French GSGN to "render" Carlos the Jackal after the French eased their own sanctions. (Courtesy of Helios Global, Inc.)

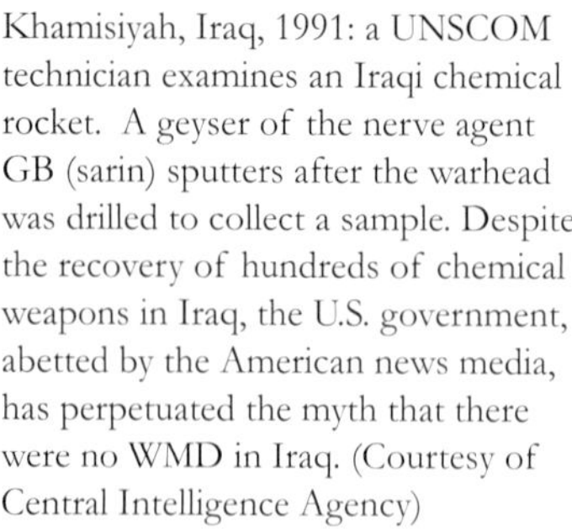

Khamisiyah, Iraq, 1991: a UNSCOM technician examines an Iraqi chemical rocket. A geyser of the nerve agent GB (sarin) sputters after the warhead was drilled to collect a sample. Despite the recovery of hundreds of chemical weapons in Iraq, the U.S. government, abetted by the American news media, has perpetuated the myth that there were no WMD in Iraq. (Courtesy of Central Intelligence Agency)

155 mm artillery shells containing vesicant war gas sulfur mustard (HD). These shells were photographed by UNSCOM weapons inspectors at the cache discovered at Khamisiyah, Iraq, in 1991. Since 2003, coalition forces have recovered almost six hundred chemical weapons from dozens of similar "stash sites." Al Qaeda exported Saddam's chemical weapons to Afghanistan and attempted to use them against U.S. troops. (Courtesy of United Nations UNSCOM)

Osama bin Laden lived in this house in Haripur, Pakistan, for seven months until he relocated his family into the compound at Abbottabad, a mere dozen or so miles away. Ayman Zawahiri gave his blessing to the move even though Faraj al-Libi had been captured in Mardan while passing information about the move. (Author's Collection)

(Above left) Al Qaeda's third in command, Faraj al-Libi, was captured on May 2, 2005, after conducting a meeting with Osama's son Khalid regarding the June move of the Bin Ladens into the Abbottabad compound. Despite this dangerous breach in security, Bin Laden decided to move into the compound. (Courtesy of Helios Global, Inc.) *(Above right)* May 11, 2010, one year before Operation Neptune's Spear, U.S. Secretary of State Hillary Clinton told an interviewer that she believed Osama bin Laden was hiding in Pakistan and that he was under the protection of the ISI. Clinton's statement was widely commented upon in the Pakistani media. Ayman Zawahiri read Clinton's statement but did nothing to change Osama bin Laden's security arrangements. One year later, Bin Laden would be dead, leaving Zawahiri in undisputed control of Al Qaeda. (Courtesy of AFP)

Pakistani police examine the car of abducted Iranian intelligence officer Hashmatullah Attarzadeh. Kidnapped on November 13, 2008, Attarzadeh was eventually exchanged for Al Qaeda members being held in Iran, including Osama's wife Khairiah Sabar bin Laden. U.S. intelligence was aware of the exchange, and when Sabar was eventually moved to Abbottabad, the net began to close on Bin Laden. (Courtesy of Tariq Mahmood/AFP/Getty Images)

After being fired from a public health position in the Khyber Agency, Shakeel Afridi, a Pakistani medical doctor, was recruited by the CIA. Pretending to offer hepatitis screenings, he canvassed Abbottabad in an attempt to locate Osama bin Laden. After Tariq Khan's cell phone was electronically "gathered," Afridi was directed to knock directly on the compound gates. Realizing that that he was involved in an important manhunt, Afridi demanded ten thousand dollars to call at the residence. The CIA's pre-mission reconnaissance was so poorly compartmentalized that Afridi and a dozen other CIA assets were rolled up less than forty-eight hours after the raid. Afridi was sentenced to thirty years by a Pakistani court. (Courtesy of Associated Press)

(Above) Operation Neptune's Spear was planned for multiple contingencies. Here, SEAL operators practice HBVI (helicopter-borne vehicle interdiction). At Abbottabad, one of the SEAL elements was prepared to capture Bin Laden if he attempted to flee by vehicle. (Courtesy of Helios Global, Inc.) *(Below)* Assault elements practiced for Neptune's Spear at secret locations and a full-scale mock-up of Bin Laden's compound. They continued to rehearse as they awaited final mission authorization at Forward Operation Base Fenty in Jalalabad, Afghanistan. The 160th Special Operation Aviation Regiment's Ghost Hawk helicopters were considered so secret that they were not used in daylight mission rehearsals. (Author's Collection)

Osama bin Laden's compound at Abbottabad. On the evening of May 2, 2011, an American Stealth Hawk helicopter landed on the roof of the main house. The assaulters jumped from the roof onto the walled terrace visible on the right of the third floor. Bin Laden was shot dead within ninety seconds. (Courtesy of Helios Global, Inc.)

The White House situation room during Operation Neptune's Spear. Administration spin to the contrary, the situation room was able to watch only an overhead view of the target beamed down from an RQ-170 drone. For all its drama, the photograph has been revealed to be a photomosaic cobbled together and heavily Photoshopped. The main part of the picture is believed to have been taken ten to fifteen minutes into the operation, when the lead Stealth Hawk helicopter was seen to lift off the roof of the main house and crash into the livestock pen adjoining the annex. (Courtesy of U.S. Government)

Pakistani television interviews Bin Laden neighbor Mohammed Bashir. An eyewitness, Bashir stated to journalists and Pakistani military investigators that ten to twelve Americans jumped from a helicopter onto the third-floor terrace of Bin Laden's residence. His story contradicts the administration's "crashed on insert" version of events. (Courtesy of SAMA News)

(Above left) President Obama reveals Bin Laden's death hours after the raid. The announcement not only alerted Al Qaeda, but rendered moot the priceless intelligence taken from the target. (Courtesy of White House Press Pool) *(Above right)* Deputy National Security Advisor John Brennan at first claimed that Osama bin Laden had been killed after a forty-minute firefight. This story was later "clarified" by the White House. Over the next several days, the administration had to walk back several key details in its narrative about the raid. (Courtesy of White House Press Pool)

Adm. Bill McRaven assumed command of the Joint Special Operations Command in June 2008, the first U.S. Navy SEAL to ever hold the job. A brilliant tactician and well-liked team player, McRaven is a scholar who wrote the definitive book on special operations. He would oversee planning and execution of Operation Neptune's Spear. (Courtesy of Department of Defense)

(Above left) A case of déjà vu. On the left, the wreckage of a U.S. Air Force HH-56 left behind after the U.S. special operations raid at the North Vietnamese prison camp at Son Tay on November 22, 1970. *(Above right)* On May 2, 2011, forty-one years later, the successful operation against Osama bin Laden would also leave the tail section of the crash-landed American helicopter on the target. Both missions had been so meticulously planned that they succeeded despite the loss of one of the insertion platforms. SEAL Team Six had pulled off one of the most spectacular special-operation successes in military history. (Courtesy of Helios Global, Inc.)

At approximately 12:30 p.m. on the afternoon of July 22, 1946, a truck containing more than half a ton of high explosives was parked in front of the lobby of the King David Hotel in Jerusalem. At the same time, a small explosive device was detonated across the street as the drivers of the truck scrambled into a getaway car.

It was a textbook Irgun operation. The smaller blast attracted a crowd. As lunchtime spectators milled around in the street, the larger truck bomb was detonated. At 12:27, an explosion shook the earth and smashed windows as much as a mile away. The detonation sheared off the southwest corner of the hotel, killing ninety-one people and wounding almost a hundred more. Scores of deafened, bleeding survivors staggered through the streets. Dozens of people were buried alive in the wreckage. It was one of the most vicious bombings in history, and horrendous in its calculation to maximize casualties.

British and Arab rescuers worked for three days pulling bodies from the rubble. Thirteen of the victims were never found—they had been vaporized by the explosion.

Not one to rest on his laurels, Begin continued to assassinate Palestinian officials, rob banks, and murder passengers in train stations. As a rule, the Irgun preferred soft targets, like officers' clubs. Sometimes, they resorted to attacking civilian neighborhoods—as on April 9, 1948, when the Irgun attacked Palestinian civilians at the village of Yassin outside Jerusalem, killing at least a hundred people at a loss of fewer than ten to themselves.

In 1945, the British urged Saudi Arabia, Iraq, Lebanon, Syria, Jordan, and Yemen to form the Arab League to coordinate policy regarding Palestine. They held meetings and issued proclamations but accomplished nothing.

Two years later, in 1947, the United Nations General Assembly partitioned Palestine into two states, one Arab and the other Jewish. No one was happy with the outcome. Comprising approximately 35 percent of the population, Jewish settlers were given approximately 55 percent of the land. The area under Jewish control contained almost half a million Jews as well as four hundred and fifty thousand Arabs. The agreement stipulated that Jerusalem was to become a *corpus separatum,* and was to be administered by the United Nations.

Representatives of both the Arab League and the Palestinians furiously rejected the UN plan and questioned the authority that the United Nations had to partition their country.

On May 14, 1948, Israel declared itself a sovereign nation. The next day, Arab forces blockaded Jerusalem and attacked Jewish settlements throughout the countryside. Syria, Lebanon, Egypt, and Iraq invaded. Saudi Arabia and Yemen also sent combat units into the fray. Their military mission was to establish a unitary Palestinian state, though the secretary of the Arab League, Azzam Pasha, clouded the issue when he declared that the Arabs were launching a war of extermination.

Joining the Egyptian army in its attack across the Suez Canal were thousands of members of the Muslim Brotherhood. On May 15, four thousand Jordanian troops entered Jerusalem. Bloody house-to-house fighting ensued. As many as ten thousand artillery shells a day were fired into Jewish urban centers and rural settlements. Arab attacks and Jewish counterattacks surged. Hundreds of thousands of Palestinians began a nationwide evacuation, fleeing from the combat areas and crowding the highways north and east into Lebanon and Syria.

On the twenty-third of May, the American consul general, Thomas C. Wasson, was assassinated in West Jerusalem as he attempted to broker a cessation of hostilities. A tentative cease-fire was reached on June 11; it was a sham. Both sides used the pause to reinforce their positions and make preparations for further attacks. At the behest of Moscow, the communist government of Czechoslovakia sent more than twenty-five thousand rifles, five thousand machine guns, and fifteen million rounds of ammunition to the Israelis.

The truce held until the eighth of July, when the Israelis launched an offensive on three fronts. The Arab forces retreated. A second UN truce lasted from the eighteenth of July until the middle of October, when the Israeli army again came out swinging, attacking the Arabs on a broad front. In combat, the Israeli forces tended to better their foes, and in December 1948 the Arabs had suffered enough. The United Nations General Assembly passed Resolution 194, mandating an end to hostilities.

In the months that followed, Israel concluded separate truce agreements with Egypt, Lebanon, and Syria. Armistice demarcation lines expanded territory under Israeli control by approximately a third. As a sop, the Gaza Strip remained in the control of the Egyptian army, and the West Bank was ceded to Jordan. The Israelis would seize control of both these territories in the next twenty years.

To the Arabs, the Israeli War of Independence was called *al Nakba,* "the Disaster." More than a million Palestinians fled from their homes or were expelled by the Israelis. Across the nation of Israel, more than four hundred Arab villages were depopulated and bulldozed. In the years following the 1948 war, seven hundred thousand Jews immigrated to Israel and were settled mainly in territory captured from Egypt and Jordan.

The reverberations of *al Nakba* tore through the Arab world like an earthquake. In a matter of months, coup d'états would be staged in Egypt and Syria, the king of Jordan would be assassinated, and Yemen would disintegrate into an appalling civil war. It is impossible to overstate the effect of *al Nakba* on the Arab psyche. The nation of Palestine had been wiped off the map. The combined armies of seven Arab nations had been crushed and driven like cattle back across their frontiers. And this humiliation was kept bitter by a series of armed conflicts fought with the Israelis in 1967, 1973, 1982, and 2006. In all but one of these wars, the Israelis fired first, destroyed all opposing forces, and occupied ever-widening expanses of Arab land. From the Arab point of view *al Nakba* was not a single catastrophe, but a string of disasters heaped one atop the other.

In 1948, for the first time in fifteen hundred years, the city of Jerusalem was occupied by a conquering army. The Arabs blamed each other, and they blamed the rest of the world. Their sense of grievance over the loss of Palestine would continue unabated for the next half century.

When Osama bin Laden was born in March 1957, the nation of Israel was less than ten years old. Its very existence rankled Arab and Muslim sensibilities. The Arab press poured out hatred against Jews, and, increasingly, on the nation that was seen as Israel's principal prop and ally: the United States of America.

As Osama grew to manhood, the problems posed by almost a million displaced Palestinians affected the entire Arab world. Within the Palestinian Diaspora, more than a dozen terrorist organizations reared their heads. Principal among them was the Palestinian Liberation Organization, headed by an Egyptian named Abdel Raouf Arafat al-Qudwa al-Husseini; the world would come to know him as Yasser Arafat. Though he was a non-observant Muslim, Arafat's strategy of global terror would have a profound effect on the tactics used by Osama bin Laden. The PLO's bloody playbook of international mayhem would become a legacy to Bin Laden and Al Qaeda.

Osama bin Laden would become a "distance learner" of the PLO's terror training camps. As Arafat bombed, hijacked, and murdered, Osama drew two important conclusions: First, that it was possible for a small, secretive organization to fight globally against a superpower; and, second, that by attacking "soft targets" like airliners, and groups of civilians, it was possible to provoke an enemy into massive retaliation, brutal counterviolence that swayed world opinion against the aggressor and joined the oppressed into a cohesive determined whole.

From Arafat, Bin Laden also learned how to organize. Arafat ruled the PLO through a maze of committees, fronts, armed factions, and splinter groups. He was a terrorist, an apologist, a dissembler, and an old-fashioned Arab sheik who took care of a "tribe" of subordinates and supplicants. He was a master manipulator, who sowed discord among his people, his competitors, his allies, and even his enemies. He could have a rival knocked off on Thursday and show up to his funeral on Friday, sobbing openly. Arafat was a chameleon and master of the grand gesture; an archetypal Arab hero to some, complex and resourceful.

In the 1960s, Lebanon was peaceful and prosperous. Osama bin Laden attended the Brummana academy in the hills above Beirut, and he continued to visit Lebanon throughout the seventies with his family. Though its central government was congenitally weak, the Lebanese pound was strong and the beautiful city of Beirut was considered the Paris of the Arab world, and also its financial capital.

Sent packing from Jordan, when that country's army had inflicted more than three thousand casualties on PLO fighters and Palestinian civilians, Yasser Arafat arrived in Beirut with suitcases full of cash and thousands of heavily armed PLO fighters. In Beirut, as Arafat practiced his tyranny, he founded a covert arm of Fatah called Black September. He selected the most battle-hardened and ruthless of his subordinates and ensured their loyalty with cash bounties. He arranged for them to receive the best training he could—often from intelligence agents from the Warsaw Pact. He made sure they were extravagantly equipped. With this paid gang of killers, Yasser Arafat would make his wrath felt around the world. Based out of Lebanon, Black September terrorists assassinated Jordan's prime minister, sent letter bombs, sprayed the Athens airport with gunfire, and gunned down Israeli diplomats in London.

The Arab world was desperate to strike any blow it could against Israel. The Arab people were so downtrodden and humiliated, they were willing to overlook that Arafat's "victories" were often scored against unarmed people. He was fighting back, and that was all that mattered.

Hundreds of millions of dollars streamed into PLO coffers, and the nations of the Warsaw Pact offered diplomatic status to PLO representatives. Communist East Germany was especially helpful—providing Black September with safe havens, weapons storage, explosives training, and travel documents. Arafat returned the favor by sabotaging electrical plants in West

Germany and scarring the 1972 Munich Olympics by murdering eleven Israeli athletes in cold blood.

Despite Arafat's frantic urging, Lebanon wisely declined to participate in the second Arab-Israeli war in 1973, but the PLO joined in, staging attacks from southern Lebanon. As the Lebanese government lost control, militias flourished in the countryside, and the rule of law bowed down to the Kalashnikov.

Largely because of the disruptive presence of Arafat and the PLO, civil war erupted in Lebanon in 1975. An estimated one hundred thousand Lebanese civilians would be consumed in a senseless paroxysm of violence. In almost a thousand years of human history there is no parallel to the violence that destroyed Lebanon. Armed with twentieth-century weapons, the citizens of Lebanon turned on each other with unfathomable barbarity. Brutal militias rained rockets and artillery shells on Beirut, killing thousands of men, women, and children as they huddled in the basements of their homes. Atrocity followed outrage and massacre followed murder until the reason for the violence was lost in a bottomless pit of human depravity. Yasser Arafat presided over a bizarre six-sided war, raining rockets and mortars around the compass, hitting "enemy locations" that included hospitals and elementary schools.

PLO fire was returned by Lebanese militias who retaliated in kind, shell for shell, rocket for rocket, sniper kill for sniper kill. It was like the end of the world—except that it would not end. Month after month, and year after year, the war continued, the lines never changing, the antagonists content to merely pump artillery shells into each other's neighborhoods. An entire generation of Lebanese children were made into trembling, shell-shocked PTSD victims. Many Beiruti survivors adapted by inuring themselves to brutality. Many of these children would grow up to become members of a violent religious militia called Hezbollah—but that would be twenty years in the future. The mayhem of the Lebanese civil war went on for almost a decade.

Osama bin Laden carefully followed the war in Beirut from his home in Riyadh, Saudi Arabia. As a boy and teenager, he had traveled many times to Lebanon, and knew the country and its people well. As a religious man, Osama cared very little for Yasser Arafat, a wholly secular and political being, who rarely, if ever, mentioned his Muslim faith. Arafat put the creation of a Palestinian state before everything else in his life—including God. Arafat is alleged to have said that "fighting wars over religion was like arguing about who has the best imaginary friend." If Osama bin Laden heard those words, he would have been incensed.

Though Osama was sympathetic to the plight of the Palestinian people, and took a secret delight in the successes of Palestinian terror operations, he could not thoroughly embrace Arafat or the PLO because they had not made Islam part of their solution.

Broadcasts from the Middle East were a monotony of violence and a bewildering array of causes, combatants, countries, and catastrophe. Osama bin Laden was shocked and infuriated by the implacable apathy of the American people to the plight of the Arabs. In his mind America's indifference was taken as proof of a cold and calculated plan to destroy the Arabs and erase fifteen hundred years of Muslim history and culture. Through the prism of his increasing religiosity, Osama began to see America not merely as the ally of Israel, but as an enemy of Islam.

Throughout 1981, Christian militias did battle both the PLO and the invading Syrian army. The Israelis could not resist getting in shots of their own. In retaliation for continued PLO attacks, the Israeli air force pummeled Beirut at will. The airport was destroyed, power plants were bombed, and hundreds of "PLO headquarters" were reduced to rubble. Parts of Beirut began to resemble the surface of Mars.

Lebanon became the prototype of the "failed nation." Through it all, Arafat ordered his forces to escalate attacks on Israel, launching raids and terror attacks from PLO bases in south Lebanon.

Finally, the Israelis had had enough. They launched an invasion.

Menachem Begin, architect of the King David Hotel bombing, inventor of the truck bomb, former head of the terrorist group the Irgun, had been elected prime minister of Israel in 1977. He decided to get tough on terrorism.

On June 6, 1982, Begin ordered the Israeli army to invade Lebanon. IDF armored columns quickly swatted aside whatever forces could be put in front of them. Their goal was Yasser Arafat in Beirut. Soon, the Israelis controlled the coast roads and had surrounded Lebanon's capital on two sides. Using U.S.-supplied aircraft, artillery, and bombs, the Israelis put Beirut under a ring of fire.

Two months after the Israeli invasion, a Christian, Bashir Gemayel, was elected president of Lebanon. He prevailed upon the U.S. to try to rein in the Israeli army. President Ronald Reagan brokered a cease-fire, and the U.S. landed a small amphibious force to embark the PLO onto ferryboats and cargo ships. In a Dunkirk-like evacuation, thousands of PLO gunmen were flotillaed to Cyprus. On August 20, 1982, Yasser Arafat and the high command of the PLO were allowed to step onto a cruise ship and also depart. During his extraction from Beirut, Yasser Arafat was protected by a detachment of U.S. Navy SEALs.

With the PLO gone, the Americans withdrew, but it took a year for the Israeli army to pull out of Beirut. It was long, fateful, and bloody year.

On September 1982, President Bashir Gemayel was assassinated by a car bomb that took out an entire city block. The crowning atrocity of the Lebanese war was set into motion.

Following the death of President Gemayel, three companies of the Christian Phalangist militia crossed Israeli-occupied territory in south Beirut and entered the Palestinian camps of Sabra and Shatila. The PLO was gone, and the refugees were defenseless. The Lord told the Christians to take an eye for an eye and the destruction they visited on the two camps was biblical.

On the nights of September 16, 17, and 18, 1982, Christian militiamen killed more than two thousand Palestinian men, women, and children in an orgy of destruction. The Israelis watched the murderers come, and then they watched them go. Israeli artillery units fired flares over the camps so the murderers could set about their work. It was one of the most cold-blooded massacres in human history.

News cameras found the victims. Some had been hacked to death and mutilated. Women and children had been tortured, raped, and murdered. Men were found with their hands tied, lined up before walls, and machine-gunned in heaps. Their homes had been ransacked, their stores looted, and even their animals slaughtered in their pens.

The news story was carried in *Time* magazine, but Jewish groups in the U.S. insisted that the story was "PLO propaganda." The sheer scale of the barbarism boggled comprehension. The American public ignored the suffering of the Palestinian people as it had ignored the horrors of the Lebanese civil war.

America turned a blind eye, but the Arab world was shocked and disgusted. The images of Sabra and Shatila did more to fuel anti-Israeli and anti-American feelings than any other event in the twentieth century. Yet it hardly blipped in Western media.

International condemnation fell on Israel's then minister of defense, Ariel Sharon. An Israeli commission found that Sharon bore "personal responsibility" for the massacre. He resigned his post and the condemnation faded. Nineteen years later, rehabilitated as a patriot, he would be elected prime minister of Israel.

The martyrs of Sabra and Shatila were forgotten, piled into garbage trucks, and bulldozed into a mass grave in a rubbish dump north of the Beirut airport.

Tens of thousands of Arab men, those who considered themselves religious and those who were purely secular, vowed revenge for the innocents killed at Sabra and Shatila.

One of those men was Osama bin Laden.

In March 1983, largely to prevent further atrocities, the United States again sent Marines into Lebanon, this time as part of a multinational peacekeeping force. France, Britain, and Italy also sent contingents, but it was U.S. Marines who did the heavy lifting.

Trouble started almost at once. On April 18, 1983, a suicide truck bomb destroyed the American embassy in Beirut, killing sixty Americans. It was the first time since the Empire of Japan initiated kamikaze attacks that a suicide operation had killed Americans overseas.

The Israeli army eventually skulked out of Beirut, leaving behind a ruin. When the Israelis departed, the Lebanese civil war exploded again in all its ferocity.

One member of the multinational peacekeeping force described what happened next: "Finally there was nothing left for the Israelis to burn. When they pulled out, it was like the last fifteen minutes of *Blackhawk Down,* all day, every day."

Once again Beirut descended into anarchy. Traffic accidents would set off fistfights, which turned in minutes to gun battles, then firefights, then artillery duels. Thousands more civilians were killed. The peacekeepers of the multinational force, especially the Marines, found themselves the targets of a dizzying array of Lebanese militias, as well as the armed forces of Syria and Iran.

Dug into bunkers at the Beirut airport and a short strip of sand called Green Beach was a battalion of U.S. Marines augmented by Navy Seabees and a platoon from SEAL Team Four. They could do nothing to stem the violence, and very little to defend themselves. The SEALs hunted snipers and took out Syrian artillery spotters in the Shouf Mountains above the city. By September, it became too crazy for the Americans to even attempt to leave their positions.

Again the American media was curiously silent about what was going on in Beirut. Marines who returned from Lebanon were surprised to learn that though they had been through six months of combat, no one back in the United States seemed to know or care. Before the year 1983 was over, more Marines would die in Lebanon than were killed in the 120-day siege of Khe Sanh during the Vietnam War. But much worse was to come for the Marines in Lebanon. Looming for them would be America's greatest military defeat since Pearl Harbor, and the single deadliest terrorist attack mounted against the United States until the horror of 9/11.

Ronald Reagan would describe Beirut as "the biggest tragedy of my presidency."

Although the Israelis were gone, those determined to strike back for the massacres at Sabra and Shatila still had targets to strike . . . namely the French and American peacekeepers hanging on to outposts within Beirut.

Members of the Iranian Revolutionary Guard Corps were serving as military advisers to a small but determined Lebanese militia called "Hezbollah," or "the Party of God." Orders came from Tehran to blow up the American and French headquarters with suicide truck bombs. The idea was to strike the French and Americans simultaneously and force their governments to withdraw their peacekeepers from Lebanon.

On a tactical level, the operation would be payback for the massacres at Sabra and Shatila. With the only credible armed force in Beirut withdrawn, the Lebanese people could be counted on to descend again into anarchy. This would enable the Shiite religious party, Hezbollah, to rise to the occasion and establish a theocratic government—along the lines of the Islamic Republic of Iran.

It was an audacious, even grandiose plan. Astoundingly, it worked.

On the morning of Sunday, October 23, 1983, a pair of identical truck bombs were driven toward the headquarters buildings of the American and French peacekeeping forces in Beirut. They detonated twenty-eight seconds apart, killing 243 U.S. Marines and sixty French paratroopers. It was the first time in history that a peacekeeping force had been massacred in their beds.

The man who designed the truck bombs was an Iranian trained member of Hezbollah named Imad Mughniyeh. The intrepid Mughniyeh went on to specialize in attacks on U.S. bases, putting together another truck bomb that would devastate a U.S. Air Force barracks in Saudi Arabia in 1996. By then, Osama bin Laden would be so impressed that he would send his own bomb makers to train with Mughniyeh in Lebanon's Bekaa Valley.

Most scholars agree that these two explosions were the opening shots of what has been called the Global Salafist Jihad. They were also a turning point in the evolution of warfare. The use of unconventional weapons and proxy militias is an aspect of fourth-generation warfare. Sometimes called "asymmetrical combat," these techniques allow a small foe to fight a very much larger enemy. This new type of war uses special operations forces, unconventional weapons, advanced technology, and social media to attack an enemy simultaneously in military, political, and social spheres. Its tactics include the use of proxy organizations, state-sponsored bombings, transnational terror organizations, information warfare, and the manipulation of media. Fourth-generation warriors operate against nontraditional points of attack—especially soft and symbolic targets like monuments and large assemblies of people. The goal is to obscure the authors of the violence, shift the blame from attacker to victims, and frame debate for the causal factors in the media. It is in the media where the real effort is expended, in an attempt to "control the narrative," so the smaller, attacking foe can "fight the fight" in the information space—on the news and the Internet—rather than on the battlefield, where open combat would be impossible.

When the Marine barracks were bombed in Lebanon, Osama bin Laden was a twenty-six-year-old college dropout. He watched as the United States folded its tents and went home, taking the French, British, and Italians with them. Osama's religious studies and political beliefs had made him enthusiastically anti-Zionist, and increasingly anti-American. And to him the twin truck bombings in Beirut were a "David defeats Goliath" moment of glory. The innocents at Sabra and Shatila had been avenged, and the United States had been humbled.

Osama bin Laden drew the conclusion that martyrdom operations could defeat a superpower and force it to turn tail. It was a lesson he would never forget.

Though it was the Iranian government that planned and executed the Marine bombing, their local proxy, Hezbollah, took the credit. To Lebanese Shiites, and the victims of Sabra and Shatila, the bombings were the justice of God. Iran and Hezbollah created the narrative that America had killed Muslims at Sabra and Shatila, and that Islamic martyrs from Hezbollah had punished the Americans. The Iranians had won the battle of the narrative as well.

The Iranians, increasingly media savvy, made certain that Hezbollah was depicted as valiant, religious, and patriotic. This was classic fourth-generation warfare. Iran did not wish a direct military confrontation with the United States. They wished only to needle it.

Over the next two decades, the Iranians would pour arms, men, money, and weapons into Lebanon. Hezbollah would exert its muscle, eventually becoming the supreme military and political power in the nation. By 2011,

Lebanon had become a near vassal state of Iran, no longer a failed nation, but a state taken over from within. The government in Beirut may not have been working, but Hezbollah was doing just fine. And wherever Hezbollah's mullahs governed, the Iranians could claim to have successfully exported their Islamic revolution.

As a boy, Osama learned to read and write in Lebanon. And it was by watching war tear apart that beautiful, tragic nation that Osama thought he saw a way to force justice and peace upon the world.

THE MAKING OF A JIHADI

1979–1984

YOU CAN SUM UP THE skewed geopolitical views shared by Osama bin Laden and members of the Muslim Brotherhood in the following way: American politicians walk a tightrope between the Christian religious right, which embraces Israel, and the Hollywood elite, who espouse Zionism for their own reasons. It is often claimed that Israel is America's only friend in the Middle East; if that is true, it might be because Israel has made all the enemies that the United States could possibly accommodate. Starting with the 1967 Arab-Israeli war, the perception on the Arab street was that the United States was in the business of propping up Israel. The face the Israelis show to their neighbors is a catalog of American military hardware: Phantom jets, HueyCobras, Hellfire missiles, M-16 rifles—these weapons are emblematic of the United States. An examination of U.S. foreign aid between 1949 and 2007 could not persuade any thinking Arab to believe otherwise. Since the establishment of Israel, the U.S. government has given more than $100 billion to its Middle Eastern ally. This includes military grants totaling $55.6 billion, economic grants of nearly $31 billion, and almost $20 billon in miscellaneous programs. In Arab eyes, the United States arms and funds a thin-skinned and expansionist regional bully. Islamic radicals might only add that in addition to being a stooge of international Zionism, the United States is a godless, corrupt, warmongering, satanic parasite whose imperial pretenses are sucking dry the world's resources, while murdering and enslaving the Muslim people.

While attending Abdul Aziz University in Jeddah, Osama read Sayyid Qutb's *Signposts* and *In the Shade of the Koran.* He attended lectures by Mohammed Qutb, the martyred Jihadi's brother. Osama would later credit both with sharpening his anti-Semitism, which was firmly based, he maintained, on Koranic principles. Osama bin Laden hated the nation of Israel, and he came also to hate the United States of America. He would wage a war of terror to set right what he saw as fundamental wrongs. But unlike Yasser Arafat and an entire generation of PLO terrorists, the mainspring of Osama's violent designs had little to do with the establishment of a Palestinian homeland. His motivations were at first, and would always remain, religious. When Osama bin Laden took up the sword, he did so to propagate the faith of Islam. It was Osama's belief that where Islam was established, justice and peace would follow.

In a country as secular as a United States, it seems unthinkable to murder people in the name of God. It is almost irresistible for Western intellectuals to invoke the doctrine of cultural relativism in regard to Islamic terrorism. We are predisposed to equate self-sacrifice with altruism. In Western culture, a captain goes down with his ship; the fireman risks his life to save others; a mother gives her life to protect her child. The Western mind is compelled to find in every act of Islamic self-murder some readily understandable motive, some root cause that is simple, pure, rational, and valid. Why are they sacrificing themselves? What is the higher purpose? And why are they targeting innocent people?

The answer is simple and terrifying: Islamic fundamentalists hate. And they hate profoundly. They hate Jews, and Christians, and Shiites and Buddhists. They hate women. What has been misnamed the "Global War on Terror" is actually a struggle not between Islam and Christianity, but between religious bigotry and Western secular liberalism.

It is inappropriate to measure Islamic violence with a yardstick notched with occidental ideas of altruism. To do so, to conceive that terrorist martyrs must be motivated toward some collective goal is to fundamentally misunderstand the nature of Islamic religious violence, and to misapprehend the process by which "martyrdom operations" are planned and carried out.

The views of Osama and his ilk are not those of the world's Muslims. They are the beliefs of a handful of twisted psychopaths who have had to claw out a justification for murder by distorting the Koran. For every Koranic injunction they cite that tells them to smite the infidel, another says to regard both Christians and Jews as the children of God. Islamic martyrs do not spring unbidden from crowds of Muslim believers. The men and women who are used up in Islamic terror operations are cultivated, steeped in hatred, armed, and sent on their missions by cynical men who have cloaked their own hatred and venal ambition in the robes of religion.

Osama bin Laden was not born to be a monster. He was raised in an affluent and moderately religious Saudi family. He was a soft-spoken, retiring, impressionable boy who lost his father at a tender age. Like thousands of other Muslims who became extremists, Osama bin Laden came under the influence of men who were ruthless, brutal, and amoral. The only difference between Osama and a teenage body-bomber in Palestine is that Osama bin Laden had money—lots of it. And because he had money, Osama was sought out by men with extremist views. Hate requires capital to manifest itself in violence. Osama was flattered, he was cajoled, he was praised. He was told he was a sheik, a religious visionary, and a man whose deeds on earth would earn him a seat in paradise. He listened. He believed. He joined the Muslim Brotherhood, and came over to their belief that violence was necessary to set the world right.

It was all in the Koran, they said, and they could find it and point to it. Osama believed them, as did thousands of others. He bought in.

Suicide bombers are invariably sold the same bill of goods: seventy virgins will attend them in cool gardens and they may be joined by seventy more members of their family. It is almost impossible for a Westerner to grasp that these words would be adequate to convince a grown man to throw away his life—to blow himself to pieces—and worse, to take the lives of as many other human beings as he possibly could.

One intelligence analyst called Osama bin Laden "the Madonna of jihad," meaning that he had a little talent and a lot of money. Osama never received any formal military training. He didn't know how to wire a bomb, disassemble a rifle, or hijack an airplane. He was not a religious scholar and he possessed few skills either as a tactician or a strategist. What he had in abundance was cash.

Osama used his money, and he learned to use people as well, convincing others to embark on one-way missions to strike down godless infidels in great heaps. Like all terrorist leaders, Osama lacked personal courage. He never considered actually hijacking an airliner himself—that was for someone else. Mere *shaheeds* could do that. He was a sheik, a leader; it was for others to die. Osama would provide the means by which his dedicated followers could realize their own dreams of martyrdom. Osama was like a travel agent, selling one-way all-inclusive trips to Paradise.

Money is almost always power. Cash can buy weapons, rent muscle, and buy ideas from intelligent people. Osama was raised by a family that made its living by doing all of the above. Hiring immigrant labor and paying the salaries of Western-trained architects and civil engineers, the Bin Ladens transformed Saudi Arabia from a swath of desert to a country filled with palaces, superhighways, airports, and state-of-the-art petroleum facilities.

It was natural that a son of Mohammed bin Laden would think it possible to remake society. His father changed the face of a nation. Osama set his sights not on one country, or a region, but on the world. Mohammed bin Laden changed Saudi Arabia by working in concrete and steel; his son would try to remake the world in blood.

Osama might be forgiven for coming to the conclusion that the United States was a paper tiger. He had no idea of the vastness of the United States, nor could he conceive of its military and technological reach.

Until 1983, Osama bin Laden had no worldview. His education had consisted of three years of business college. Few of his classes interested him much, and the hard science he needed for a degree in engineering had proved to be beyond his scholastic ability. Osama never in his life had to work at anything—cars, houses, hunting trips, business jets, women—these things came to him because he was a millionaire's son. As an upper-class Saudi, Osama might also have felt that hard work, even academic work, was somewhat demeaning. He'd come from a family of high achievers and he withdrew from Abdul Aziz University before his academic failure became too spectacular. He'd lived a sheltered life, surrounded by servants. As a child of privilege he was unused to either effort or contradiction. When he pronounced an opinion, people agreed.

Osama bin Laden followed the progress of the Iranian Revolution intently; he believed, as many extremist Muslims did, that what the Iranians were seeking to create was the rule of God on earth. The face of the Iranian Revolution would eventually be revealed in starker terms, but at its inception the Ayatollah and his gang of mullahs and imams were greeted by the Iranian people with ecstasy.

Close upon the success of the Iranian Revolution came a reminder that the faith of Islam was not secure. On December 26, 1979, the Soviet Union invaded Afghanistan. And it was there, in Afghanistan, that Osama bin Laden would begin his career as a leader of Jihad.

The heroic struggle of the Afghan people to throw off the Russian invaders was not at first a particularly religious endeavor. Despite myths of his own making, Osama bin Laden did not immediately travel to Afghanistan to join the Jihad. No one did. It would take several years for the struggle of the Afghan people to take on the religious character with which it is seen now. The first leaders of the Afghan resistance were not particularly devout men. They did not ask the Muslim world for assistance—only for weapons.

Though some Afghani warriors invoked the name of God and declared Jihad against the occupying Russians, most Afghan citizens saw their struggle in more down-to-earth terms—they had been invaded by the Russians and now did what they had always done when they found a would-be conqueror at their door: they waged total, bloody, and unmerciful war.

Like the Americans before them in Vietnam, the Russians would be defeated by an enemy that did not seek major engagements, had no standing armies and few fixed bases. They were up against ghost soldiers who struck their enemy at times and places of their own choosing and melted away whenever the Soviets tried to concentrate their forces.

Afghanistan has been aptly called the graveyard of empires. In twenty-five hundred years of recorded history, Afghanistan has never fielded a unified coherent army, yet it has defeated in turn the Macedonians under Alexander, the Mongols, the Huns, the British at the height of their imperial power, and the combined might of the entire Soviet military.

In 1973, King Mohammed Zahir Shah was overthrown. Earlier, in 1963, his introduction of a parliament, civil rights, free elections, and the vote for women were taken in stride, but the king was neither charismatic nor popular. A decade passed.

In quick succession, the Afghan government was headed by an ever more brutal series of Soviet puppets. In 1979, to stabilize their unruly protégés, the Soviets invaded, and the first Jihad of modern times began.

Thirteen thousand Russian soldiers were killed in the Soviet-Afghan war, and another fifty thousand were maimed or wounded. Afghan civilian casualties were incalculable, but probably number close to three million. More than five million Afghani civilians were made homeless and fled into Pakistan and Iran. During nine years of Soviet occupation, Muslims from all over the world came into Afghanistan to fight. Some were little more than adventure tourists, coming for a week, learning to shoot weapons at Jihad training camps, and coming home to Bahrain, Saudi Arabia, or Yemen to strut about in their new Pashto trousers. But others were serious and bloody-minded men. And a smaller portion of them were religious zealots.

It was the Afghan people themselves who defeated the Soviets. They were helped by U.S.-provided weapons that were funneled through the Pakistani intelligence service, the ISI. Fewer than ten thousand "Afghan Arabs" joined the Afghanis.

For almost a decade the Soviet Union provided a battle laboratory where Jihadists from all over the world learned how to fight. They gained combat experience and training in explosives, clandestine military work, small-unit tactics, and the simple business of killing efficiently. The Soviet-Afghan war had several world-altering consequences: The first was that the Soviet juggernaut would shudder and creak and wheeze back across the border, broken and defeated. Soon after its defeat in Afghanistan, the Soviet Union would collapse. No one in NATO or the West could predict this outcome when the Soviets landed on the day after Christmas at the Kabul airport in 1979.

No one in the West could foresee that because of the Soviet defeat, a new class of warrior would emerge into history. The West had armed, trained, and encouraged Jihad fighters against the Soviets—it would now find itself fighting these same men. It was blowback on a global scale. Skilled in the use of state-of-the-art weapons, computer literate, technologically adroit, and media savvy, these new war fighters did not fight for a nation, or a region, or even necessarily for a religion. Sunni and Shia both were warriors of an Idea.

That idea was to remake the planet: one world, one people under Islamic domination and the will of God. To accomplish this, these new Jihadists would use any means, however bloody, nefarious, or cruel. Women and children were fair game, as were the enemy's ships, trains, and airplanes. These men would do the work of God. The time had come to make way for the coming of the Mahdi, the prophet of God. They would fight to bring about the end times as predicted in the Koran.

Riding out of the dusty plains of Afghanistan, galloping past the wreckage of Soviet tanks and the bleaching bones of Russian soldiers, Jihad had come.

HERO OF THE LION'S DEN

AROUND 1982, OSAMA DECIDED THAT he would become a polygamist like his father. Osama purchased a small, four-unit apartment building about a mile from his mother's home and decided to fill it with three new families. His objective, he told his friends, was to show that polygamy was a thoroughly Islamic way of life, and, as practiced by the Prophet, could be a fair and equitable arrangement for all involved.

Osama's choice for second wife was surprising. She was seven years his senior, the daughter of a wealthy Jeddah family who had earned a Ph.D. in child psychology from the women's college of Abdul Aziz University. Soon he courted and married another highly educated woman—wife number three. She also held a doctorate, this one in Arabic grammar. Osama's third wife was known as Umm Khalid. She moved into unit number three, and raised a son and three daughters. Osama's fourth wife was from Mecca, a daughter of the prominent Gialani family. After celebrating their nuptials, she, too, moved into the apartment building and there bore him three children, eventually giving birth to a son and assuming the title Umm Ali.

Osama had taken a job with the family business. His duties at the Bin Laden Group's headquarters in Jeddah did not take up very much of his time, and Osama found himself playing host to a series of visiting fund-raisers, fresh from the war in Afghanistan.

Some were rough, military men who had little time for the gangling, soft-spoken Bin Laden. Others were polite, accepted his hospitality, and enthralled him with tales of battles with the Russians. They needed money to buy weapons and found that the young millionaire was willing to write checks. Just as important, he made introductions to the upper echelons of Saudi society.

Later, in his own mythmaking, Bin Laden would claim to have traveled to Afghanistan the day after the Soviet invasion. This is nonsense. During the early 1980s, he spent his days raising a gaggle of children, seeing that they were home-schooled, and playing host at the hospitality tents offered by his family's company at religious events such as the Haj. It was not until after the success of the Beirut bombings that Osama bin Laden decided to get involved in the "holy war" then evolving in Afghanistan.

Despite Beirut, or perhaps because of it, the United States was now pouring money into the Afghan war. The major route for U.S. funds and weapons was through the Pakistani ISI (Inter Service Intelligence). Pakistan became the clearinghouse for American cash, and that made the ISI the powerbroker among the Afghan-manned groups who did the actual fighting of the Soviet invaders.

The Saudis were anxious to open their own direct channels to the Mujahideen. Osama told several stories about his path to Jihadi stardom, but things probably didn't begin to click until he reconnected with Ahmed Badeeb, his old teacher. After leaving the faculty of Al Faqr University, Badeeb started to work for Saudi intelligence, eventually becoming an aide to Prince Al Tarqi. Osama met his teacher at one of the Bin Laden Group's sponsored events. They exchanged pleasantries and the older man sized up his former student. Osama was wealthy, he was connected, and he was eager. Thus began Osama's cultivation by Saudi intelligence. Prince Al Tarqi saw Bin Laden as a conduit and cutout for funding Afghan Jihad.

Wealthy people like to surround themselves with others who are either beautiful or interesting—this is the case in New York and Paris, and it is also the case in Mecca and Jeddah. Osama was introduced to thirty-four-year-old Sheik Abdullah Azzam, then the most dashing of Arab Afghans fighting the Soviets. Osama came under the sway of this highly educated, articulate, and fearless Mujahideen. Lawrence Wright pointed out that the romantic image of the warrior priest is as strong in Islam as it is in the Japanese culture of Shinto. Abdullah Azzam was the quintessential Arab manifestation of this spiritual, resolute, and determined warrior.

Azzam was a religious scholar with a degree in sharia law. Born in Palestine, Azzam found that his fiery sermons got him kicked out of both his native land and Jordan and Egypt before he landed in Saudi Arabia. He eventually drifted to Pakistan and Afghanistan to fight the Soviets. Azzam was a tall, handsome man, and had a beard streaked with gray. He was an articulate, even mesmerizing speaker, and he wore the black and white checked Palestinian kaffiyeh that marked him as both a combatant and a man determined to fight for freedom.

Azzam's message was simple: Islam would come to its rightful place when Muslims no longer played the victim. The caliphate had been won by force of arms, and Islam's first caliph, the Prophet Muhammad, was a prophet of the Lord and was a military leader. It was the duty of all Muslims to resist infidel invaders when they intruded on Muslim lands. Tape cassettes of Azzam's sermons included his motto, "Jihad and the rifle alone. No negotiations, no conferences, no dialogue."

Azzam was a Jihad rock star.

Osama frequently provided hospitality when Azzam visited Saudi Arabia. Osama and his friends would listen as the sheik amazed them with stories of battling Soviet tanks. Azzam maintained that the participation in Jihad was not an option for able-bodied Muslims—it was an obligation. It was their duty to fight the Soviets. Azzam was there to raise money, but also to recruit men. Osama was enthralled.

Preachers like Azzam convinced many Saudis that communism was a threat to their region, and a menace to their religion. Should the Soviets be allowed to remain in Afghanistan, Pakistan would surely fall, then Iran, Iraq, and Saudi Arabia. It turns out that there are not just geopolitical dominoes, but religious dominoes as well.

During this time, Osama was being tested by Saudi intelligence. His recruitment followed a time-honored pattern. He was first asked to do small favors, then perform slightly more involved tasks. When he had successfully fulfilled that request, he was given slightly more responsibility and eventually larger tasks, such as providing cover jobs for radicals recruited from abroad. The Cairo offices of the Bin Laden Group was soon funneling Algerians, Libyans, Moroccans, and Yemenis into Saudi Arabia, and then facilitated their transportation into Afghanistan.

Osama was himself a member of the Muslim Brotherhood, and it's likely that at this time he made contact with Egyptians who were part of the mother organization in Egypt. Prince Turki al-Fisal noted Osama as a man who might do some good.

Osama bin Laden, the mediocre son of a Saudi millionaire, had finally found his métier. His star was on the rise.

Both the United States and Saudi Arabia believed that the Russians' aim was to conquer Afghanistan and destabilize the countries in the Persian Gulf region. There was oil in the region but the Russians had plenty of their own. What was really in question was the Strait of Hormuz—the opening of the Persian Gulf to the Indian Ocean. Through this narrow body of water, almost 40 percent of the West's petroleum passes by tanker. The Russians wanted the Strait of Hormuz, and the West needed it. That is what raised the stakes of the Soviet-Afghan war.

These were geopolitical considerations and in 1984 they were way above Osama's pay grade. The prime mover and shaker in Saudi Arabia's Afghan affairs was Prince Turki al-Fisal. A month after the Soviet invasion, the prince flew to Pakistan to coordinate aid to the Mujahideen. Prince Turki would become the pivot man in a secret alliance between Saudi Arabia and the United States to vector weapons and money to aid the Afghan resistance.

This alliance would eventually defeat the Soviet Union, but spawn the hell child of international Jihad.

Prince Turki and the Saudis had to tread carefully. If the extent of the Saudi and American aid did not remain secret, the Soviets might easily use it as an excuse to invade Pakistan itself, bringing the bear one step closer. For these reasons the Pakistanis insisted that all money and weapons, both Saudi and American, be transferred through the ISI.

Almost five years after the Soviets first invaded, Osama bin Laden made a trip to the battle area. Incredible as it seems, he had not gone earlier because he could not secure his mother's permission. Armed with the arguments of Abdul Azzam and his personal assurances that her boy would be well taken care of, Osama traveled on one of the family jets to Islamabad.

On June 26, 1984, accompanied by Azzam, Osama slipped across the Afghan frontier at a place called Jaji. He found a squalid camp surrounded by shallow, hastily dug trenches. Morale was high, but the fighters' weapons, clothing, and equipment were in pathetic condition. Yet these men were happy and eager to fight. There was a major Soviet encampment quite close by. Osama found himself on the front lines.

He would later recall a shame he felt for not participating earlier in the struggle against the Soviets. "I asked forgiveness from God Almighty, feeling that I had sinned because I'd listen to those who advised me not to go. . . . I felt that this four-year delay could not be pardoned unless I became a martyr."

He almost got his wish—that morning. Just after dawn, Soviet jets appeared over the camp. They bombed and strafed but did little damage. It was the first time in his life that Osama bin Laden had stood in the sights of an enemy's weapon, and it thrilled him. He claimed later that Mujahideen antiaircraft fire downed four Soviet planes. That part was unlikely, but the effect the strafing had on Osama was galvanizing.

"Not one of our brothers had been injured, thank God. This battle gave me in fact a big push to continue in this matter. I became more convinced of the fact that no one could be injured except by God's will."

Osama's baptism by fire had energized him.

According to Abdullah Azzam, Osama returned to Saudi Arabia and started to raise money in earnest. Ten million dollars poured into the coffers of Azzam's group; two million of it came from members of the Bin Laden family. Money put Osama on the map. Until now, Osama had been seen as a disciple of Sheik Abdullah Azzam. He was now beginning to emerge as his own man.

In September 1984, during the Haj in Mecca, Osama bin Laden and Abdullah Azzam officially joined forces. Azzam had the Jihadi credentials and Osama had the cash. At the time there were very few Arabs fighting in Afghanistan. Those who were there were treated as "glorified guests" by their Afghan hosts.

Azzam and Bin Laden set out to form a new fighting organization, with its own recruiting pipeline, financing, and logistical support. Azzam published a book entitled *In Defense of Muslim Lands.* In it was a fatwa that declared that Jihad in Afghanistan was obligatory for every Muslim. Azzam's call to arms was issued to Muslims around the world: Bosnians, Malaysians Turkmen, and Filipinos all were needed. Osama's connections ensured that the first editions of *In Defense of Muslim Lands* included a foreword written by Sheik Abdul Aziz bin Baz, the chief cleric of Saudi Arabia. This amounted to an official endorsement.

Osama and Azzam returned to Pakistan and established a string of guesthouses they called *Makhtab al Khadamat,* the Services Bureau. They established a main office in the university town of Peshawar, and their first efforts involved printing copies of Assam's books and producing a glossy magazine extolling the manly virtues of armed Jihad.

They started recruiting. Osama sweetened the deal by offering airline tickets, living arrangements, and a $300-a-month stipend to anyone willing to sign up and fight in Afghanistan.

The Saudis had been pouring money into the Afghan insurgency through the conduit of Pakistani intelligence. In addition to the funds transferred directly from Saudi intelligence, Osama remained the conduit through which wealthy donors in Saudi Arabia and the Persian Gulf could show their support for the Mujahideen. These monies are now estimated to have amounted to hundreds of millions of dollars.

Such funds, raised covertly and held in Swiss banks, put the Services Bureau on the map as a major player in the Afghan resistance. Neither Osama nor Azzam had yet to fire a shot in anger. For a while, they collected men and money, directing both to training camps across the border.

Arriving fighters pledged loyalty, *al bayat,* to Sheik Azzam, but everyone knew who was paying for the show. Eventually arriving fighters would render *al bayat* to Osama himself—but that was in the future. Osama was content to be treated obsequiously by both his Pakistani hosts and his employees at the Services Bureau. He visited wounded fighters in the hospital and contributed money to start the University of Dawa and Jihad (the university of Outreach and Struggle) across the border in the tribal areas. Run by Abdul Sayyaf, the school would later gain notoriety as the world's premier training facility for terrorists.

To Pakistani and Saudi intelligence, the charismatic Azzam was the brains of the outfit, both a military leader and a religious scholar. Osama was reticent and soft-spoken; he had soft hands and a cryptic smile on his face that struck more than one person as being hopelessly naïve.

The several hundred Arabs who assembled under the auspices of the Services Bureau were christened "the Brigade of Strangers." They did not seek to integrate themselves into the Afghani forces they had pledged to help. Of almost one million Afghans who would give combat to the Soviet juggernaut, these "Afghan Arabs" never comprised more than 1 percent of the total armed force. They didn't do much fighting, either. Most of them never left Peshawar.

Many were Islamic radicals on the lam from their own governments at home. Some were merely seeking adventure, but a small number actually believed that fighting the Russians was a firm religious duty. They all found that as soon as they joined the Brigade of Strangers, they were unwanted at home. Many Arab governments used Bin Laden's offer of free transportation to rid themselves of troublesome fundamentalists.

Bin Laden and Azzam had established a suicide travel bureau and disaffected Muslim drifters came from all over the world. They were Sunni, mostly, and tended toward the absolutist, Wahabi strain of Islam. Theirs was an underground and revolutionary existence. It was not uncommon for comrades not to know each other's real names. In the Brigade of Strangers, no one really asked where a man came from— it didn't matter. And besides, they had all come to Peshawar for the same thing, to martyr themselves.

Osama bin Laden did not create the Jihad movement or contribute in any real way to its cultural, religious, or intellectual underpinnings. That was for men like Abdullah Azzam and later, Ayman Zawahiri. Osama was an impresario. By all accounts he was not a particularly charismatic person, nor did he speak well in public. Why, then, did Muslim men answer this call to doom? What compelled them to travel to a faraway land and throw down their lives in what seemed to be an almost hopeless struggle against a Russian superpower?

Since the first days of the Soviet invasion, preachers in Wahabi mosques thundered that the rewards for martyrdom were an eternity in paradise. Most of the men who heard these sermons were not unintelligent. The vast majority wondered that if paradise were so readily at hand, why didn't the preachers just get on an airplane and rush into the fight?

So who answered this call to Jihad?

Radicalism can only take root in the absence of hope. The Nazis rose to power in the poisonous environ forced upon the German people by military defeat and economic crisis. In a like manner, the Global Salafist Jihad was a siren call to a generation of Muslim men who felt thwarted and embittered.

From Pakistan, the Gulf states, Lebanon, Syria, Egypt, and North Africa, Azzam and Bin Laden gathered lost Muslim souls who had given up on both themselves and their futures. These were men who lived on the margins of society—beaten down by military dictatorships, or frustrated and thwarted by rigid monarchies where freedom of expression and social mobility was vastly curtailed. In these dark corners of the world, there was no art, literature, or theater. There was no indigenous cinema, and there was little music or entertainment that was not prepackaged and state approved. But there were sociological and cultural reasons why they joined as well. Across the Muslim world a stifling, priggish culture was spreading; a new, all-consuming, religious masochism that forbade young men and women from socializing. And in Lebanon, where it was still possible for men and women to meet each other, they could not; almost the entire country was a battlefield.

In the 1980s, there was not one functional democracy in the Arab world. The humiliation of continuous defeats at the hands of the Israeli army engendered a simmering hatred that was palpable. The heat was on, and the pot's lid was screwed down tight.

Azzam's books and sermons promised a quick and painless fix to these multifarious problems: martyrdom. The world could not be fixed—it was too evil, too corrupt, too sinful. The answer lay on the other side, in paradise.

At first, not many answered this mournful call to death, but they came, in ones and twos and then in dozens. Men with nothing to lose, and no other dream than to give up their lives. These men would later become the nucleus of Al Qaeda—but first, they had to defeat the Russians.

In 1985, Osama bin Laden began his short, star-crossed career as a combat leader. Together with sixty of the Brigade of Strangers, he crossed into Afghanistan, hoping to join forces with Afghan warlord Gulbuddin Hekmatyar, then engaged in battle with Soviet forces near a place called Jihad Wal.

They arrived in the middle of the night, lights blazing on their vehicles, weapons unsafe, chattering among themselves, their pockets full of raisins and chickpeas by way of rations. They were not an inspiring sight, these Jihadi reinforcements, and promptly the next morning the Afghani commander told them their services were no longer required.

Abdullah Azzam was quick enough to understand that they presented a ridiculous spectacle, but Bin Laden was not used to being told what to do. He wanted to enter the fray.

When told that the Russians had retreated, Osama asked why they all did not give chase. Gulbuddin Hekmatyar explained to the eager young Saudi some of the realities of combat with a superpower. The Soviets had the advantage in numbers and possessed both helicopter gunships and fighter-bombers armed with guided missiles. Their midnight arrival might easily have brought down an air strike. In the light of dawn, Hekmatyar got a glimpse of Osama's troops. Some had brought white-colored tents—and when asked about them they said that they wanted to become targets: martyrdom was their goal. The Afghanis have traditionally practiced a moderate form of Sunni Islam; over the course of their military history they have not enthusiastically endorsed suicide as a military tactic. What Gulbuddin Hekmatyar needed on the front lines were trained and disciplined fighters, not instant heroes.

Azzam and Bin Laden handed over their weapons and ammunition to Hekmatyar's fighters, plodded onto a trio of buses, and were driven back to Peshawar.

The Afghanis started to call them the Brigade of the Ridiculous.

Osama and Azzam continued to take in money and direct volunteers to training camps and combat across the border. This is what they were good at, and for a while they stuck to it. Azzam made frequent fund-raising trips far afield, and in 1986 he went on a speaking tour of the United States, collecting money in mosques in Dallas, Kansas City, and Los Angeles. He told stories of miracles on the battlefield—of a single determined Mujahideen who scattered a platoon of Soviet tanks, of bullets that bounced off copies of the Koran and left fighters unharmed, of martyrs' corpses that never decomposed, of bombs sent astray by clouds of birds that were the heaven-bound souls of Jihadists. Azzam's words brought in money and new recruits. His sermons resonated where the rewards of living were few and hard to find; Mujahideen came from Saudi Arabia mostly, but also from the oppressive military dictatorships of Yemen and Syria. Some even came from the United States.

Money rolled in and the Services Bureau grew. Hassan al Banna, the founder of the Muslim Brotherhood, had written that "Martyrdom is art." Osama's art was luring fighters through the publication of his glossy magazine *al Jihad*, studded with photographs of burning Soviet tanks and dead Russian soldiers. Volunteers came, many of them Saudis on school vacations who flew to Pakistan on discounted airfares for a week or two spent at the Services Bureau guesthouses. The money kept coming.

Bin Laden eventually brought his wives and children to live with him in Peshawar. It was 1986, and the Soviets were discovering what the British had learned in 1839: Afghanistan was not to be conquered.

America had added to Russia's nightmare by providing shoulder-launched Stinger antiaircraft missiles to the Mujahideen. These man-portable heat-seekers were death to Russian helicopter gunships, and kept Soviet fighter-bombers at altitudes that made precision bombing impossible. Stinger missiles contributed to the Soviet's looming defeat, but they were not the war-winner that some military pundits would claim. The toughness of the individual Afghan is what won the war.

Thirty years later, when it came America's turn to invade Afghanistan, the Stingers would be gone, but the fight would be just as unwinnable.

The Soviets were on the ropes and arms from around the world arrived in the port of Karachi in cargo containers filled to bursting. The Pakistanis had to find a place to store this embarrassment of weapons, and a great number of rifles and rocket launchers were hidden in a cave complex excavated by Bin Laden southwest of the Khyber Pass. The area was called the Parrot's Beak.

On the northern slope of the Khyber Pass, Osama made for himself an underground lair consisting of barracks, field hospitals, food and fuel storage, and of course, armories containing weapons and magazines for explosives and ammunition. The hard rock made the caves practically unassailable, and years later, during the American invasion, Osama would make a stand there. The place was called Tora Bora, meaning "Black Rock," and it was one of the most secret and important supply centers for Mujahideen during the war.

In May 1986, Osama made his third combat foray, returning again to Jaji, in an area then controlled by the warlord Abdul Sayyaf. The deployment again descended into black comedy.

Bin Laden and a small group of fighters were tucked into pup tents overnight, and failed to detect when a passing Soviet aircraft sowed their camp with "butterfly bombs." These are green, plastic antipersonnel mines that fall to earth spinning like the seeds of maple trees. They contain just enough explosive to blow off a man's foot—they are designed to wound, rather than kill, on the theory that one wounded man takes three people out of the fight: the casualty and two men to carry him.

At dawn, a cook stepped on one of the mines. There was a flash of light and a thud, followed by a scream and someone yelling "God is Great! God is Great!" Osama and his men were thrown into a panic. The light revealed that hundreds of butterfly bombs littered the camp. As they tried to pick their way out of the mined area, crawling on hands and knees, a second air strike thundered into a cliff face near by, spraying the confused men with shrapnel and splinters of granite.

Osama and his men were engulfed in a roiling, black cloud of cordite. The blast turned their tents inside out, scattered men and equipment, and killed a Jihad tourist from Egypt. When the dust cleared, four men had been seriously wounded, and all were badly shaken.

Abdul Sayyaf took Bin Laden aside and gently suggested that he take the wounded back to Peshawar. It was not necessary to add that they had made asses of themselves.

Three times Osama had tried to join in the fighting and three times he had succeeded only in making a target out of himself. Bombed out of thin air, he had yet to fire a shot in anger, or even point a rifle at a Russian soldier. Word of his haplessness preceded him, and soon no Afghan commander would allow Osama's Arab Mujahideen anywhere near the front lines.

There are few people who will speak truth to power, or say no to money. In December, Osama arranged to have an "all Arab" base camp constructed near Jaji. He would call it "The Lion's Den." It was badly situated, exposed to the elements, and in close proximity to an active and alert Soviet encampment.

Abdul Azzam tried to talk Osama out of having a frontline base and he encouraged Osama not to keep Arab fighters sequestered from the Afghan-commanded combat units—those who were doing the actual fighting.

A rift was forming between Osama and Azzam, and it was bigger than the tactical importance of a single encampment. Abdul Azzam had issued a call to Jihad, and had done so to all Muslims. It was his aspiration to bring together the *ulma,* all of the Muslims together, to drive the Soviets from Afghanistan. Wherever possible, Azzam preferred to disperse Arab volunteers into Afghan units. This made military sense. Azzam knew that the Arab volunteers were fervent, but they lacked basic military skills. They did not speak the local languages. Azzam felt that concentrating the Arab fighters in a fixed base was to invite catastrophe. This was, after all, a guerrilla war. Bases were targets.

Azzam was thinking in the here and now, but Osama was thinking of the future. The Soviets were already crafting an exit strategy. Osama was looking ahead to a fight that he thought would come with Islam's second enemy: the West. Bin Laden was planning the creation of an Arab legion of Mujahideen, a private army of fighters that could carry Jihad to the world. Azzam was an intelligent man, and knew that Bin Laden's funding was vital to his own plans and to the Afghanis' continuing struggle against the Soviets. He pleaded with Bin Laden not to place himself in needless danger. Osama would not listen.

Finally, Azzam enlisted the aid of Bin Laden's brother-in-law Jamal Khalifa. Khalifa was married to Bin Laden's sister. He was a shadowy character with ties to Saudi intelligence, and ran a series of front companies and sham Islamic charities that would later finance Khalid Sheikh Mohammed's worldwide network of terror. Together with local warlord Abdul Sayyaf, they went to talk sense to Osama at the Lion's Den.

No one found the location salubrious. The base was situated on a mountainside unshielded from a merciless wind. The squalid camp was scattered under pine trees, its entrenchments shallow and badly positioned. A few mortars and Chinese rockets were perched about with more of an eye for picture-posing than military utility.

Worse, much worse, was that there was a Soviet base in a broad valley less than three kilometers away. Spitting distance in military terms, and well within the range of Soviet guns. One well-worked mortar battery could obliterate the camp in a matter of minutes.

Osama seemed oblivious to the danger he had placed himself in. A single vehicle that made a long journey up a twisting mountain road to smuggle in supplies during the night supplied the camp.

For three days, Azzam, Sayyaf, and Khalifa tried to talk sense into Osama. Bin Laden fobbed them off on his new "military aides," a cadre of Egyptian hard-liners who had worked their way into his confidence.

Though he was not present at the Lion's Den, chief among Osama's new friends was a thirty-five-year-old Egyptian-born physician named Ayman Zawahiri.

Dr. Zawahiri is a caricature straight out of a Faustian nightmare. His apocalyptic worldview would change the life of Osama bin Laden, and cut short the lives of hundreds, if not thousands, of innocent people around the world.

Born in 1951, and raised in a middle-class Cairo suburb, Zawahiri's father was a professor of medicine at Cairo University, and his mother was from a distinguished political family. Ayman Zawahiri's maternal grandfather served as the Egyptian ambassador to Pakistan, Yemen, and Saudi Arabia. His uncle was one of the founders of the Arab League, and served as its first secretary general.

Like Osama, Ayman Zawahiri was close to his mother. As a boy, attending the state's elementary and secondary schools, Ayman was a bookworm who was sometimes bullied. He liked Walt Disney movies and cartoons and watched them at an outdoor movie theater near his home. As he grew to manhood, he hated violent sports and thought they were "inhumane." His twin sister, Umnya, would also become a physician, as would a younger sister, Heba. Two younger brothers, Hussein and Mohammed, would become architects.

Ayman Zawahiri's mother inculcated in him a love of literature, and he often wrote love poetry to her.

The patriarch of the Zawahiri clan was his uncle, Mahfouz, who served as Sayyid Qutb's lawyer when he was put on trial for conspiring to assassinate Egypt's president, Gamal Abdel Nasser. Mahfouz Zawahiri had been one of the last people to see Qutb alive before he was hanged.

As a boy, Ayman grew up listening to his uncle tell stories of Sayyid Qutb's intellectual brilliance and resilience of character. Qutb had been brutalized in Nasser's prisons, but had gone to the gallows unrepentant. When Qutb heard that he was sentenced to be hanged he said, "Thank God I have performed Jihad for fifteen years until I have earned this."

Ayman Zawahiri was fifteen years old when Qutb was executed. He joined the Muslim Brotherhood soon afterward and was an active member until he fled Egypt in 1984.

Zawahiri was one of the plotters who murdered Anwar Sadat in 1981.

Furious that Sadat had sold out Palestine by signing the Camp David Accords, and dissatisfied with Egypt's secular, socialist government, the Muslim Brotherhood planned a very public end for Egypt's first Nobel Peace Prize laureate. Dressed in Egyptian army uniforms, a hit squad boarded a military vehicle during a dress parade. When the truck passed the presidential box, the attackers jumped down, lobbed hand grenades into the crowd and sprayed the reviewing stand with automatic weapons fire. Anwar Sadat was standing at attention, saluting, when his murderers emptied an AK-47 assault rifle into his chest.

As Sadat fell, one of the shooters bellowed, "I have killed the pharaoh!"

Immediately following Sadat's assassination, Ayman Zawahiri took part in a plan to attack Sadat's funeral. When the shooters were arrested before the plan could be carried out, Zawahiri went into hiding. After a few weeks on the down low, he tried to flee to Pakistan. He was arrested on his way to the airport.

Egyptian police kept the arrest secret and held Zawahiri in a dungeon cell in the medieval citadel overlooking Cairo. They knew from the start that Zawahiri was no small fish. Authorities evicted his family and tore his home apart looking for evidence. They found enough to implicate Zawahiri and several others. In police custody, Zawahiri was stripped naked, and beaten with electrical cables. His genitals were shocked with coat hangers attached to car batteries and he was worked over by attack dogs. In a crowning debasement, he was sexually abused, and then raped with a wooden baton.

He broke.

In exchange for his life, Zawahiri informed on his coconspirators and helped Egyptian intelligence to arrest Essam Al-Qamari, a fugitive Egyptian tank commander and key member of Gama'a al-Islamiyya. In exchange for this Judas bargain, Zawahiri was spared his life. Fearing restitution, Zawahiri fled from Egypt first to Tunisia and then to Saudi Arabia.

It is doubtful that Osama bin Laden knew of Zawahiri's collaboration when they met in Jeddah, sometime in late 1984. Bin Laden was just then beginning his trips to Pakistan, and was not yet an icon of Islamic fundamentalism. Zawahiri's speeches while in the defendant's cage had made him well known in Jihad circles. While Zawahiri had withered in prison, the world had changed. Israel had invaded Lebanon, American Marines had been slaughtered in Beirut, and the Afghani insurgents had turned the tide against the invading Russians. Suspected of his treachery, Zawahiri had been eased out of the leadership of al Jihad. He was a broken man, tortured by nightmares. Had he not met the Saudi millionaire, Zawahiri would have probably resumed his career as a physician.

Psychological studies show that protracted exposure to beatings and physical brutality fundamentally alters human personality. Some survivors are made into loners. More resilient souls pass through the experience and transcend violence, forgiving their torturers, and trying their best to get on with their lives. Ayman Zawahiri had been abused and demeaned in Egyptian custody. He had been beaten and raped by his jailers; they had done him violence, but he had done worse to himself. He had betrayed the things he believed in and helped the government capture several of his companions and coconspirators. The abuse he had undergone was inexcusable and vile. Zawahiri hated what had been done to him and he hated the men who had had their way with him. But now, he also hated himself. He would turn that self-loathing outward and turn it onto the world.

It's not known exactly when Osama met Zawahiri, but it was very likely in Jeddah at this time. What is also likely is that Osama gave the Zawahiri family money to rebuild their lives. Osama was a generous man, and regardless of how he felt about the murder of Anwar Sadat, Zawahiri was a Muslim Brother and Osama was obligated to render assistance. The financial aid was sufficient to allow Zawahiri to establish a small practice, and continue to pay rent on his other clinic back in Cairo—certainly things he could not do without a substantial loan.

After he moved to Jeddah, the doctor was quick to insinuate himself into Bin Laden's Jihadi entourage and in 1986 he joined Osama when he moved his own family to Peshawar. Zawahiri soon ran afoul of the Brotherhood by arranging to have published an elegantly bound, beautifully printed screed called *Bitter Harvest.*

In this magnum opus, Zawahiri poured out the hatred in his soul. He lambasted the Muslim Brotherhood as a bunch of wimps. He castigated them for "collaborating" with infidel regimes and he condemned the Brotherhood as "tools of the western powers," and demanded that they "renounce man-made laws, democracy, elections and parliaments." Copies of Zawahiri's book were given away in restaurants and markets free of charge all over Peshawar. It was bloodcurdling stuff, and most of those who picked it up quickly put it back on the shelf. It was too radical for even hard-line Jihadists because it pointed out that there were enemies to be fought both outside and inside the Muslim faith.

The history of mankind has been darkened by a number of physicians who turned from medicine to politics. Jean-Paul Marat of the French Revolution and communist guerrilla leader Ernesto "Che" Guevara are but two bloody examples. Ayman Zawahiri joined them in the pantheon of world terror. Jean-Paul Marat sent hundreds to the guillotine as "the people's friend," and Guevara murdered capitalist stooges as a "revolutionary doctor." Zawahiri planned to out-slaughter them both. And he would answer to a higher authority—he would kill in the name of God almighty.

Zawahiri had embraced a heretical concept in Islam called *Takfir. Takfiri* doctrine holds that Muslims who are judged *not Muslim enough* are apostates—worse than nonbelievers—and may be killed with impunity. A corollary to *Takfir* is called *al-Takeyya*, and it grants its practitioners a license to carry out religiously sanctioned dissimulation; a get-out-of-jail-free card that allows them to lie, cheat, and steal, as long as they do so for religious purposes.

If this seems counter to a basic concept of right and wrong, that perception is shared by most of the Muslim world. *Takfir* and *Takeyya* are considered to be wicked and ridiculous heresy by almost all mainstream Islamic theologians. Dr. Zawahiri, like most other Salafist Jihadis, played fast and loose with both the Koran, Islam's divinely revealed foundation, and the Hadith, the sacred body of sayings and traditions of Islam's founder, the Prophet Muhammad.

Like Marat and Che Guevara, Dr. Zawahiri would take it upon himself to decide who needed to be excised from the diseased carcass of a world that *he alone* could cure. To bring his world-altering visions to reality, Zawahiri could decide who was a good Muslim and who was not. Unhinged by violence, this broken, emotionally crippled little man was a megalomaniacal sociopath bent on destroying the world.

Osama and Zawahiri needed each other. They were never to become fast friends, but they offered each other the means to a similar end. Theirs was a utilitarian and symbiotic relationship. Zawahiri needed capital, and Osama needed intellectual and religious justification for a global campaign of violence.

Zawahiri inveigled a cadre of Egyptian fanatics into Osama's organization. It was simple; he told Osama what he wanted to hear: that the time was right to expand the Jihad he was waging against the Soviet Union. Zawahiri told Bin Laden that he should continue his war against the Russian occupiers, and then expand the horizons of his campaign to embrace both the enemy close at hand, the Soviets and the apostate Arab governments, and the far enemies, the United States and its aggressive Zionist progeny, Israel.

Bin Laden's creation, the Services Bureau, was a cash cow. It possessed a fortune that had been gathered from donations from all over the world; this treasury was the prize that Zawahiri coveted, and he moved closer to it on two lines of march.

First, Zawahiri sowed discord among Osama's followers, raising the specter of *Takfir,* and sorting out Jihadis according to his own estimation of their fitness as Muslims. Second, Zawahiri cynically encouraged Osama to lead from the front, and involve himself personally in combat with Soviet forces.

Zawahiri knew well that Osama was a tactical incompetent—the cunning doctor encouraged Bin Laden to expand the base he was building right under the Soviets' nose. Zawahiri, himself, seldom visited the frontlines. He knew his own importance to the cause, and kept himself safe in Peshawar. He agitated, spreading *fitna,* discord, and he bided his time.

All it would take was one well-placed Russian mortar shell and Osama bin Laden would become the martyr that he'd always hoped to become. This was Zawahiri's simple plan. A Soviet bullet might kill Osama, but not his money or his organization: That would be Zawahiri's, ripe for the plucking. He encouraged Osama on an ever-more ridiculous series of military actions and hoped for the best.

On that cold winter morning when Abdullah Azzam, Abdul Sayyaf, and Jamal Khalifa went up to the Lion's Den to retrieve Osama from the frontlines, they found him surrounded by Zawahiri's handpicked minders.

He had changed.

Osama refused to listen to his friend Azzam's pleas that this was not a place to make a base, and that the point of the spear was no place for a person so important to the cause. There was an argument. Osama told them that he planned to form an Arab Special Forces command that could strike the oppressors of Islam anywhere in the world. Those enemies included what Bin Laden called the *kafir* leaders of all the Arab governments: Egypt included.

Azzam was shocked.

The word "*kafir*" is an ugly word to Muslims. It signifies infidels or unbelievers. Osama had been converted by Zawahiri to the doctrine of the *Takfiri.* Now, he was not only willing to fight the Russians but other Muslims as well.

Jamal Khalifa urged his brother-in-law again to leave the frontlines. Bin Laden told him: "This is Jihad! This is the way we want to go to heaven."

Zawahiri had become Osama's puppet master. The doctor encouraged Osama to expand the base at the Lion's Den, and dig increasingly intricate tunnels, bunkers, and air raid shelters. There was no tactical or strategic point to this useless feat of engineering. How the activity of bulldozers, road graders, and tunneling equipment failed to attract the attention of Russian helicopter gunships is anyone's guess. The base expanded, and the Russians were either blithely ignorant or unwilling to leave the security of their own bunkers.

As the base expanded, Osama's would-be commandos were anxious to kill Russians. Osama was content to build his base and wait. In March 1987, Osama returned to Saudi Arabia for another round of fund-raising and consultations with Prince Turki, the head of Saudi intelligence. They would discuss, among other things, what was to happen in Afghanistan after the Soviet departure, which was now foreseen as inevitable.

In Osama's absence, a subordinate planned an ill-conceived attack on the nearby Russian base. It would have stirred a hornet's nest. Osama returned to the Lion's Den just as the attack was nearing fruition—he called it back and chastised the instigators.

The attack was canceled, but there was grumbling in the camp—his men wanted action and Osama was not secure enough as a military leader to tell them that the time was not yet right to bring on a general engagement.

The complaining got worse, with Zawahiri's henchmen agitating for another move against the nearby Russians. Osama was goaded into action. On April 17, 1987, Osama put himself in the point element of one hundred fighters chosen to hit an Afghan Army outpost near the city of Khost. One can imagine Zawahiri waiting for the result.

The operation was the worst-kept secret of the Soviet-Afghan war. Zawahiri made certain that news of the attack was spread all over Peshawar. Bored Jihadis took it upon themselves to take buses up to the base camp at Jaji and insert themselves into the attacking column. One intrepid American-born Jihadi, Abu Rida, drove his own car from the city and found the gathering column by asking a mule driver where to find Osama bin Laden.

The staging area was a chaos of hallooing troops, braying mules, crackling radios. Orders and counterorders were shouted down the valley. First, the cars carrying ammunition were delayed and the attacking troops were without rifle bullets. Rocket launchers and mortars had to be manhandled into positions to cover the attack—something that could have been done days in advance. No provision had been made for food or water, and some men wandered back to base camp for something to eat. The electrical devices and wires necessary to fire the artillery rockets got left back at base. A rider was sent galloping back up the mountain to retrieve them.

Osama's collegial leadership style did not seem to empower officers to give orders. There was a lot of standing around. By twos and threes, some fighters went back to their bunkers and went to sleep. No one seemed to have thought to stop them.

All of this was in broad daylight and in plain sight of the objective.

The Afghan army soldiers manning Osama's target also slipped away, leaving one man behind with an obsolete Gorjunov machine gun. He was either very brave, or just wanted to see what would happen next. He stayed at his gun, held his fire, and waited.

Somewhere in the massing body of troops, Osama was sick—a thing that happened regularly before contact with the enemy. He did his best to buck up in front of his men, but his languid demeanor and sulky expression did not engender confidence.

Osama allowed one of his lieutenants to give a preattack oration. The pep talk was cut short when the sole remaining Afghan defender decided to open fire. He'd had a long time to aim.

A stream of tracers ripped into the milling throng, splattering one of the attackers cold dead, and seriously wounding two others. Belt after belt of 7.62 mm bullets spanged over the rocks, tearing long sparks in the gathering dusk. Mules heehawed and threw off their loads, horses bolted, and troops without orders flattened or scattered. No one called for covering fire, or ordered any maneuvers. Somewhere, Osama took cover behind a rock and froze. Fighters ran away, and their officers scuttled after them.

The single defender kept firing until the barrel of his weapon glowed red and then white hot. One man kept a hundred leaderless Jihadis pinned down until darkness fell. When he ran out of ammunition, the Afghani soldier sauntered back to rejoin his unit, already a mile back from the point of attack.

It was over. Disgusted, Osama's men returned to the Lion's Den. Some gathered their remaining equipment and left, never to return. It was a flat-out fiasco, and amazingly only one man paid for it with his life. Osama's reputation as a military commander was at rock bottom.

The Afghan fighters who witnessed the debacle spread the word—one soldier had defeated the Arabs. Word got back to the Pakistani army, who began closing down Osama's guesthouses in Peshawar.

It seemed that Osama bin Laden's Excellent Adventure was over.

He returned to Peshawar where, quite predictably, Ayman Zawahiri advised him that it was necessary to show more resolve. What was necessary for morale was for Osama to lead another attack. This one would be better planned, and Osama would be assisted by one of Zawahiri's trusted Egyptian commanders, Abu Ubaydah.

In May, Osama accompanied a nine-man reconnaissance against a Russian rifle squad. That he would again risk his life in direct combat says something either about Osama's personal valor, or the hold that Zawahiri had over him.

It is unthinkable that anyone who cared about the emir's safety would willingly put him in direct contact with a technologically superior enemy.

The nine men wobbled forward, made contact and exchanged fire. The Russians withdrew in an orderly fashion. For the Soviets, it was a routine firefight. Zawahiri's pal Abu Ubaydah persuaded Osama that it had been a resounding success.

It was a success—if the intent was to show the Russians where to find the base.

The Soviets organized a battalion-sized block-and-sweep operation against the Lion's Den. They assembled dozens of trucks and armored vehicles and closed in. Osama was in a well-covered and camouflaged position. The camp had been greatly improved over the past months, and hundred-foot-long tunnels had been bored into solid rock. The place could have withstood anything short of a nuclear attack, and the Russians were coming at them with a lackadaisical, slow-moving operation in the full light of day.

It would be a turkey shoot. Or so Bin Laden thought.

Abdullah Azzam, eager to get back into Osama's good graces, later would spin a mythical version of the "battle," claiming that the Russians attacked with more than ten thousand troops against a mere seventy determined Jihadis.

Osama dramatically yelled "Allah'u Akbar" and the three mortars at his command opened fire. They were aimed with enough precision to stop the Russians' commanding officer and temporarily halt the attack.

The Russians dialed in their mortars. Osama, expecting the attack, ordered his troops underground, and accompanied a personal protection unit to a bunker on a nearby hill. He watched as a rippling barrage sent geysers of dirt up from the Lion's Den. Osama's men were safely underground, and he was on a different peak. He thought, as did his bodyguards, that he was safe from harm.

They had been spotted and the Russians shifted fire onto their position. He took cover and waited out the barrage. By nightfall the Russians lost interest. Osama and his men scuttled back to the deep tranquility of the bunkers in the Lion's Den.

Day and night the Soviets rained 120 mm mortars on the camp. Napalm strikes set the tall pines ablaze. The ground was churned up and craters pockmarked the mountainside. Though no one was killed or even wounded, some of Osama's more high-strung fighters began to show symptoms of shell shock. One ran out into the barrage waving a Koran over his head as the shells screamed in around him. He lived through the experience and would tell the tale frequently.

Osama had never in his life been under a sustained artillery barrage. His cover was solid—rock solid—but he feared that the Soviets might be maneuvering under the covering fire and take the camp by main force. Consulting his own safety, Osama ordered the Lion's Den abandoned.

During a lull a van pulled up to take Osama and his men to the rear. As he drove away he rather dramatically ordered the rearguard to put the camp to the torch. A small detachment tossed the mortar tubes and base plates off a cliff and lobbed hand grenades into the mess hall.

When the evacuees reached the headquarters of Abdul Sayyaf, the regional Jihadi commander, he was furious. The cover at the Lion's Den was truly bombproof—Sayaff was incensed that so strong and impregnable a position had been cowardly abandoned.

Osama and his men had been under a spectacular barrage but their cover had been solid. However loud it had been, it had killed or wounded no one. Sayaff immediately ordered Osama to reoccupy the position.

To make sure it happened, he sent a reliable platoon of Afghanis to chaperone the Arabs back to their position.

Bin Laden waited until the next morning to travel back to the Lion's Den, arriving after the position was deemed safe. He showed up with a small bodyguard unit in the middle of the morning. It was Eid ul-Fitr, the feast day that marks the end of Ramadan. It would be a dismal celebration.

Following Osama's orders the retreating fighters had spoiled the remaining supplies to prevent them from falling into the hands of the Russians. Now his men scrounged through the wreckage for something, anything, to eat. They found nothing but some lemons.

Upon returning to the camp, Osama seems to have undergone some sort of collapse. He gave no orders, and allowed Zawahiri's military adviser Abu Ubaydah to again dispatch him to the forward edge of the battle area.

He probably had no idea people other than the Russians might want to see him dead. He and his small group made their way to the left flank of the camp. It was daylight, and Osama had incautiously advanced with his party toward a densely wooded hilltop. There he spread them out into a ragged skirmish line.

Osama had blundered to within a hundred yards of a Russian scout team. For some unknown reason Osama climbed a tree—something that, despite what one sees in John Wayne movies—is almost instantly fatal in combat. He was immediately taken under fire and a rocket-propelled grenade was fired at him. It exploded in a fireball of bark and pine needles, shaking the tree so badly that Osama nearly fell to his death.

Osama's recollection of this contact with the enemy is bizarre but has about it the ring of truth. Lawrence Wright quotes him thus:

"It [the rocket] passed by me and exploded nearby, but I was not effected by it at all—in fact, by the grace of Allah, the exalted, it was as though I had nearly been covered by a handful of mud from the ground. I descended calmly and informed the brothers that the enemy was on the central axis and not on the left wing."

Osama made it away from the tree as a mortar strike tore apart the hillside. He somehow found cover, likely in a predug firing position. The trees and vegetation around him were sufficiently dense and he was able to hide from the Russians as they determinedly advanced, sweeping the hill with automatic weapons fire and trying to flush out Osama and his men.

Back at the Lion's Den, Abu Ubaydah showed his mettle. He led a counterattack that managed to flank the Russians and drive them back down the hillside. At one point during the engagement, Osama claims that he took a nap.

The story of Osama's battlefield slumber was told by Azzam and others of proof of his steadfast resolve and manly courage. It is more likely that he lost consciousness due to the effects of Addison's disease. Upon his death, a DNA sample would reveal that Osama suffered from this failure of the adrenal gland; it is a life-threatening condition that can cause sudden unconsciousness, especially under conditions of stress.

As the firefight sputtered on, Osama came to and had the calm presence of mind to remain hidden as the counterattack drove the Russians back. Abu Ubaydah and others would claim that thirty Russian Spetsnaz troopers were killed in the action.

Whatever the number, Osama was presented by his men with a snappy AKSU carbine they had collected from the battlefield. Called a *suchka* by the

Russians, the AKSU was a signature weapon of the Spetsnaz and is much prized for its compact firepower. Until the end of his life, Osama would keep this weapon by his side, and pose with it whenever the opportunity arose.

After five humiliating forays into combat, Osama had a real battlefield victory to his credit. The win persuaded the Pakistanis to allow the Services Bureau to continue operations. The daylong firefight was polished in the retelling into an almost mythical triumph of good over evil.

His followers, already religious men, began to attribute their survival to the intervention of angels. Osama had nearly lost his base, his reputation, and his life. His insubordinate and unskilled mob of Arab fighters had redeemed themselves—they were no longer hapless, "military guests" but had acquired a reputation for improvisation and almost reckless courage under fire.

Osama had been vindicated as well. With this one victory he reestablished his reputation as a Jihadi, an Islamic warrior and the emir of the Afghan Arabs.

Osama bin Laden had become a legend.

THE EMIR

OSAMA RECOUPED FROM BATTLE in the company of his four wives and a growing brood of children—now numbering more than ten. A man who was willing to kill boys and girls on three continents was loving and gentle to his own children. In August 1988, in Peshawar, Abdullah Azzam chaired a meeting called to discuss the future of Jihad. Also in attendance were several of Zawahiri's henchmen, including Abu Ubaydah. Bin Laden sat at the head of the table—he was the real power in the room.

Relations between Osama and Azzam were still cordial, but cooling rapidly. Osama wanted to form a three-hundred-man force selected from non-Afghan volunteers. He proposed to develop this new unit around a command element of battle-tested leaders, and the most promising recruits now graduating from training.

Though he had asked the conference to vote on his proposal, Osama had already created Al Qaeda on May 17—designating a group of approximately a dozen men to form a training cadre and nucleus around which he could grow the new organization. The purpose of the conference was to get the project out into the open.

This was the first time most of the assembled Jihadis had heard the words "*Al Qaeda*." Abdul Azzam had long suspected that Bin Laden was going to keep a "force in being" after the conclusion of the Afghan war; now he had it spelled out for him.

The founding documents of Al Qaeda divided the "military work" to be undertaken in two parts: operations of "limited" and "open" duration. "Limited duration" meant continuing Arab participation in the Afghanistan resistance. These operations would be terminated when the Russians pulled out. Ominously, military work of "open duration" implied that at the conclusion of hostilities with the Soviets, this new organization would wage Jihad against targets *outside* Afghanistan.

Placed into the minutes of the meeting were the ideal qualities of a new recruit. These included virtues that seemed lifted from a Boy Scout handbook: "good manners . . . rising early in the morning . . . and an ability to take orders." The new regulations also required that Al Qaeda members swear an oath of *al bayat* to Osama himself. The previous pledge of allegiance had been to Abdullah Azzam.

Osama would later say of the founding of Al Qaeda, "Brother Abu Ubaydah formed the camp to train youth to fight the oppressive, atheist and truly terroristic Soviet Union. We call that place Al Qaeda, in the sense that it was a training base, and that is where the name came from."

Abu Ubaydah had been continually at Osama's side since the Lion's Den fight; he and the other Egyptians were exerting greater and greater influence over Osama's daily affairs. This worried Azzam, but he felt that he could still talk sense to Osama, particularly as he felt that the Egyptian hard-liners were crackpots.

Al Qaeda's purpose was to assemble an all-star outfit; it was to be a mirror-image of JSOC—the best and the brightest. Especially prized were individuals with backgrounds in engineering, chemistry, computers, and media and those with proficiency in foreign languages.

Once a recruit passed screening, he would be put through a series of "testing camps" to gauge his determination and religious zeal. Besides a shot at martyrdom and eternal glory, Al Qaeda offered temporal rewards as well. Those who made it through training would receive a salary of a thousand dollars a month, and married men would get an extra five hundred. Medical care was provided, as was a month of vacation and a round-trip ticket home once a year.

News of the recruiting drive spread in eager whispers all over Peshawar. Soon, Jihadists from a dozen countries were lining up to fill out Al Qaeda's multipage application form and swear their loyalty. Everybody wanted in, and paradoxically, the more Osama tried to keep Al Qaeda a secret, the more widely known it became.

Abdul Azzam appears to have viewed Al Qaeda with skepticism. Would it not become a mercenary army? Could paid soldiers remain true to the principles of Islam?

Azzam was a Palestinian, and he had seen with his own eyes what happened when men put paychecks and leader oaths above a cause. The Abu Nidal Group was a cultlike splinter group of the PLO. Its members swore *al bayat* to their founder, Abu Nidal, a violent, paranoid psychopath who set himself up as a freelance operator, hijacking planes and carrying out murders for hire. Abu Nidal was also an atheist, and Azzam could at least reassure himself that Bin Laden was neither an unbeliever nor overtly insane. Still, he worried that a group of privately recruited fighters, loyal first to the man who paid them, had the potential to do evil as well as good.

Azzam was aware that his own star was waning. This was driven home when Osama won a unanimous election to head the new group. Azzam took his demotion in stride—he had been a mentor and now he was minion. He was faced with two options—he could get on the bus, or he could get run over. With some misgivings, Azzam went along for the ride.

Training facilities at the Lion's Den were expanded, and other camps were opened. Volunteers were tested and selected on a two-track system. The lucky ones were those whose applications listed Western academic training or language skills. These men were groomed for international missions and sent to an advanced course lasting three months.

Those in the second rank were Jihadists without higher education and those who had less fervent ideas about martyrdom. These men were given three weeks of infantry training, an AK-47, and a blanket and were sent into Afghanistan to harass the fleeing Russians. They were cannon fodder.

The advanced camps were open to second-tier recruits who distinguished themselves in combat, but Osama could afford to be choosy about whom he trained. No one was admitted who did not meet Osama's increasingly bigoted religious convictions.

Though he was not at the meeting, Ayman Zawahiri had been instrumental in urging Osama to form Al Qaeda. Zawahiri knew that Abdul Azzam objected strongly to both his *Takfiri* leanings and the Egyptian's growing influence over his former student.

The prize was more than Osama's esteem and affection: It was his money. For Azzam, who was less mercenary than Zawahiri, this behind-the-scenes struggle was not for capital, but for the soul and purpose of the Afghan Jihad. Azzam cared deeply about what would happen to both the Afghan people and the Arab fighters he had assembled to help fight the Russian invaders.

For Zawahiri, the squabble was not about the Afghan Jihad, but about a broader conflict—a battle for the entire world. Zawahiri did not care a fig for the Afghan people, and not much more about Osama bin Laden. He had repeatedly urged Osama to put himself into harm's way. When the Russians failed to make a martyr out of him, Zawahiri sought to convert Osama to his own opinions about global Jihad, and take over Al Qaeda from the inside, by surrounding the pliable young millionaire with yes-men and his own cronies. The prize for Zawahiri was the fortune amassed by the Services Bureau: almost unlimited cash with which to wage his own version of Jihad—first against Egypt and then against the entire world.

To accomplish these ends, Zawahiri intended to take Azzam out of the picture, politically, if possible, but physically if necessary. The doctor started a rumor that Osama decided to form Al Qaeda because Azzam's creation, the Services Bureau, had been infiltrated by the Central Intelligence Agency. In the armed and dangerous atmosphere of Peshawar, Zawahiri's rumor mongering was much more serious than mere gossip.

The currents swirling around Osama were Byzantine. Prince Turki, the chief of Saudi intelligence, also wanted Azzam taken down. Abdullah Azzam was a Palestinian, and had helped to found the terrorist organization Hamas just the year before. Saudi intelligence was always suspicious that Azzam's ultimate loyalties were not to Osama or the Kingdom of Saudi Arabia, but to Palestine. They worried that an Al Qaeda headed by Azzam would pull young Saudi fighters into the orbit of the Muslim Brotherhood, the same men who killed Anwar Sadat. Still reeling from the assassination of King Faisal, Saudi Arabia did not want a problem on the home front.

Saudi Prince Turki knew that civil war in Afghanistan was a foregone conclusion. Even as victory loomed bright, the several Afghani insurgent groups were turning on each other. The Saudis wanted an organization to see to their interests as Afghanistan was either divided up or brought to heel after the Soviet departure. Prince Turki wanted Al Qaeda in the hands of someone he thought would be compliant. Turki knew Bin Laden well enough to know that he was easy to influence—what the prince did not count on was that someone as manipulative as he was had inserted themselves close to Osama and was now pulling the strings.

As the summer burned, Zawahiri turned up the heat on his rival Azzam, this time accusing him of diverting money from the Services Bureau for his own use. These charges were false, but the principle of *al-Takeyya* allowed Zawahiri to lie about anything he wanted. The embezzlement scandal echoed through Peshawar, and redoubled when Zawahiri had placards put up around the city demanding that Azzam face trial. The personal enmity between the two men grew as Zawahiri forced Abdullah Azzam off the boards of several mosques and hospitals and continued a vindictive campaign to discredit him.

Abdullah Azzam was highly educated and politically adroit, but he did not comprehend the forces lining up against him. His underestimation of Ayman Zawahiri would cost him dearly.

On August 17, 1988, a C-130 aircraft carrying the president of Pakistan, Zia ul Huq, took off from Bahawalpur airbase three-hundred miles south of the capital Islamabad. Ground control radar tracked the aircraft as it suddenly pitched into a near vertical dive, smashed into the ground, and exploded. Killed instantly along with Pakistan's president were the American ambassador, Arnold Raphel, the chief of staff of the Pakistani armed forces, and several dozen high-ranking Pakistani military officers. There were no survivors.

The nation of Pakistan was stunned and teetered on the brink of revolution.

The public summaries of a pair of top secret investigations pointed to a catastrophic failure of the aircraft's hydraulic system. This seemed an impossibly unlikely event, as the C-130 had a decades-long record as an extremely reliable and durable aircraft, even in combat. No one wanted to call it a bombing.

The Pakistani investigation hinted obliquely that the crash might have occurred because the pilots became "incapacitated."

Just who killed President Zia may never be known, but the head of Pakistan's intelligence service, General Hammed Gul, was convinced that the crash was the result of a "conspiracy involving a foreign power."

Almost three decades later, American intelligence officials would admit privately that the Soviet Union was probably behind the crash. It was KGB payback for nine years of bloody, miserable war.

Osama, and those around him, took it for granted that President Zia had been killed by the Russians.

In May, a Soviet-made antitank mine was found in a mosque attached to a Services Bureau facility. The bomb had been intended to kill everyone in the building. Al Qaeda redoubled its security efforts, triple-screened all new applicants, and reformed Osama's personal protection detail.

The security situation in Peshawar was deteriorating: bombings, bank robberies, and politically motivated hits had become daily events and Osama thought it might be a good time to put himself beyond the reach of Soviet retaliation. He packed up to go home.

Abu Ubaydah took over the supervision of Al Qaeda's training. Zawahiri could not go back to Egypt where it was likely that he would be killed as an informer. He surrounded himself with bodyguards and stayed on in Peshawar, solidifying his grip on Al Qaeda and stirring up trouble. Abdullah Azzam bravely started a round of shuttle diplomacy, trying to defuse tensions between a half-dozen Afghani warlords who now seemed more willing to fight one another than combine forces and take on the pro-communist government the Russians had left behind.

On the day of his departure, Osama said a tearful good-bye to Azzam. He was so distraught that Azzam also wept. Perhaps he knew who had placed the antitank mine at the Services Bureau mosque. Azzam's security team had discovered the bomb on a morning he had been scheduled to lead Friday prayers. Osama and Azzam parted, never to see each other again. Bin Laden loaded his family aboard a chartered jet and flew back to Saudi Arabia.

On Friday, November 24, 1989, Azzam's son Ibrahim turned the family car onto Gulshan Iqbal Road, in the University Town section of Peshawar. His father was to deliver a sermon at a mosque near their home. Abdullah Azzam was in the backseat, chatting with his second son, Mohammed. A car carrying bodyguards preceded them, and another trailed behind. The guards stopped at the mosque and the men deployed as Azzam and his sons turned left into the parking lot.

There was a flash—the noise was so overwhelming that the survivors could not even remember it—a white-orange-yellow ball of fire, then a searing, burning fist of heat. A one-hundred-pound bomb had been placed at the intersection of a narrow street adjoining the mosque. The concussive force shattered windows and blew the mosque's front doors off their hinges. The explosive charge had been specially designed to concentrate the blast, and it tore through Azzam's car, ripping his son Mohammed limb from limb and blowing his brother into pulp. The explosion tore off the car doors, peeled away the hood, bent the chassis, and sent human debris sailing a hundred yards to smash through shop windows and dangle off power lines. Azzam's corpse was found, intact, lying against a wall.

It was said that the body had emerged from the blast without the least disfigurement. Perhaps it was a miracle.

It was certainly no accident.

A detonation wire was found across the street, leading to a hidden firing position near an open storm drain. Azzam's killers had watched him arrive and set the bomb off electronically as his car slowed to enter the mosque. The murderers walked away in the confusion after the blast.

The next day, November 25, Ayman Zawahiri attended Azzam's funeral. He was smiling.

Osama returned to the kingdom of Saudi Arabia as its most famous citizen. Stoked by media outlets controlled by the royal family, and wafting into town on a PR campaign of his own making, Osama returned to Jeddah and threw open his doors to the rich and powerful. Princes and Arab business magnates, most of them bearing checks, visited him. The last Soviet soldier had been withdrawn back in February, but recruits and money still poured in to Osama's Services Bureau. Absurdly, now that the Russians were gone, more Arab fighters than ever flooded into Pakistan and Afghanistan.

They were carrying out Jihad, not against the godless Soviets, but against the last remnants of the Afghan army. The last, and most brutal farce of the Afghan war was unfolding, and now Osama bin Laden and Ayman Zawahiri were pitting Muslims against Muslims.

Back in Peshawar, Zawahiri was settling old scores with other Egyptian radicals. One who still remembered his treachery was Sheik Omar Abdul Rahman, the blind cleric who'd marked Sadat for death with a fatwa sanctioning the murder of apostate political leaders.

Zawahiri fended off the truth about his collaboration by pointing out the obvious fact that Sheik Rahman was blind—and that the Jihadist movement could hardly be led by a man who couldn't see. The irony in this seemed to be lost on Zawahiri, who himself wore a set of heavy-rimmed, Coke-bottle glasses.

Both men battled over Osama's official endorsement. Zawahiri won the mudslinging contest, and from Jeddah, Bin Laden wired $100,000 so the doctor could form a new organization called al Jihad. Eventually, Zawahiri would merge his organization with Al Qaeda when its brand name proved easier for Western media outlets to pronounce.

Back in Saudi Arabia, Osama made a show of rejoining the construction business, commuting between his ranch, his multifamily apartment complex in Jeddah, and a place in Mecca. Osama lived modestly, a stark contrast to the ostentatious lives of dozens of Saudi princes who roared around in Lotus convertibles, partied on the French Riviera, and prayed hungover under the soaring minarets built by Mohammed bin Laden.

To thousands of Muslims, Osama bin Laden was a larger-than-life hero. He combined for them, as Abdul Azzam had earlier, the allure of a warrior with a mystical sort of religious intensity.

He began to see himself as a man in the grip of destiny. His gestures were wan, almost feline, and his voice was so quiet that a listener had to pay close attention to hear what he said. Osama spoke this way deliberately, and began to affect the languid gestures and lingering gaze of a person who was talked to by God. His reedy voice was in contrast with a message that was increasingly apocalyptic.

One night after his return, Osama rose to speak at the end of evening prayers at one of the family's mosques in Jeddah. His audience was male, some of them had already answered his call and given combat to the Russians in Afghanistan. They had seen that enemy thrown into retreat, and now watched as the Soviet empire slouched toward dissolution.

Osama had convinced himself that his tattered band of Jihadis had been the deciding factor in the Russia's nine-year war and eventual defeat. He believed, utterly, that it was the military contributions of the Afghan Arabs that had turned the balance and sent the Soviet Union back across the border.

Now he drew a bead on the world's other superpower. Osama told his assembled audience that it was time for the United States to be brought to account.

"America went to Vietnam thousands of miles away and began bombing them in planes," Osama told his rapt listeners. "The Americans did not get out of Vietnam until they had suffered great losses. Over 60,000 American soldiers were killed until there were demonstrations by the American people. The Americans won't stop their support of Jews in Palestine, until we give them a lot of blows. They won't stop until we do jihad against them."

In later pronouncements, Osama would maintain that his hatred for the United States began when U.S. forces came ashore in Lebanon in 1982.

"America permitted the Israelis to invade Lebanon and the American 6th Fleet helped them." That was true enough. American Marines had been landed under the guns of America's Mediterranean fleet, but they had come to provide security for Yasser Arafat's withdrawal.

It is one of the ironies of history that Navy SEALs were deployed as countersnipers to prevent the Israeli army from killing Arafat as he boarded a ferry for Larnaca, Cyprus.

But Osama could not know that; it is unlikely that he would have cared, for a second group of Marines and another SEAL platoon were landed in September of the same year, as part of a multinational peacekeeping force. British, Italian, and French troops took up positions in the city of Beirut, to prevent a repeat of the massacres at Sabra and Shatila.

Osama preferred to remember differently: "Blood and severed limbs, women and children sprawled everywhere. Houses destroyed along with their occupants and high-rises demolished over their residents. . . . The situation was like a crocodile meeting a helpless child, powerless except for his screams." What Osama was describing was an inaccurate portrayal of

Lebanon's sectarian civil war and the carnage meted out by Menachem Begin's 1982 Israeli invasion.

For Osama, the massacres at Sabra and Shatila were the start of a genocidal, Western-backed assault against Islam. He not only blamed the Lebanese Christian militiamen who laid waste to the camps, but also the Israeli soldiers who stood by and did nothing as a crazed gang of psychopaths wasted more than two thousand unarmed people.

Though an Israeli investigative commission would find Defense Minister Ariel Sharon "personally responsible" for the massacre, and dismiss him from office, Osama would feel hatred toward Jews and Israel for the rest of his life. Until he drew his last breath, Osama blamed Israel for the massacre and he blamed the United States for arming Israel. It was Osama's belief that the bloody hand of the United States had been lopped off by the valiant sacrifice of two Lebanese martyrs. When the multinational peacekeeping force was withdrawn from Lebanon, Osama drew the conclusion that two truck bombs had defeated the combined forces of the United States Marine Corps and the French Army.

What he proposed now was for the Muslim world to gather together, under his leadership, and again strike the United States. Osama thought that if enough Muslim martyrs attacked the United States at home and abroad, it would collapse, just as the once mighty Soviet Union was doing now.

No one told him differently, certainly not Ayman Zawahiri, and Abdullah Azzam, the one man who had dared to speak to truth to Osama, was dead.

Saudi Arabia makes no pretense about allowing its citizens the freedom of speech. Its media is tightly controlled, so when Osama bin Laden declared Jihad on the United States, his words took on a semiofficial resonance. He was wealthy, his family called princes their friends, and because he was not disavowed for his speech and because the government did not contradict him, the "truth" of his words cast a long shadow.

In the 1990s, Osama would speak often of how the United States had murdered Muslim men, women, and children. In the days before American troops invaded Iraq and Afghanistan, these pronouncements left Americans baffled. To their recollection, they had never engaged in warfare against the Arab people or the Muslim faith. But this was to overlook that American weapons had killed Arabs, in the tens of thousands. Flown by Israeli pilots, American-made airplanes dropped American-made bombs. Israeli gunners fired American-made artillery pieces that scattered American-made cluster bombs on Arab soldiers and civilians alike.

No one in Saudi Arabia contradicted him, and nobody in the United States could bring themselves to take Osama bin Laden seriously.

That he was anti-Israel was no surprise. King Faisal had called Jews "monkeys." That Osama thought the U.S. was to blame for Israel's career of military aggression was a perception that was shared, even among Western leftists. Hugo Chávez, the darling of Latino progressives, has compared Israeli military operations to "genocide." Asked by the French newspaper *Le Monde* to comment about Israeli retaliation against Hamas militants in the Gaza strip, he said, "What was it if not genocide? . . . The Israelis were looking for an excuse to exterminate the Palestinians."

Osama bin Laden agreed. Talking to the men sitting and kneeling in rows on the floor of the mosque before him, he told them it was time to leave *Dar Islam,* the place of Islam, and enter the labyrinth of *Dar Jihad.*

It was time to abandon their jobs, their lives, the families that loved them; they should give away all their possessions and enter with him into *Dar Jihad*: the place of war.

Bin Laden was as good as his word.

Taking a page from the Lebanon's terror group Hezbollah, Osama bin Laden ordered that two martyrs be selected, trained, and sent to Africa. On the morning of August 7, 1998, a rented Mitsubishi Canter truck turned toward the gate of the American embassy in Nairobi, Kenya. Built to Hezbollah specifications, the truck bomb contained more than a ton of gas-enhanced high explosives, stacked and configured to maximize blast effect and concussive shock. Like the bomb that struck the Marine barracks, a firing wire had been installed between the explosive payload and the passenger compartment. It was a "dead man's switch" that allowed the driver to actuate the bomb without taking his hand from the steering wheel.

It was 10:30 in the morning. Grinding gears, the Canter truck rolled up to the embassy gate. In quick succession, a grenade was thrown, shots were fired, and the bomb was detonated. The explosion melted the concrete façade of the chancellery building, blasting out windows and starting fires. But the real carnage was done to the buildings surrounding the embassy. The multistory Ufundi Building was torn apart by the shock wave and collapsed, killing hundreds of students and teachers at a secretarial college—most of them women in their twenties. A ten-foot chunk of white-hot shrapnel flew down Haile Selassie Street, and tore through a packed commuter bus. It burst into flames, incinerating dozens of passengers in their seats. Throughout the city of Nairobi, windows shattered in high-rises, raining glass down on panicked citizens, maiming and blinding many scores of people.

Nine minutes later, and four hundred miles away, another Al Qaeda truck bomb, configured with both high explosives and cylinders of compressed oxygen, was detonated at the American embassy in Dar es Salaam, Tanzania. It tore a five-foot-deep crater into the Bagamoyo Road, and sent a swirling, mushroom-shaped cloud five hundred feet into the sky.

When the smoke wafted away, almost a hundred Tanzanian citizens were struck down, eleven killed instantly and eighty-five more suffering second- and third-degree burns, blast effect, and shrapnel injuries. The bomb in Nairobi had been even more devastating. In the smoke-choked swirling chaos after the explosions, buildings collapsed on either side of the American embassy, trapping hundreds of people. Four thousand Kenyan civilians were injured, and two hundred and twenty-two people had been killed.

Many of the victims in both Nairobi and Dar es Salaam were innocent Muslims.

On October 12, 2000, another pair of Al Qaeda martyrs brought a speedboat loaded with explosives alongside an American destroyer, refueling at a pier in the harbor at Aden, in the country of Yemen. A sophisticated charge exploded next to the warship's hull—blasting a fifteen-foot-wide hole into the ship, killing seventeen sailors and burning and wounding thirty-nine more.

Osama had only begun to pay back the United States for its crimes against Muslims. In February 2001, the Israeli minister of defense who was found personally responsible for the massacres at Sabra and Shatila was elected to the office of prime minister of the nation of Israel. Osama's anger grew cold and implacable.

In September 2001, nineteen years after the attacks on the Lebanese camps, Osama would order the 9/11 attacks on the United States. This time he would command four near simultaneous attacks, using hijacked airliners to smash into what he considered symbols of American arrogance and greed: the Twin Towers of the World Trade Center in New York City and the Pentagon in Washington, D.C.

Three thousand innocent, unarmed American men, women, and children would be consumed in the attacks—almost the same number who perished at Sabra and Shatila.

Osama had brought Jihad to America.

WEAPONS OF MASS DENIAL

MAY 2003: IT COULD BE SEEN PLAINLY through binoculars: an artillery shell, angled up onto the side of the curb, in a position to maximize blast effect and shrapnel—a fairly typical roadside bomb. For an improvised explosive device, the design was crude, the fuse appeared to be wired to a wristwatch and battery, but it was surely a Humvee killer. The patrol had seen it a hundred yards away, stopped and called in the Explosive Ordnance Disposal guys from battalion. Everyone was now hunkered under cover, and they were impatient; the sun was beating down and they wanted to get going, but the bomb technicians were in no hurry to go forward.

The IED was too obvious. No one had tried to cover it with trash, or bury it by the roadside—it was just sitting in the open, taunting them.

What the bomb techs worried about was a trap. Not even the laziest insurgent left an IED out in the open—it was likely that under the artillery shell there was another explosive, maybe even a five-hundred-pound bomb, laid and waiting. The goal was to lure the patrol forward to the obvious threat, then destroy them with the buried charge, or wait until an EOD tech lumbered out in a hundred-pound bomb suit, and simply kill him with a sniper. That was a guess. The head game was played daily between insurgents and bomb disposal teams. The bomb techs peered through their laser-range finders and stared. Maybe it was, after all, just the work of an amateur.

An unmanned aerial vehicle snarled overhead, a small, light, miniature airplane. It scanned the rooftops around the IED with thermal and high-resolution video, beaming the pictures to a laptop in the lead Humvee. There seemed to be no one waiting in ambush. There were no obvious wires or leads pointing to a hidden firing position. The patrol leader had already waited too long. This was after all Saddam Highway, the main road leading into the Baghdad airport, and it wasn't a good place to stay.

The technician donned her bomb suit, a hundred pounds of Kevlar and ceramic armor plate, checked the audio and video connection to the laptop, and waddled toward the patiently lethal object at the side of the road. This simple, selfless act of valor was committed a dozen times a day all over Iraq.

The tech quickly identified the improvised explosive, a 155 mm artillery shell, painted with a faded yellow band. The shell was maybe twenty inches long, a steel cylinder truncated into a tapering arch. A digital clock taped to the shell had stopped at 11:30. Without incident, the bomb tech attached a "disrupter," a countercharge designed to separate the main explosive shell from the smaller, electrically activated blasting cap connected to the clock. The tech returned to cover, radioed "fire in the hole" and set off the disrupter using a remote firing device. There was a small, sharp crack as the disrupter blew off the clock and battery, rendering the roadside bomb safe.

The bomb technician doffed her protective suit and walked forward with her partner to inspect the IED. Per standing orders, they would collect what was left of the shell, watch, and battery. The pieces would be studied and logged, and details of the incident would be added to the growing catalog accumulated by the FBI's Bomb Data Unit.

As they approached the curb, both technicians could smell a sweet, flowery odor, not unpleasant, something like the smell of Juicy Fruit chewing gum. The first tech was close enough to see a puddle of amber colored liquid rolling against the curb. He knew immediately what it was, and he waved his partner back. By now, there was a ringing in his ears and his vision started to wash out—the sunlight seemed suddenly blinding, the result of his pupils dilating uncontrollably. The artillery shell placed against the curb did not contain high explosives, but a deadly nerve gas called sarin. And now both techs had been exposed.

The bomb tech tried to yell a warning, but could only stumble backward and fall. His partner grabbed him under the arms and dragged him back toward the Humvee. She laid him out and fumbled in the cargo pocket of her trousers for an atropine serette. The serette was a spring-loaded syringe containing valium, atropine, and obidoxime. It was now her only hope of saving him. His eyes rolled wildly, the pupils huge and black, and his hands began to shake and clutch as the muscles in his body locked up. The tech slammed the serette into his leg, and then pushed a second one into her own thigh. She told the infantry guys to get away from them—they were both now contaminated. She told the lieutenant to lead the patrol away, upwind, and radio battalion they had been exposed to nerve gas.

If they were lucky, very lucky, they all might still be able to get out of this alive.

This event was not taken from a Hollywood thriller. It happened on May 16, 2003, in the al Baya neighborhood of western Baghdad. The 155 mm shell discovered on the airport highway contained slightly more than a gallon of the nerve agent called GB or sarin—enough to kill ten thousand people.

The meteorological conditions were perfect—the nerve gas canister had been placed upwind of the target and the location had been chosen for maximum effect. Had the shell functioned as intended, it would have spread a mortal, invisible cloud over a dozen city blocks. Death would have come quickly for ten thousand Iraqi civilians living around the airport, and the three thousand coalition troops stationed at nearby Camp Victory. This attack, using a state-of-the-art nerve gas artillery shell, had been intended by Osama bin Laden to deal a humiliating defeat on the American forces stationed in Iraq.

That the bomb failed to detonate was due to the malfunction of a cheap, ten-dollar wristwatch.

Although the attack blipped on the media's radar, the story was quickly quashed. The press wasn't interested in stories about WMD in Iraq: They had already convinced themselves, and most of the American public, that Saddam Hussein didn't have any chemical weapons. Since Saddam had none, Osama bin Laden couldn't possibly have any.

That was the story line they were invested in. And it was dead, flat wrong.

Is a chilling fact that thousands of chemical weapons have been uncovered in Iraq. What's worse, chemical weapons of Iraqi provenance have been transported through Iran and Pakistan into Afghanistan. These weapons have been used by Al Qaeda against coalition and NATO forces on dozens of occasions.

What's so important about a handful of overlooked chemical munitions? To put these weapons into perspective, if two nerve gas artillery shells were detonated in a crowded football stadium, say, any Nebraska home game, the casualties could exceed those suffered by the United States during the *entire* Vietnam War. One artillery shell could fit easily into a large duffle bag. Nor do the means of delivery need to be overly complex: Concealed as a business delivery and wired to a cellular phone, an improvised chemical device could be delivered to the target by Federal Express. It is only a matter of time before improvised chemical weapons are used to produce a mass casualty incident within the continental United States. Bad actors do not need access to complex military hardware in order to stage a chemical attack. Chemical agents taken from warheads, shells, and bombs can be recycled.

Terrorists have improvised chemical weapons using plastic bags, aerosol sprayers, and commercially available smoke generators. The technological barrier to entry is the production of effective and lethal chemical agents. Saddam has supplied the chemicals, in abundance; the means of delivery is left to the imagination of Al Qaeda. To be fair, this first use of terrorist chemical weapons was reported in the media. Both *The New York Times* and BBC reported that a chemical weapon had been used at al Baya. The story wafted over to academia, where it has been discussed in counterterrorism journals. Then nothing.

What is to be made of the deafening silence surrounding chemical weapons in Iraq? Why was the American public deliberately left with the impression that there were no weapons of mass destruction in Iraq? The story lost traction in mainstream news for a number of reasons, some of them political. The media turned a blind eye to continued reports of chemical weapon attacks partially because its own credibility was threatened. Several major outlets were deeply invested with the story line of an "unjustifiable war."

What happened at al Baya was a paradigm shift in world history. The use of nerve gas by Al Qaeda in Iraq was the first time in the history of mankind that strategic weapons (in this case a chemical weapon) had been used on the battlefield by a nonstate actor. But editors and news producers did not bestir themselves. They hoped the story would go away. Not many people can bear to admit they were wrong, especially in print, and especially if they have been *very* wrong for a *very* long time.

To perpetuate the myth of "no WMD in Iraq" the media and the U.S. government has had to scrupulously ignore facts on the ground, the testimony of victims, half a dozen United Nations reports, and medical journal articles discussing the treatment of soldiers exposed to nerve gas. Clearly, big media in the United States wanted nothing to do with the issue. Presented with facts, it ignored them. The facts wouldn't go away. Confirmation of the chemical attacks would come from a very unlikely source: the U.S. military itself. Enter Julian Assange and the WikiLeaks Papers.

In July 2010, three years after the nerve gas bomb fizzled in al Baya, WikiLeaks released 492,000 classified U.S. documents relating to the war in Afghanistan. WikiLeaks' publicity-conscious director Julian Assange was quick to compare his disclosure to the 1970s publication of the Pentagon Papers. The WikiLeaks trove dwarfs its historical counterpart—both in vastness and in lurid detail. If the Pentagon Papers revealed a military leadership in disagreement about the Vietnam War, the WikiLeaks documents paint a picture of a pair of schizophrenic U.S. administrations who say one thing, do another, and continue to deny a terrifying and potentially world altering truth. Since 2004, Al Qaeda has carried out at least one hundred chemical attacks on coalition forces in Iraq. Most attacks used "repurposed" chemical warheads from Saddam's arsenal—nerve gases and mustard gas. Although these incidents briefly found their way onto page one, pundits have failed to grasp their significance. The Obama administration, like the Bush administration before them, ignored the attacks and hoped no one else would notice.

If one believes the WikiLeaks trove, it confirms that Al Qaeda is in possession of chemical weapons, and they have been used against U.S. troops in both Iraq and Afghanistan. The largest part of the WikiLeaks documents consists of message traffic from forward-deployed U.S. forces to higher headquarters. These messages state that some of the chemical weapons discovered by U.S. troops were judged so dangerous that they had to be neutralized on site by "Technical Escort." Also called TEU, Technical Escort Units are a top secret outfit trained in nuclear, chemical, and biological warfare. Technical Escort Units are not sent willy-nilly into the field; they deploy only when a chemical, biological, or nuclear threat has been confirmed. Technical Escort is mentioned eleven times in the WikiLeaks documents.

The "no WMDs in Iraq" myth has been allowed to persist because the truth is much more disturbing. Flaunting UN sanctions, and baffling UN inspection teams, Iraq maintained a considerable stockpile of biological and chemical warheads—up to and after the U.S. invasion in 2003. Saddam's failure to account for his weapons of mass destruction was the *casus belli* of the Second Gulf War.

Where did these weapons go? What happened and where are they now?

Following the first Gulf War, UN resolutions demanded that Iraq surrender, dismantle, and destroy its Weapons of Mass Destruction. For almost a decade, television was filled with the Keystone antics of UN inspectors chasing down Iraqi military convoys, battling obstinate gate guards and launching surprise inspections at "Baby Milk" factories. Saddam's farcical efforts to thwart UN compliance teams were, never the less, effective. The UN Special Commission (UNSCOM) and its successor, the United Nations Monitoring, Verification and Inspection Commission (UNMOVIC) both had little to show for months of digging. The UN discovered no nuclear materials, only a few leaky chemical shells, and a number of dented biological warfare bombs and warheads. It was hardly an arsenal.

Early, cursory searches for Saddam's weapons came up empty-handed.

The conspicuous failure of UN inspections and sanctions was ridiculed in two high-profile books, one by former Chief Weapons Inspector Hans Blix, and the other by ex-National Security Council staffer Richard Clarke. Both expressed the opinion that Iraq's Weapons of Mass Destruction had been destroyed. Their arguments were well turned out but pivoted on the same dangerous piece of illogic: "We looked for weapons and didn't find any—that means they don't exist."

If the WikiLeaks papers are searched for under the term "chemical warfare improvised explosive device (CWIED)," more than six hundred documents offer themselves for inspection. "Suspected chemical" yields an additional eighty-five. These are battlefield reports of hundreds of Al Qaeda chemical attacks. These include some of the deadliest substances known to man: VX, a persistent nerve agent; varieties of liquid and powdered mustard gas; the war gas phosgene; and blood agents like cyanogen chloride. By 2004 it was clear that Saddam's "legacy" weapons were being repurposed as improvised explosive devices and that several Iraqi insurgent groups were working to create their own chemical and biological weapons—*for export.* Yet the chorus droned on: "There are no WMD in Iraq."

Until the WikiLeaks confirmation, no dissenting analysis was to be heard in the commercial and mainstream media. In the face of such blithe indifference it was easy for many to forget that Iraq's terror weapons were not a matter of speculation—they were historical fact. During the Iran-Iraq War, over 100,000 Iranians were killed, blinded, or mutilated by Saddam's chemical weapons. From 1980 to 1988, these weapons were produced in Iraqi factories by the tens of thousands—then used on the battlefield. Iraq's own paperwork indicates that it developed chemical and biological weapons to include nerve and mustard gas, anthrax, bubonic plague, and ricin. These were not samples burbling in some petri dish. Saddam produced bombs, missile warheads, and remote control aircraft to scatter these pathogens. In hindsight, it should have been obvious that Saddam would not, indeed he *could* not, destroy his arsenals. His military had been thrashed and scattered after the First Gulf War. Following his calamitous retreat from Kuwait, Saddam faced grave internal threats—Shiite uprisings in the south and Kurdish rebellion in the north. More ominous was the continued hostility of his well-armed neighbor and mortal enemy, Iran.

Even after defeat in the First Gulf War, Iraq concealed and sustained a wide-ranging chemical and biological warfare program. Despite UN Resolutions, surprise inspections, and crushing economic sanctions, Saddam continued to manufacture chemical weapons, and repeatedly used them against his enemies. In March 1991, Mi-8 Helicopters swooped over the cities of Najaf and Karbala; the anti-riot agent CS and the nerve agent VX were used to kill thousands of Shiite insurgents who had attacked Iraqi police outposts and Ba'ath party headquarters. Saddam kept his arsenal topped off. Documents discovered in 2003 indicated that Iraq stockpiled 21,000 chemical warheads following the Iran-Iraq war, and during the period of UN sanctions.

Despite mixed signals from the Obama administration and the continuing indifference of the press, the number and type of WMDs being recovered in Iraq has been *increasing*, rather than decreasing. Again, if the WikiLeaks documents are correct, Saddam's WMD were not destroyed, but simply dispersed. These weapons are presently in the hands of Al Qaeda. Since the 2003 invasion of Iraq, U.S. and coalition forces have located and destroyed more than five-hundred chemical weapons. Most of these have been 155 mm artillery shells. Most contained varieties of the vesicant HD, mustard gas. VX, sarin, tabun, cyclosarin, including advanced binary weapons, chemical aircraft bombs, mortar projectiles, sprayers, and bulk-produced agent have also been recovered and destroyed. It can be assumed that these weapons systems, too, are in the hands of Al Qaeda.

How did this happen? How are these weapons permitted to fall into the hands of Al Qaeda? In the chaos of the U.S. invasion in 2003, Saddam Hussein lost control of both his government and the widely scattered caches where he had dumped his WMD and chemical weapons. As American forces poured across the Iraqi frontier, members of Saddam's intelligence services buried more than ten thousand serviceable chemical warheads. As the Iraqi insurgency coalesced, the location of these hidden caches was communicated to Osama bin Laden, who ordered the weapons to be collected and rehidden. A portion of these munitions were shipped secretly through Pakistan and Iran, then stockpiled near Bin Laden's underground lair in Tora Bora, Afghanistan.

As recently as the twenty-second and twenty-third of February 2008, Osama bin Laden ordered truck bombs containing chlorine gas to be detonated in Baghdad. These were test runs for similar devices to be employed against U.S. cities. The effects, though horrendous, disappointed the Al Qaeda leadership. Casualties from the poison gas and from the blast effect killed or wounded slightly more than a hundred people in sequential attacks.

Bin Laden had been hoping for casualties in the thousands. Al Qaeda bombers went back to the drawing board, to design the more devastating weapons.

The WikiLeaks documents and the events of the past thirty-six months suggest first, Saddam did *not* destroy his chemical arsenal. And second, Al Qaeda is manufacturing its own chemical weapons using legacy materials from Iraq's stockpile as well as material produced in their own clandestine laboratories. Instead of preventing Weapons of Mass Destruction from falling into the hands of terrorists, the 2003 invasion of Iraq has accelerated the acquisition, manufacture, and use of chemical weapons by Al Qaeda.

In a scathing article in the British magazine *The Spectator,* dated April 2, 2007, journalist Melanie Phillips summed up the entire WMD mess:

> The Republicans won't touch this because it would reveal the incompetence of the Bush administration in failing to neutralize the danger of Iraqi WMD. The Democrats won't touch it because it would show President Bush was right to invade Iraq in the first place. It is an axis of embarrassment.

If the purpose of the American intervention in Iraq was to remove the threat of Saddam's WMD it has backfired, dreadfully.

Clearly, there is a major disconnect between public perception, media reporting, government admissions, and truth on the ground. For the administration and the media, the mantra "we didn't find any" remains preferable to the admission "we have armed the enemy."

History is marked by military turning points: the battles at Cannae, Waterloo, the German Blitzkrieg through Europe, and America's defeat in Vietnam stand as examples. In each case, a radical, epoch-making change in tactics led to the defeat of a world power. On May 16, 2003, in al Baya, Iraq, the world changed forever. Until that day, weapons of mass destruction had been the sole prerogative of superpowers.

Al Qaeda has chemical weapons. This nightmarish fact is why the wars in Iraq and Afghanistan have dragged on for more than a decade. Osama bin Laden, an ascetic, religiously self-educated multimillionaire, had declared war on the United States, and he meant to see it destroyed root and branch. His was no idle boast—Osama bin Laden had financed and directed the most horrific acts of terrorism in history. At his behest Al Qaeda had bombed embassies, beheaded journalists, and plotted the assassinations of President Clinton and Pope John Paul. He had sent airliners hurtling into the World Trade Center, and watched gleefully on a satellite dish as three thousand people were incinerated. Now he had chemical weapons—and he intended to use them against the United States.

Only one thing stood in his way: SEAL Team Six.

NEPTUNE'S SPEAR

CONTINUE TO PLAN, PLAN TO CONTINUE

ON A COLD JANUARY MORNING in Virginia Beach, the STE telephone rang in Scott Kerr's office at SEAL Team Six. It warbled three or four times a day, direct from JSOC's headquarters, and it usually meant that someone was going somewhere. When the SEAL officer detailer notified Scott that he would be the new CO of SEAL Six, he was delighted: it was the most coveted command in the SEAL community—the top of the heap. He had now been on the job seven months, and had started to wonder occasionally if it had been such a great idea to come aboard. Six was engaged worldwide, and doing some seriously cool stuff, but he was stuck most of the time in Virginia Beach. Scott used to kid his wife, Martha, that he'd been hired as a travel agent.

The caller, JSOC's chief of staff, asked Scott to fly down for an afternoon meeting. *Right now?* But before he could ask for a postponement, the chief of staff made the issue moot. *The meeting size is at three,* he said, *you, the admiral, and some guy from the agency*. Scott leaned back in his chair. The admiral meant William McRaven, the boss of JSOC, and the agency, perennial and spreading as rapidly as poison ivy, was the CIA. This was important, and Scott found a starchy uniform shirt on the back of the private shower adjoining his office and called for his briefcase. Buck Buckwalter stuck his head into the office. Buck was the master chief of the command, its senior enlisted man. He functioned not only as Scott's direct liaison to the troops, but his right hand for operations and planning. Sometimes he also played butler.

"What do you need in the briefcase, Skipper?" Buck asked. "What'cha want me to draw?" Buck was referring to contingency plans, of which the command had a thousand. What-ifs for everything from presidential kidnapping to how to take an embassy back from rioters in Estonia.

"No subject," Scott said. "Not yet." Scott buttoned up his uniform blouse, checked the shine on his jump boots, and found his starched Navy cover. "Just fill me up with the admin flight, so I can do some tree killing on the way down."

Travel to and from headquarters was so routine that Scott Kerr had a special briefcase prepared for what he called "the admin flight"—work he could do as the helicopter traveled between bases. It was the stuff that made him feel like a travel agent: reports on fuel and ammunition consumption, travel orders, per diem and rental car receipts, performance evaluations, and the reams of paper that torture commanding officers in every branch of the service. As the Team's blue and silver Hughes 500 flew over Albermarle Sound, Kerr rarely looked out the window as he signed, edited, and "chopped" has way through an Augean stable of administrative horseshit.

The conference room at JSOC is three stories underground, and sits behind a foot-thick, soundproof steel door with both an electronic card reader and an old-fashioned combination lock, like a bank safe in a spaghetti western. Actually there are about six of these rooms at JSOC, but Scott was heading for the one called "Flag"—the one deepest underground and closest to the admiral's office.

At JSOC, no one calls any of these places "conference rooms," unless a civilian has been invited. Civilian invitees are usually senators, or secretaries of defense or deputy directors of the CIA or occasionally the FBI or Department of State. Everyone else, everyone military, calls them "the vaults."

These steel doors outnumber regular doors in the intricately connected basements of JSOC headquarters. All of the conference rooms and most of the working offices have the same gray, oppressive, electronically secured doors. The most important vaults, like Flag, also have an armed guard standing in front of them.

The first hint Scott had that something was afoot was when he walked into Flag A and found only two attendees: Vice Admiral Bill McRaven, JSOC's commanding officer, and a short, thin-lipped man whom the admiral introduced as Walter Youngblood, an intelligence officer from the CIA's Counterterrorism Center. The admiral and the agency man each had a pair of thick folders in front of him.

When the guard closed the vault door a red light panel switched on: BRIEFING IN PROGRESS. When no one else came into the room, Kerr knew this was going to be interesting. The room was locked and guarded and would stay that way until their meeting was over. Kerr sat when the admiral did. He had known Bill McRaven for more than twenty years, and the six-foot three-inch Texan was known throughout the community for his poker face. The CIA guy was an unknown. He was keeping his expression a near blank, but unlike McRaven the man from Langley was showing a giddy sort of happiness under the surface, like a school kid who'd brought a frog to school in his lunch box. Kerr thought he might have seen the agency guy before, at some conference or another, but he didn't place him right away.

The admiral came right to the point, "We're going to need some of your guys for a while. To set up a planning cell."

"How many?" There were never enough Jedis to go around, and CIA was famous for wanting Team guys to advise their own "experts" on a host of tactical matters. The job was so routine and disliked that the shooters had long ago christened the trips to Langley as "Pet SEAL" operations.

"It looks like we've got a line on a high-value individual. And a location this time. It's firming up, and I want to have an immediate action plan in hand if he looks like he's going to move."

Scott Kerr didn't blink. High-value individual didn't necessarily mean Osama bin Laden. But the fact that there were only three people in this brief added a lot of gravity. Osama had been the most hunted man in the world for almost a decade—and the SEALs had been close more than once: In September 2008, Scott had participated in a raid launched deep into Waziristan, to a one-goat town called Angoor Ata. CIA provided intel stating that Osama was in residence, but the SEALs came up empty. Since the 9/11 attacks, Osama had been seen everywhere from Tehran to Tripoli. One lady clairvoyant kept sending perfumed letters to JSOC, stating that she had "visions" of Osama hiding out at the Ritz in London.

Clairvoyants aside, there was some very serious speculation within JSOC that Osama was dead. No one thought anymore that Osama was hiding out and living on Pashtun hospitality. There was a $25 million bounty on his head. Hospitality or no hospitality, for $25 million most people will turn in their grandmothers. Many people in JSOC thought that Osama was being sheltered by a government, either dead or alive. The "He's Dead" theory went that Osama had been murdered by the Pakistani ISI, and that they had concealed his death to make sure that the "boogeyman" of international Jihad kept the money flowing to the Pakistani armed forces. It was starting to make sense to a lot of people, especially since more and more of Al Qaeda's intercepted communications indicated a simmering power struggle between Osama and Ayman Zawahiri. Zawahiri had turned back up in late 2003, crossing into Pakistan. Like Bin Laden, he was figured to be in the tribal areas, or maybe southern Iran.

Scott Kerr looked across the table to the CIA guy, a perfectly anonymous-looking person in a suit that you wouldn't remember either. That's where he remembered him from—Angoor Ata.

"All right," Kerr said. "Tell me what's up."

Kerr knew better than to ask exactly where they thought this high-value individual might be. Operators know better than to ask noun-verb-object questions when they are first being "written in" on a project. They listen first. And strange as it might seem, for most of Kerr's intents and purposes, exactly where the HVI might be located was irrelevant. If this was Osama, his geospatial location mattered only to the extent that it affected a SEAL Team's insertion and extraction. McRaven knew, and Walter had a pretty good idea how SEAL Team Six conducted actions at the objective.

McRaven was leaning back in his chair and had one hand on the edge of the table. Kerr noticed he wasn't touching the files yet. The admiral said, "I talked to the DCI yesterday, he wants us to open the file and start the planning cycle."

The DCI, director of Central Intelligence, was Leon Panetta. McRaven dropped this name as an overture to what Walter would now tell Scott Kerr. It made Scott pay attention, perhaps more than he normally would to another CIA theory on Bin Laden's secret hiding place.

"There's a compound," Walter said. "We've had it under surveillance for a couple of weeks now. We're certain there's a high-profile individual inside."

Maybe they weren't talking about Osama at all.

"How high profile?" Kerr looked at the admiral.

"He's in a walled compound," McRaven answered. "Maybe an acre and a half, photographs are in the target folder. The best we can tell, he's in there with about two dozen people. There's no telephone lines into the building, and no Internet. These guys burn their own trash, keep their gates locked, and homeschool their kids."

"How many kids?"

"A dozen. Something like that," Walter said.

That complicated things immensely. It's one thing to hit a high-value target—that's pretty straightforward. But to hit a target that is also an elementary school would be a lot different.

"How heavily defended is this place?"

Walter spoke. "There doesn't seem to be much overtly defensive behavior."

Kerr looked at McRaven again. "Overtly defensive behavior" was not a term in the SEAL Team lexicon.

McRaven's voice was even. "We haven't seen any armed guards, uniformed or not. The defenders keep a low profile. That doesn't mean people aren't in there with guns. There are at least five military-aged males in the compound and the guesthouses. They are certainly armed."

Walter said, "What we've been seeing are some women and children in the compound. We think they are all related. Multiple families."

"How many people total?"

"Twenty or so. Twenty-five."

"There's a structure on the roof of the main building. A three-sided box, open at the top. It looks like it was built for some antiaircraft equipment, a machine gun probably. The gun isn't mounted now and they haven't seemed to be putting it up at night. It's not impossible that there are some Strela missiles in there."

"That's not good," Kerr said aloud. Strelas were helicopter killers.

"CIA is going to start putting some assets in on the ground. They're going to start seeing if we can get a make on the occupant."

Scott Kerr looked at his boss. In the days of digital camouflage uniforms with slant pockets and Velcro, Bill McRaven still wore an old school green woodland-pattern battle dress uniform. It made a statement about how he approached special operations. That's not to say he wasn't innovative—fresh tactics and out-of-the-box thinking are what make special operations succeed. Bill McRaven's Naval Postgraduate School thesis had blossomed into a three-hundred-page survey of ten of the most important special operations in military history. Like most other SEAL officers, Scott had read the admiral's book. Bill McRaven generally knew what he was talking about.

"So is this Bert or Ernie?" Kerr asked.

Over the last couple years, SEAL team intelligence analysts had christened Osama bin Laden as "Bert" and Ayman Zawahiri, his second in command, as "Ernie." One was tall and taciturn and the other was a short, round yapper. They were named after the famous Muppet characters on *Sesame Street.* Some wag in intel had come up with the handle, and it stuck.

Walter didn't get the reference to *Sesame Street.* JSOC's official handle for Osama was "Crankshaft."

"Our technical people got a voiceprint," Walter added quietly. "The recordings were a little sketchy, but the voiceprints are telling us at about sixty or seventy percent that this is probably our guy."

"Technical" meant listening devices or communications intercepts. A voiceprint was a pretty good hook to hang an identification on.

"National Reconnaissance Office has parked a satellite over the place. They got a measurement on his shadow," McRaven added. "He's over six feet tall."

For the first time in the meeting, Scott Kerr felt his pulse quicken. Putting a satellite over a target was not something that just happened. Reconnaissance satellites were national assets. They didn't just get pointed over places of routine interest. This was beginning to look like the real deal.

McRaven was as good at reading expressions as he was at controlling his own.

"I've got another meeting with the president on March fourteenth. I am looking at three courses of action. One is a JDAM." A JDAM was a smart bomb with a range of thirty or forty miles. They were relatively low tech, and had a better ability to penetrate hard targets than a cruise missile. Unlike cruise missiles, a JDAM couldn't get shot down, and very seldom went off course. JDAMs were usually dispensed by Stealth bombers, and whatever they hit usually stayed dead. Really dead. There was the strong possibility that if a couple of JDAMs were used to take out Osama there wouldn't be much left, of him, his house, or the neighborhood.

McRaven continued, "The second option is a combined operation with the host nation."

The words "host nation" were another tripwire.

"Host" implied that this six-foot person was a "guest" somewhere. If Kerr were being tasked to conduct an operation in Iraq or Afghanistan, no one would have implied that a host-and-guest dynamic might be involved. As a rule, JSOC confined combined operations to trusted NATO allies. What SEAL Team Six did might be fairly well guessed at, but how they went around getting it done was a zealously guarded secret.

Kerr's next question would narrow the possible locations for him considerably. "Is this a permissive or a nonpermissive environment?"

"Nonpermissive," Walter said.

Nonpermissive environments were ones in which the governments were hostile to the United States. A special operations team entering a nonpermissive environment could count on being shot at. At this point, Kerr's possibilities for a host nation included Syria, Lebanon, and Iran—with Libya and Somalia as long shots. Semipermissive environments would have included Yemen and a couple of other places without zip codes.

At this point Scott Kerr was thinking Iran, but he kept his mind open. He didn't expect to be told exactly where they thought Osama was. It was not at all unusual for SEALs to train for a mission, even extensively train, and not be told until the last minute where the target would be. Scott looked again at the thick folder in front of Admiral McRaven.

"How am I going to insert?" Kerr was not asking for advice. This was another question that would help him to both narrow down the target list and start to train his guys.

"160th SOAR," McRaven said. "Range from doorknob to doorknob will be about two hundred miles."

That meant helicopters. A hundred miles into the target and a hundred miles to get back out. Kerr's operators would be limited in their time on target, and they would be in hostile territory. Helicopters need a lot of fuel to fly two hundred miles, plus whatever loitering time it took to wait for a SEAL Team to do its thing. A two-hundred-mile trip would involve refueling, a tricky process in a combat zone.

"Plan on inserting with Ghost Hawks," McRaven said.

That clinched it for Kerr.

If he had any doubts whether this might be an elaborate sort of exercise, they vanished in this instant. The Ghost Hawk helicopters were among the most highly classified aircraft possessed by the U.S. military. SEAL Six used them routinely and they were only used by Six and Delta. They were Jedi rides, so secret they were only flown at night, and kept in locked, guarded hangars during the day. The Ghost Hawks were so low noise that the SEALs joked that they flew in "whisper mode." The newest version of the Stealth helos, the GEN 3s, were even quieter than the previous editions called Stealth Hawks. The Ghost Hawks were invisible to radar and emitted zero electromagnetic radiation. They had shielded exhausts so they put off not much more heat than a Harley motorcyle. They were only used on the most important missions.

"Who's standing down now?" McRaven asked.

"The Red Men," Kerr answered. During "stand down," a squadron went for a month performing weapons and equipment refurbishment and sent operators to various schools to keep their skills sharp.

"All right," McRaven said. "Start bringing them back from their trips. I'm looking at a ninety-day planning and ranging window." McRaven pushed one of his folders across the table, and Walter added one of his to McRaven's.

"Read yourself into the target. Who's the Red squadron leader?"

"Frank Leslie."

"Okay, send him up, with his master chief, and we'll give them some offices . . ." McRaven broke off. "Walter will give them some offices, up in Langley.

"I am going to want a tentative full-mission profile. Be ready to brief it back to me in forty-eight hours. The object of the mission is close hold. Nobody knows about who you're going after or where it might be. No speculation."

"Check."

"You can have your Seabees build a mockup to these specifications and then we'll run a cycle of rehearsals at Tall Pines."

Tall Pines was a sprawling, secret Army training facility tucked in Camp Pickett, which was itself put off into the far corner of a national forest in an eastern state. Lots of spooky things happened in Pickett, and the SEAL Teams have trained there for years. Far from the prying eyes of the public, surrounded by tens of thousands of acres of woodland, dozens of target mockups dot Tall Pines' rolling hills. Some nights, strange, silent lights are seen over the forest and UFO calls are made to the sheriff. Camp Pickett is SEAL Six's playground.

"What's the time frame on this?" Scott asked.

"If you mean when will this go down, that's up to the president," McRaven said. "Get your guys up to Langley, and start in on a detailed plan."

It was a pretty tall order to prepare the full battle plan in two days, but Scott knew his guys could do it. Their entire career had been full of planning, intense, complicated work often done at the last minute because when orders come down from on high, the suits usually want it done ten minutes ago. The full mission plan would take weeks to craft and would be informed by more intelligence as it came to light.

Scott lifted the files and stood. "Easy day," he said.

He shook McRaven's hand and thanked him, nodded to Walter and walked back out into the low-ceilinged corridor. Walking back toward the stairwell was a bit like passing down the passageways belowdecks on a ship. There were no windows.

At the stairwell Scott ran into Colonel Jim Overall, a friend, and his opposite number from 160th SOAR, the "Night Stalker" helicopter squadron. Jim Overall commanded the Ghost Hawk squadron as well as the rest of 160th SOAR. They'd worked together on hundreds of operations, and hosted each other at barbecues and the family birthdays. Now they passed each other with only a nod.

Jim Overall looked down and saw the files in Scott's hand, and heard Admiral McRaven's deep bass voice welcoming him from the door of the conference room. Kerr knew that it was Jim Overall's turn next—they were going to brief the pilots separately.

Scott and Jim exchanged a look that meant *Good luck and I'll talk to you later.* Nonverbal communication skills are vital in special operations.

Scott started up the stairs as the vault door closed behind him. The red BRIEFING IN PROGRESS light again switched on. Scott knew that Jim Overall would be getting pretty much the same brief, but with a little more geographic information. Jim would have to plan flight operations, and one of the first things a pilot needs to know is where he is going. Keeping the information in separate pipelines was called compartmentalization.

The wires of this operation would be kept apart until the last minute.

At the top of the stairs Scott Kerr pushed open the door and emerged into daylight. The sunshine made him blink his eyes. *Jesus Christ,* Kerr thought, *this might really happen.*

First in the manner of planning are the five Ws: Who, What, Where, When and Why. In an intelligence package called a "target folder," the SEALs are told who and where. Based on those parameters, they plan how and when. But the most important part of any SEAL tasking order is a paragraph called "Commander's Intent." Most of the time, it includes the why, the reason behind the operation, but not always. The why of an operation is sometimes too obvious to mention, and occasionally the real reason why is too highly classified to put out on the operator level. The reason why is sometimes only known by one person.

A mission being undertaken for purposes of deception isn't always told to the men sent forward to perform the operation. The Rosetta Stone of the operational plan comes under the heading "Commander's Intent," a clear sentence that sets forward exactly what it is that higher authority wants accomplished.

JSOC is a black program. Deception is involved in every JSOC mission and the SEALs know that wheels turn within wheels, and the civilian portion of the chain of command is a hall of mirrors designed to deflect the stigma of failure, and maximize the rewards of success.

Functioning as a "national asset," JSOC and SEAL Six have a direct chain of command. Scott Kerr, commander of SEAL Team Six, answers only to one person, Admiral Bill McRaven, the commander of JSOC. And

Bill McRaven answers to only two people: the secretary of defense and the president of the United States.

So what was it that SEAL Team Six was being ordered to do? What exactly did the commander in chief want to happen when the SEALs made it to their objective? Admiral McRaven and Captain Scott Kerr both understood that this assignment had not only military requirements but political ramifications as well.

When a man decides to accept a position above the rank of commander in the SEAL Teams, he makes a compromise. Above the rank the Navy calls "0-5," SEAL officers lead Teams and Groups and it becomes rare for officers above the rank of commander to "loot and shoot" with the SEALs under their control. It happens sometimes that a commander will suit up and go out, but not often. By the time a SEAL makes the rank of commander (after fifteen years of service) he is still physically capable of undertaking missions—almost all of the operators at SEAL Team Six are in their mid-thirties or older—but the days of piloting mini-subs, kicking in doors, and rescuing hostages are usually over. Commanders are eased into desk jobs, off the frontlines, and into staff and planning work. They have distinguished themselves leading SEALs in combat—that is how they became commanders—but above this rank, they assume more of a managerial role. In any organization, the skills of a manager are increasingly those of a politician.

SEAL Team admirals, if they are not themselves politicians, are certainly able to translate between politicians and the men who wear the trident. When the mission came down from the White House to interdict a high-value target who was a member of Al Qaeda, Scott Kerr knew, as Bill McRaven did, that not only would the lives of their men be placed in jeopardy, their own lives and careers might possibly hang on the precise legal definition of a term used in their orders.

If they are ordered to "interdict" a target, SEALs may apply the amount of violence necessary to destroy it, as stipulated in the operation's written "Rules of Engagement." If SEALs are assigned to "neutralize" an individual, they are wise to ask, and receive, precise clarification as to what that means. Do they unplug his phone or kill him? If they are told to "take someone out," do they capture that person or apply lethal force?

At the top of the military food chain, admirals and generals consult attorneys. Orders to tactical subordinates are passed through the hands of JAG lawyers who check to make sure that the orders do not contravene the rules of war, the rules of engagement, the Geneva Convention, and a host of other directives including, incredibly, environmental impact. Increasingly, politicians are on hand to second- and third-guess the decisions made by SEALs under fire.

Scott Kerr flew back to the Death Star and his orders slid hot out of a laser printer. They stated that he was to plan to "interdict a high-value individual in a nonpermissive environment" and that he was to detach two officers for "TAD, temporary additional duty" at CIA headquarters to begin the planning cycle. As the operation began to come together, Scott Kerr and the officers of Red Squadron had several cautionary examples to guide them.

On March 31, 2004, three military contractors guarding a food convoy were ambushed in Fallujah, Iraq. One of them was a former Navy SEAL. After the contractors were shot dead, their bodies were dragged from their vehicle, stripped naked, dismembered, and set on fire. Fourteen months later, a SEAL Team captured the man responsible, Ahmed Hashim Abed.

After he was taken into custody, Abed claimed that he had been punched during his capture by one of the SEALs. *Punched.* Major General Charles Cleveland, the commander of the Army's Special Operations Command Central, a politician if ever there was one, insisted that charges of abuse and assault be brought against all the SEALs who captured Ahmed Hashim Abed. The Obama administration concurred, and allowed the matter to proceed to trial.

The SEALs who captured Ahmed Abed were court-martialed in San Diego. They were acquitted and returned to duty. But the White House had no comment and issued no apologies. It was a gratuitous slap in the face that the SEAL community would not forget.

In 2006, during a firefight in Ramadi, Iraq, Navy SEAL Michael A. Monsoor threw himself on a hand grenade that had been lobbed into his position, giving his life to save two other SEALs who had taken cover with him. Three years after Monsoor gave his life to save the lives of others, Major General Cleveland and the Obama administration carried out a determined prosecution of his teammates for "abusing a prisoner."

For his valor, Petty Officer Michael Mansoor was posthumously awarded the Congressional Medal of Honor, becoming the second Navy SEAL to receive his nation's highest decoration since 9/11. The medal was handed to his mother and father in a White House ceremony.

No wonder SEALs have an aversion to politicians.

As Scott Kerr gathered together the leaders of Red Squadron to plan the mission, he had good reason to move forward carefully. Because the bad thing about politicians is that some of them wear uniforms.

VANISHING ACT

IT MIGHT BE ARGUED THAT America's longest war—the invasion and occupation of Afghanistan—started out as an effort to kill one man. After the 9/11 attacks, the United States demanded that the Taliban government of Afghanistan hand over Osama bin Laden and dismantle Al Qaeda's bases. When Afghanistan's head of state, Mullah Omar, refused, air strikes hit Kabul and Kandahar. Taliban and Al Qaeda forces were swept first from the major cities and then gradually south toward the Pakistani frontier. Operation Enduring Freedom began on October 7, 2001. American troops began to arrive by helicopter and parachute, then by flotillas of troop planes, until tens of thousands of U.S. and coalition forces were engaged in battles all over the country. Soon, U.S. Army Special Forces and Northern Alliance troops closed in on the last remaining Al Qaeda stronghold at Tora Bora. As B-52 strikes and Navy and Marine fighter-bombers pounded Al Qaeda and Taliban positions, a grim joke soon made the rounds of Special Operations Forces—Afghanistan was being bombed from the Stone Age into the Gravel Age. It was not very far from the truth.

On December 13, 2001, CIA eavesdroppers at Tora Bora identified Osama bin Laden's voice on the radio as he ordered his men to dig rifle pits and prepare for a suicidal last stand. Dalton Fury, Delta Force's on-scene commander, has stated that he was preparing a final assault when the Afghan militia units with whom he had been operating suddenly balked. Though Osama bin Laden was almost completely surrounded, the Afghans refused to attack. Haji Zaman, the Afghan commander, told the Americans that he had negotiated a local cease-fire with Al Qaeda. When Fury and his men tried to press home the attack on their own, the Afghans drew their weapons.

A tense twelve-hour standoff ensued, with the Afghan militiamen refusing to budge and the Americans prevented from closing and finishing

Al Qaeda's leadership. This bizarre incident came to an end when, as suddenly as they had ceased fighting, the Afghans announced that they would resume operations. Had Haji Zaman been bribed? Fury thinks so—but whatever the reason for the delay, when the Tora Bora caves were finally reached on December 17, Osama bin Laden was nowhere to be found.

Another incident should have been instructive to American war fighters. On November 29, 2001, in an event called "the airlift of evil," a dozen Pakistani Air Force transports landed at the Taliban-controlled airfield at Kunduz. There, the Pakistani military rescued hundreds of non-Afghan Taliban and Al Qaeda fighters. Despite initial American denials (and later protests), this evacuation repatriated hundreds of Pakistani military advisers who had been training both Taliban and Al Qaeda fighters in Afghanistan prior to September 11. Also returned to Pakistan were more than six hundred Pakistani and Arab Al Qaeda volunteers, hard-line fighters who made up the bulk of Osama bin Laden's boots on the ground in Afghanistan. These Jihadis would form a nucleus around which Al Qaeda and the Taliban would reconstitute and continue to fight. From the outset, America's ally Pakistan played by its own set of rules.

It's now believed that Osama bin Laden slipped across the Pakistani frontier near Khair-ud-din during the night of December 16, 2001. As he fled to safety, Osama stayed in radio contact with the last of his Arab Jihadis, who, in covering his retreat, found their own martyrdoms under a hail of American bombs and missiles. Once across the Pakistani frontier, Bin Laden was as safe from the Americans as he had been from the Soviets twenty years before.

Osama knew that the United States was monitoring all electronic means of communication. For the next ten years, Bin Laden would depend on a group of trusted couriers to communicate his orders and to relay both funding and supplies to him. Principal among Osama's bodyguards were two Pakistani nationals born in Kuwait, brothers Ibrahim and Abrar Khan. Ibrahim, the elder, came eventually to be known to U.S. intelligence by his nom de guerre, Abu Ahmed al Kuwaiti. By all reports, the Khan brothers were intelligent, discreet, and multilingual, speaking Urdu, Pashto, and Arabic. Their allegiance to Osama bin Laden and to the cause was absolute. As personal protectors, aides-de-camp, and couriers, the brothers would eventually accompany Bin Laden and his family members to half a dozen safe houses that spanned the length and breadth of Pakistan.

Sometime around December 20, 2001, Osama sent Abrar Khan to Karachi, Pakistan, to make contact with Khalid Sheikh Mohammed, the mastermind of the 9/11 attacks. The portly terrorist had declined an invitation to join the glorious stand at Tora Bora, and was living comfortably in Pakistan's sprawling port city on the Arabian Sea. Bin Laden's courier asked that KSM reestablish communications with Al Qaeda's number two, Ayman Zawahiri, as well as members of the *shura,* or council, some of whom had been airlifted from Kunduz as coalition forces pushed deeper into Afghanistan. A few days after the meeting, Abrar Khan made contact with Amal Ahmed al-Sadah, Bin Laden's fourth and favorite wife. Amal had been sent to take refuge in Karachi, Pakistan, immediately following the 9/11 attacks. On orders from Osama, Abrar Khan guided her back to Bin Laden's safe house in Parachinar in early January.

From the outset, Osama hid in plain sight. Soon after his escape from Tora Bora, he settled into a smart, two-story home in a walled compound just outside of the city of Parachinar—only a dozen or so miles south of the cave complexes at Tora Bora. Al Qaeda had a decades-old network in Pakistan, and Osama had extensive personal contacts with members of the military and intelligence organizations. During the ten-year hunt for Osama bin Laden, it was often said that he had been able to remain hidden because of the iron-clad custom of Pashtun hospitality. Once he had been received as a guest, the assumption went, it was a host's moral duty to keep him safe and his location secret.

This proposition is nonsense. Bin Laden was only able to remain hidden because he received coordinated assistance from the Pakistani Intelligence Service, the ISI, and the Pakistani Armed Forces. The effort to hide him was neither accidental nor sporadic, nor the result of rogue elements within the Pakistani security apparatus; providing safe haven for Taliban and Al Qaeda leadership was the product of a deliberate and calculated national security strategy. Pakistan saw Bin Laden, Zawahiri, and other prominent members of Al Qaeda and the Taliban as insurance policies. It was not in Pakistan's interest for Afghanistan to become a peaceful, prosperous, and self-determining nation. Such an Afghanistan might well drift into the orbit of Pakistan's mortal enemy—India. Bin Laden, Ayman Zawahiri, and the Taliban's Mullah Omar were all "hostages to fortune," men who, Pakistan believed, could have a role in what Afghanistan would become, even if they were only to be spoilers. Afghanistan was too important to Pakistan to let it drift into independence.

Once across the border, Bin Laden and Ayman Zawahiri were "hidden" in plain sight—placed into safe houses in medium-sized military towns in proximity to the border with Afghanistan. During his ten years on the run, only once did Bin Laden ever seek refuge in an isolated rural community. The rest of the time he was in military cantonments, where his ISI handlers could closely coordinate his logistics and communication requirements. Then, as later, the decision was made to hide Bin Laden and the other high-profile Jihadis in the shadow of credible military force, both to facilitate their operational requirements and as a deterrent to cross-border action by American forces. U.S. officials may perhaps be forgiven for not immediately apprehending the staggering duplicity of their Pakistani allies.

There is evidence that Bin Laden suffered some sort of medical emergency soon after his wife Amal's arrival in January 2002. How it was handled was indicative of the freedom of movement Bin Laden enjoyed while in Pakistan. Traveling with an entourage that included his wife, child, and bodyguards, Bin Laden arrived in the city of Peshawar for medical treatment. While there is an army presence in the frontier municipality of Parachinar, Peshawar is an *army town.* The city is the divisional headquarters of Pakistan's XI Army Corps, and home to more than thirty thousand combat troops, as well as sizeable detachments from the ISI, Military Intelligence, and the Frontier Forces. After his medical treatment, Bin Laden convalesced for almost a month at the Khan family residence in Salman Talaab, a small village a short fifteen-minute drive from downtown Peshawar.

According to Amal bin Laden, Osama met with Khalid Sheikh Mohammed in Kohat in late January 2002. It may be assumed that Osama congratulated KSM for the two most spectacular terrorist acts in history. During their meeting in Kohat, KSM communicated the details of several spectacular terror plots. These included plans to attack World Cup soccer matches in Korea in 2002, and a series of operations targeting Western tourists in Africa. It is unknown if Osama had foreknowledge of Khalid's unfolding plan to kidnap and murder an American journalist, but it is likely he was informed of it during their January meeting in Kohat. In any case, it would have been necessary for Bin Laden to approve the plan, and there is no question what happened next.

Soon after KSM's return to Karachi, on January 23, 2002, *Wall Street Journal* reporter Daniel Pearl was abducted on his way to an interview. Pearl was held for a month under brutal conditions, and was forced to read a statement as video cameras rolled. He was then beheaded by Khalid Sheikh Mohammed himself while terrorist companions filmed the entire grisly scene. The video was posted on the Internet and an unknown organization called the National Movement to Restore Pakistani Sovereignty took credit for the murder. The organization was a transparent front. It was KSM's desire to kill a Jew, and it was an Al Qaeda operation from start to finish.

As Osama's health improved, he traveled from Kohat back to his comfortable house in Parachinar. There, he also gave final approval for an attack targeting Western tourists in Tunisia. On April 11, 2002, a propane-enhanced truck bomb was detonated at an ancient Jewish synagogue in Ghriba, Djerba, Tunisia. The blast killed forty Western tourists and critically burned several dozen more.

In the summer of 2002, Osama ordered Khalid Sheikh Mohammed to transfer money to Jemaah Islamiyah, an Al Qaeda–associated terror group based in Indonesia. Members of Jemaah Islamiyah had trained at Osama's camps in Afghanistan, and they'd found a soft target. On the night of October 12, 2002, Jemaah Islamiyah terrorists sent a body bomber into a crowded bar called Paddy's Pub in Bali, Indonesia. The place was filled with Western tourists, many of them Australian surfers who had come to the beautiful and peaceful beaches of the island paradise. A man carrying a backpack waded into the crowd and touched an electrical switch hidden in his pocket. The bomb detonated, sweeping the dance floor with shrapnel, overturning amplifiers, scattering musical instruments, and shattering the mirrors behind the bar. Panicked, the crowd rushed out of the bar into the street—and into a diabolical ambush. A truck bomb containing the equivalent of over a ton of high explosives was driven straight into the crowd and detonated. A one-hundred-foot-wide fireball tore through the block, ripping open buildings, lifting parked cars from the pavement, and killing more than two hundred people instantly. Torn to pieces were eighty-eight Australians, about two dozen Britons, and seven Americans. Hundreds more were wounded, and many of the injured died in a massive fire that consumed a city block. It was the deadliest attack in the history of Indonesia. Jemaah Islamiyah claimed credit, but this was an Al Qaeda operation approved by Osama and coordinated by Khalid Sheikh Mohammed.

While in Parachinar, Bin Laden received plans for another KSM atrocity, this one designed to be even more spectacular and deadly than the Bali bombing. Osama arranged for the transfer of two Soviet-manufactured Strela surface-to-air missiles that he had taken with him from the armory at Tora Bora. These lightweight shoulder-fired missiles are a Russian knockoff of the American Stinger, slightly less effective in range and tracking ability, but never the less deadly, and some of the "Crown Jewels" of Al Qaeda's weaponry. Khalid arranged for the missiles to be smuggled across Pakistan and into Africa.

Mombasa, Kenya, is a tropical city on the southeastern coast of Africa. Its beaches are frequented by Israeli citizens seeking a cheap and exotic getaway under the palms. On November 28, 2002, approximately two hundred Israeli tourists were packed into the lobby of the Paradise Hotel, watching as a troop of native dancers performed a welcoming ceremony. Just as the dancers finished, a green truck smashed through the hotel's outer gate and crashed through the plate glass of the lobby.

The truck bomb exploded and seconds later a suicide bomber who had hidden himself in the crowd set off an explosive vest. Sixteen people were killed instantly, including three children. Seconds later, at Mombasa's Moi International Airport, two more Al Qaeda terrorists stepped from behind a truck parked at the end of the runway. As an Israeli Arkia Airlines jet completed its takeoff roll and roared over their heads, the terrorists pointed their Strela missiles and fired. The missiles streaked upward, trailing behind them a silver plume of rocket exhaust. One missile passed behind the airliner, narrowly missing its starboard engine. The other warhead missed the airliner completely and headed off toward the sun, exploding harmlessly a mile into the sky.

The aircraft landed safely in Tel Aviv. Osama's rocketeers had missed, but only by the smallest of margins. Had either of the missiles struck the airliner, it would have been the worst aviation disaster in Israel's history.

By now, Osama was living and moving about using the "cover" that he was a wealthy Pashtun Afghan who had come over from Khost, fleeing the authorities. As all spies know, a cover should be as close to the truth as possible. Pretending to be a man on the run—in this case an Afghan, not an Arab—worked on several levels. It explained the close presence of bodyguards, and also why their patron could not speak Urdu, the national language. Crucially, it also explained why the tall, quiet stranger preferred houses with high walls. It is a Pashtun custom, *Parda,* to conceal female family members from outside viewers. In 2003, while in Parachinar, Osama's wife Amal gave birth to their second child, a baby girl named Aasia. The child was born in a government hospital and soon disappeared behind the walls of Bin Laden's compound. Despite the ample military presence in Parachinar, Osama's security remained airtight.

While in Parachinar, Osama came up with his grandest and most terrifying plan yet: to attack the Pakistani nuclear site at Kahuta, and steal a nuclear weapon. Pakistan is the fourth largest nuclear power in the world, and is estimated to possess more than one hundred warheads. Pakistan's strategic weapons program is centered in a rural, mountainous area fifteen miles east of Islamabad. The nuclear facility at Kahuta is surrounded by earthen berms and a twenty-foot concrete and razor-wire wall. The nuclear lab and weapons storage areas are heavily defended and the roofs of its several dozen key buildings are painted with digital patterns to obscure them from satellite observation. Only a single road leads into or out of the laboratory, and it is studded with checkpoints. Kahuta is the most heavily defended site in Pakistan—the exact opposite of the soft targets that were Al Qaeda's specialty.

As harebrained as a raid on the weapons facility might at first seem, Al Qaeda had developed contacts with several key scientists working inside the nuclear laboratory, including Sultan Bashiruddin Mahmood and Chaudiri Abdul Majeed. According to reports, in August 2001, a month before the 9/11 attacks, both scientists met with Osama bin Laden and Ayman Zawahiri at a compound in Kandahar, Afghanistan. Later, both were reportedly detained by Pakistani authorities but subsequently released. What information they revealed is unknown, but plans by Al Qaeda went forward for a raid on the facility at Kahuta soon after.

Khalid SheikhMohammed was enthusiastic about the Kahuta operation—but others within Al Qaeda's *shura,* or ruling council, were not. Ayman Zawahiri, in particular, saw the Kahuta attack as suicidal. The Kahuta episode was one of the first signs of Osama's growing estrangement from reality. Still, no one dared stand up directly to the Emir—and after the successes of 9/11 and the Bali bombings, Osama's stock was running high with Al Qaeda's rank and file. During the initial planning stages, Zawahiri pretended to go along with the scheme. The unctuous doctor knew better than to oppose Bin Laden's wishes directly.

Zawahiri consulted Al Qaeda's *shura,* including Mustafa Abu Yazeed al-Misri, and shared his opinion that the consequences of this operation were potentially devastating—not for the innocent people who might be consumed in a nuclear conflagration—but for Al Qaeda as an organization. Bin Laden had seemed utterly to forget that he, as well as Zawahiri, were all in Pakistan on various degrees of permission from the ISI. Any move against Pakistan's strategic weapons would bring the hammer down on them all. Zawahiri worked behind the scenes to derail the Kahuta operation, referring it repeatedly to the *shura,* who took weeks to add a few cosmetic changes to the plan.

In late February 2003, with the go date looming, Zawahiri found he could not dissuade Osama bin Laden, but did not yet want to risk outright disobedience. So how was Zawahiri to foil an operation he saw as a real threat to his own security? As he had so often in the past, Zawahiri got his way by taking down a rival. In intelligence parlance, the doctor "dropped a dime" on Khalid Sheikh Mohammed, meaning that he informed the authorities of his whereabouts. Zawahiri did this by arranging for a mid-level Al Qaeda operative to volunteer the information to the CIA. Zawahiri's plan was ingenious—and it worked.

Khalid Sheikh Mohammed was captured after a previously unknown Al Qaeda member walked into the American embassy in Islamabad, Pakistan. The CIA does not have a very good record with walk-in spies. During the Cold War, many a Soviet defector found himself tossed out on his ear after trying to offer his services to the United States. In order to be taken seriously, a volunteer intelligence source has to provide actionable intelligence—something that is either so important or so time critical that he is taken seriously. After going through the usual hoops at the embassy, the Al Qaeda walk-in was fobbed off with a cell phone and told to call if he ever had anything really important. Two nights later, the walk-in called back from the restroom of a Karachi restaurant and told the CIA, "I'm having dinner with Khalid Sheikh Mohammed."

At two a.m. on March 2, 2003, CIA officers watched as Pakistani police commandos burst into a house in a comfortable Karachi suburb. They kicked down the door to a back bedroom to find Khalid Sheikh Mohammed fast asleep. The terrorist who'd beheaded Daniel Pearl declined an instant trip to paradise and surrendered in his pajamas. Not a shot was fired.

It may never be proven who sent the walk-in into the American embassy in Islamabad, but it is obvious who benefited from the capture of Khalid Sheikh Mohammed. With his only rival out of the picture, Zawahiri instantly regained his position as Al Qaeda's number two. It was Zawahiri who notified Bin Laden that he had to flee—as Zawahiri was quick to point out, KSM knew everything, not only about Kahuta and the other attacks, but about Osama bin Laden's safe house in Parachinar.

Zawahiri used the crisis not only to consolidate his position within Al Qaeda, but also to ingratiate himself with Bin Laden for the timely warning.

In the days before KSM's arrest, Zawahiri arranged a new safe house for himself in Shkai, in South Waziristan; he traveled there on March 3. If Zawahiri was able to plan in advance, Bin Laden could not. When word reached Bin Laden of KSM's arrest, it was decided to move Osama and Amal to a remote safe house in Pakistan's Swat Valley. Located in the

Khyber Pakhtunkhwa, an area formerly known as Pakistan's North West Frontier Provinces, Swat is as far away from Parachinar as one could get and still be in Pakistan.

But the journey was problematic in the extreme. Even with the complicity of Pakistan's intelligence services, a domestic journey through Pakistan from Parachinar to Swat would be too dangerous for Osama; he was after all one of the most recognizable men in the world. Osama enjoyed protection at the highest levels of the Pakistani military and intelligence services but that did not mean that every traffic cop and frontier corpsman was in on the arrangement. It was necessary to make the move both quickly and in utmost secrecy.

Ibrahim Khan recommended that Osama should cross to the Afghan side of the border, travel the length of the Hindu Kush, and reenter Pakistan at Bajaur, coming into Swat's Peochar Valley from the north. This roundabout, external route had two advantages—it was extremely remote, and much of the territory was firmly in Taliban, not Pakistani control. Even if Khalid Sheikh Mohammed spilled the beans, Bin Laden would be out of reach of the Pakistani authorities. The Taliban was, and continues to be, a creation of the Pakistani military—there would be no trouble for Osama in Afghanistan.

As he had done in Kohat, Bin Laden would again, according to reports, take refuge with the Khan brothers' relatives. Abrar Khan's father-in-law, a man named Naeem ud Dun, owned a home in a remote location in the Peochar region of Swat Valley. On March 3, 2003, Bin Laden, Amal, and the Khan brothers split into two traveling parties and headed separately for the Swat Valley. Osama and Ibrahim Khan headed north into Afghanistan, traveling first to Gandamak in Nangarhar Province. Amal and her young children, escorted by Abrar Khan, headed south and then east through Pakistan toward Swat.

While Osama moved through Afghanistan in a four-wheel-drive vehicle, Amal and her two children were transported by minivan, passing through Pakistan's main cities of Peshawar and Islamabad. As would become a pattern in future moves, Amal arrived at the new location first—in effect testing the security arrangements, and making sure the safe house would be ready to receive her husband. Amal arrived in Shangala, Swat, in the middle of March and set up housekeeping. Ten days later, Bin Laden joined her in the village of Kotkay after a five-hundred-mile journey, which took most of three weeks.

Through the spring and summer, Osama remained as inconspicuous as possible, moving once, but remaining in Shangala and maintaining a low profile. With Bin Laden in hiding, Ayman Zawahiri was able to reassert control over both Al Qaeda, and Bin Laden's security arrangements. After KSM's arrest, Zawahiri saw that Abu Faraj al-Libi, the man assigned to coordinate Osama's safe houses, was promoted and made Al Qaeda's new head of operations. Zawahiri now had his own man in the number three slot.

When news came from Iraq that Al Qaeda had come into custody of some of Saddam's chemical artillery shells, Zawahiri was overjoyed. It was al-Libi who passed the orders to Mesopotamia's Al Qaeda commander, Musab al-Zarqawi, to carry out the nerve gas attack on the al Baya neighborhood on May 16, 2003—the first time in history that a nonstate actor had used a weapon of mass destruction. The attack fizzled, but just barely. Two American EOD technicians were contaminated with nerve gas but a catastrophe was averted when the weapon failed to explode completely. Zawahiri and Bin Laden were both disappointed when the attack failed to garner much press interest. The BBC and *The New York Times* both reported on the nerve gas attack at al Baya, but then the story was relegated to the back pages. The Western press, after all, was invested in the story that there were no WMD in Iraq. Still determined to use what he had, Zawahiri began to plan for a second, much more massive attack—this one targeting the population center of a major U.S. ally.

This second chemical operation was considered so important that Bin Laden and Ayman Zawahiri both risked traveling back into Afghanistan to plan the attack. In August 2003, Osama met Zawahiri at Gandamak in the province of Nangarhar, Afghanistan. During this meeting, Zawahiri posed in a video with Bin Laden, presenting himself to both the Al Qaeda faithful and the world as Al Qaeda's undisputed number two. At their conference, Zawahiri reported on the near miss of the chemical attack in al Baya, Iraq, and informed Osama about a developing plan to use several more chemical weapons against Amman, Jordan. Also discussed were chemical and radiological attacks on the United States. After their summit, the world's most wanted men returned separately to hiding in Pakistan—Zawahiri to Waziristan, and Bin Laden back to Kotkay in Swat.

However much the pious Zawahiri hated Khalid Sheikh Mohammed, he lacked both his charisma and his ability to command the loyalty of men. Zawahiri promised Osama big things with their cache of Saddam's chemical munitions, but without the operational expertise of Khalid Sheikh

Mohammed, Al Qaeda found it difficult to get an attack through to fruition. The frustration was taking its toll. Almost all who met Zawahiri came away with the same impression—he was a deeply troubled and unbalanced man, ruthless to his subordinates and obsequious to his patron, Osama. As plans went ahead, Zawahiri knew that his clock was ticking: KSM had provided Osama with success after success—so far Zawahiri was batting zero.

Through the spring and summer of 2003, Osama remained in his remote quarters in the Swat Valley. His accommodations were adequate and comfortable, the climate was pleasant, but the location was extremely isolated. Unlikely as it might seem, the world's most wanted man was getting lonely. Bin Laden wanted his family—all of his families—around him. In his twin capacities as Al Qaeda's chief of operations and head of Osama's logistics, this Herculean task fell to Faraj al-Libi. In the summer of 2003, al-Libi was summoned to the Swat Valley and provided with a hand-drawn building plan. Turning his talents to architecture, Osama had sketched out a three-story house with multiple bedrooms, baths, and kitchenettes. What Bin Laden wanted was a permanent compound to accommodate his family as well as the wives and children of his two bodyguards, Ibrahim and Abrar Khan. Osama wanted to build, not rent, so merely finding an existing place was not an option. To complicate matters further, wherever the new compound would be located had to have easy access to medical care and to the Federally Administrated Tribal Areas, should another quick takeoff become necessary.

During the next ten months, al-Libi reconnoitered locations in Quetta, Mardan, Haripur, and Abbottabad. Osama was given the final say in where the house was to be built, and he picked the location with a practiced eye. Like the Parachinar house, Osama preferred hiding in plain sight—in the very midst of the Pakistani Armed Forces. Fifty miles from Islamabad and only a little farther from Peshawar, Abbottabad is a mid-sized town nestled in the Orash Valley. At four thousand feet of elevation, its climate is pleasant. Abbottabad was a non-Pashtun area, but a few wealthy Pashtuns did live there, and many of them dwelt in walled compounds. Osama's cover as a wealthy Pashtun would again allow him to live a publically cloistered life. In many ways, Abbottabad would be the perfect hiding place; it is home to Pakistan's Kakul Military Academy, and could be thought of, literally, as the last place anyone would look. Al-Libi considered Abbottabad so secure that he had moved his own family there. Work on Bin Laden's new home started almost at once, and al-Libi made contact with Bin Laden's second wife, Siham Sabar, who had fled to Saudi Arabia. She was told that Osama wanted her to come to him, and to bring her children and his grandchildren. She obeyed.

In March 2004, Siham Sabar traveled from Jeddah, Saudi Arabia, to Pakistan. It was considered too dangerous to bring her directly to the house in Swat, so Faraj al-Libi saw her settled in the city of Mardan, sixty miles northwest of Islamabad. Again, the Khan brothers arranged a safe house with relatives. As incredible as it may seem, the Central Intelligence Agency, while scanning the world for a trace of the illusive Bin Laden, had not yet developed any interest in the travel patterns of his family members. It was not only Osama's wives and children who jetted between Saudi Arabia and Osama's Pakistani hideouts—they were accompanied by Al Qaeda security personnel. It was surely a conspicuous and interesting sight as the Burqa-clad wives of the world's most wanted terrorist flitted through airline terminals and past customs inspectors with kids, grandchildren, and luggage in tow. Even if Siham bin Laden and her children carried false passports (which they did not) the CIA might have been on the lookout. It is another mystery that the CIA failed to detect, or apparently even suspect, that Osama would want for company while on the run.

While the permanent compound was being built in Bilal Town, a section of Abbottabad, a temporary house was rented in Haripur, midway between Abbottabad and Pakistan's capital, Islamabad. In late November, escorted by Abrar Khan, Amal and her two children arrived at a neat, two-story, four-bedroom villa in the Nassem section of Haripur. The house was surrounded by a ten-foot wall, and was unusual in that it had a full basement. Completing Bin Laden's domestic arrangements, Osama's second wife, Siham, relocated from Mardan and moved into the Haripur villa with her children and several of Osama's grandchildren. After Osama's wives and children had been given a chance to settle in, Bin Laden departed from Swat some time in December, arriving at the Haripur villa in time for the birth of Amal's first son, Ibrahim. Born in December 2003, the boy was Osama bin Laden's twenty-fourth child, and was named after Osama's increasingly indispensable bodyguard Ibrahim Khan.

On April 26, 2004, Jordanian officials announced that they had foiled an Al Qaeda plot to attack the U.S. embassy in Amman, as well as the headquarters of the Jordanian Security Services and the offices of the prime minister. The plan was ambitious, involving multiple chemical weapons as well as large quantities of sulfuric acid and vehicle-borne explosives. Officials speculated that the attack could have killed upward of twenty thousand people—dwarfing the attacks of 9/11. There is no doubt that these attacks were the same ones planned by Ayman Zawahiri and Osama in Afghanistan back in August 2003.

Abu Musab al-Zarqawi, Al Qaeda's commander in Iraq, had directed the operation from across the Iraqi border. Jordanian security officials were able not only to prevent the attack, but also to roll up several dozen operatives, and to trace the operation back to Al Qaeda in Iraq. That Al Qaeda had intended to use chemical weapons to target the Muslim inhabitants of Amman, Jordan, was a sobering revelation. The failed operation was a tactical defeat for Al Qaeda, and it was a public relations nightmare.

Khalid Sheikh Mohammed had overseen an impressive string of Al Qaeda successes: 9/11, the attacks on Tunisia, the murder of Daniel Pearl, the Mombasa Assault, and the devastating Bali bombings. In the two years since he took over, all Zawahiri had to show was the near miss at al Baya, the aborted attack on Kahuta, and now Al Qaeda's worst setback in Jordan. Relations between Bin Laden and Zawahiri began an irreversible downward slide.

After the failure of the Amman chemical attacks, Bin Laden again attempted to maintain a low profile. During a seven-month residence in Haripur, he and the family attracted little attention, and as May approached, word came from Ibrahim Khan that the compound in Abbottabad was move-in ready. As the Bin Ladens readied for the move, Faraj al-Libi was captured riding pylon on a motor scooter in the city of Mardan, Pakistan. It was May 2, 2005, and the authorities seemed to have finally started to close in on Bin Laden.

Al-Libi had been on the way to a meeting with Ibrahim Khan regarding the upcoming move to the Abbottabad compound. An intercepted cell phone call brought him to the attention of the Pakistani police. Al-Libi's capture sparked a serious row between Zawahiri and Bin Laden. It had taken almost a year to build the Abbottabad compound. Now that al-Libi was in custody, it seemed likely that Bin Laden's security arrangements would be compromised. Captured with al-Libi was a laptop computer and a coded notebook. Some of the contents were eventually deciphered and an Al Qaeda plot to use liquid explosives concealed in airline carry-on baggage to destroy airliners traveling between London and the United States had been prevented. That plot was foiled, but the Pakistanis told Washington that the notebook yielded nothing about the whereabouts of Osama bin Laden.

Of course, the ISI knew exactly where Bin Laden was, but did not inform the United States. Just to make sure that Bin Laden's path would go cold, the Pakistanis held al-Libi for more than a month before turning him over to U.S. custody in June. With the capture of al-Libi, Bin Laden might have been expected to change his plans, or to go deeper underground. Although Ayman Zawahiri did go into hiding in Southern Afghanistan, Bin Laden calmly went ahead with moving his family into the Abbottabad compound. That he would do this clearly indicates that he had been given assurances of his own personal safety.

Once again, Bin Laden sent his family ahead first to test the security arrangements. One night in late May, Amal, Siham, and more than a dozen children and grandchildren were transported up the N-15 highway forty miles to Abbottabad. As she had done previously, Amal set up house and waited for Osama to join her.

Three weeks passed. Ibrahim and Abrar Khan carefully surveyed the neighborhood, watching to see what the authorities would do. Predictably, they did nothing. By late June, assured that the coast was clear, Osama also made the trip from Haripur to take up residence in Abbottabad. He would remain there undisturbed for the next five years.

Bin Laden's new home was a three-story rectangle surrounded by cement and cinder-block walls that ranged between ten and twenty feet high. Located on a triangular-shaped triple lot in Bilal Town, it was only eight hundred meters from the front gate of the Kakul Military Academy, Pakistan's West Point.

The property had walled areas for vegetable gardens, chickens, and a couple of bullocks. A garage was built into the eastern wall, with a trellis that allowed visitors to walk from the carport to the main house without being viewed from either the street or the sky. Another long, high-walled driveway bisected the triangle and a narrow lane led to a guesthouse and a few smaller structures, which included a place for conferences and a media studio. The windows facing the street on the north side of the main building were bricked in. It was the biggest house for several miles, and everybody in Abbottabad did their best to ignore it and its strangely reticent occupants. The main house was not air-conditioned but did have central heating. Furnished to Osama's austere tastes, it had cheap furniture and beds covered by inexpensive foam mattresses. The compound seems to have been added to in an ad hoc fashion. There were bedrooms that were adjoined by kitchens and bathrooms, allowing occupants to live separately. Interior hallways and the center stairwell were transected by locking metal grate work that looked like garden gates. There were doorways leading to brick walls and hallways that went nowhere. It was an odd, lopsided house.

In Abbottabad, the Bin Laden family ménage was not in all respects a happy or equitable one. Osama lived on the top floor of the main house with Amal, and rotated Siham out of his bedroom as suited his mood. Ibrahim Khan and his wife and family shared quarters on the ground floor of the main house. His brother, Abrar, and his wife and three children lived behind the main house in a one-story building called the Annex.

The brothers did odd jobs around the compound and made purchases of bulk supplies at local stores and brought in batteries and digital tapes for the video cameras. The food served in the Bin Laden household was basic: olive oil, dates, dried meats, eggs, and fresh-baked naan from a nearby bakery. Occasionally, one of the compound's chickens would make the ultimate sacrifice and be tossed into a pot with rice and raisins. Osama insisted that his children be homeschooled, and a classroom was set up with a whiteboard and desks on the first floor. There were textbooks in Arabic, and between frequent lessons with their mothers, the kids raised rabbits and played behind the compound's twenty-foot, barbed-wire-topped walls. Osama's young sons and daughters lived in a four-walled limbo, cut off from school, playgrounds, and other children. They were as isolated and alone as their father.

Al Qaeda's operational capabilities were further diminished in June 2006 when Abu Musab al-Zarqawi, the leader of Al Qaeda in Iraq, was killed outside Baghdad. Al-Zarqawi had been betrayed by a courier and was "laser tagged" by a pair of SEAL Team Six snipers on the evening of June 7, 2006. His loss was a major setback for the terrorist organization.

The United States announced a troop surge in 2007, and kept the pressure on in Iraq. Al Qaeda's use of chemical weapons was the reason SEAL missions quadrupled in Iraq, with teams operating against as many as four or five targets a night, rolling up Al Qaeda terrorists as soon as they could be linked to one another or as soon as they turned. Within Al Qaeda, morale was failing. Martyrs who risked their lives in what were supposed to be "glorious" chemical attacks found that their missions did not strike terror into coalition soldiers and were all but ignored by Western news outlets.

In 2008, Al Qaeda tested new combinations of truck-bomb and chlorine-gas weapons in a series of bombings in Baghdad. These bombs blew more than two hundred Iraqi civilians to pieces, and choked the wounded to death with chlorine gas. The victims were two hundred Muslims that

Ayman Zawahiri had determined were *kafirs*—unbelievers. When these chemical attacks again failed to interest the American media or bring forth an Islamic government in Iraq, relations between Zawahiri and Bin Laden became brittle. Besides their operational failures, the two men argued over media strategies.

Al Qaeda itself was in no hurry to tell the world that its attempts to use Saddam's legacy of chemical weapons usually fizzled. At great expense, Osama and Zawahiri smuggled nerve and mustard gas into Afghanistan and attempted to use these weapons against coalition forces there. The WikiLeaks documents suggest that Iraqi chemical munitions were recovered from IEDs and cache sites in Afghanistan, but Al Qaeda's attempts to gas American soldiers came to nothing.

Letters and operational plans later found at the Abbottabad compound confirmed that Al Qaeda remained in possession of chemical weapons as late as 2011. In a lengthy memo written just a week before his death, Bin Laden advised operations boss Atiyah Abd al-Rahman that a plot by the Yemeni affiliate of Al Qaeda to use poison gas should go forward only after "study of the political and media reaction against the Mujahideen." Clearly, Bin Laden was concerned less for the innocent victims of a gas attack than he was that the incident might have negative public-relations effects.

Zawahiri and Bin Laden faced a pair of problems they had never expected: American cognitive dissonance and the sheer inertia of the Western media. Osama bin Laden had expected to shake the world when it became known that Al Qaeda possessed chemical weapons. Instead, even as the details of al Baya and Amman came to be known, the Western media yawned.

The U.S. military rarely confirmed when a chemical weapon was discovered—even as UN Weapons Reports and leaked WikiLeaks cables tallied these weapons in the hundreds. Ironically, if the U.S. military was trying to play down the threat posed by Al Qaeda's chemical warfare campaign, the American press assisted them—not out of patriotism or out of a desire to defeat Al Qaeda in the information space, but because they had told a different story for more than decade. Since there were no Iraqi WMD, there couldn't possibly be any Al Qaeda WMD. Lest its own credibility be sullied, the press ignored one of the single greatest strategic threats ever faced by the United States.

To the men and women of America's counterterrorism community, Al Qaeda's chemical weapons were much more real. Every year the entire U.S. government practices the response to chemical, nuclear, and biological attacks in exercise TOPOFF. Where the wires did come together, America took the threat of Al Qaeda's chemical weapons very seriously. The national counterterrorism plan has a fifty-page annex on improvised nuclear, radiological, chemical, and biological weapons. The chemical weapons in this threat-assessment document are based on designs incorporating purloined chemical munitions—just like the one found at al Baya.

As the Arab Spring rippled across the Middle East, the Muslim faithful were throwing off the chains of dictatorship and calling out not for Sharia law but for democracy. Bin Laden and Zawahiri found that they were becoming increasingly irrelevant. Repeated plans to smuggle chemical (and even nuclear) weapons into the United States had come to naught. Zawahiri's plots, proclamations, and plans came by courier and piled up on hard drives in Bin Laden's Abbottabad office. Osama was surrounded by sycophants who were eager, even anxious, to martyr themselves, but in order to attack the United States or Europe, he needed tech-savvy volunteers, men who could speak foreign languages and live in Western cities undetected. The nineteen terrorists who crashed hijacked planes into Manhattan and Washington represented an increasingly hard-to-find commodity: educated men who still bought into the myth of mayhem in this life and of peace and pleasure in the world beyond.

As he failed to sell his mythology to others, Osama became increasingly involved in his own. Locked into the second floor of his home, he spent hours watching himself on television. In the study attached to his home, he took months to produce carefully staged video recordings of himself. Osama's health was worsening; the Addison's disease that wracked his body made him lethargic. It became increasingly obvious to him and those around him that he had set out to change the world, but instead was trapped in a prison of his own making. His Pakistani hosts might've wondered, as his family did, if he was going insane.

Despite his operational failures, Bin Laden had succeeded, incrementally, in bringing his family to him. That in itself had been an operational feat that had required careful planning and extreme operational security. In Abbottabad, Amal shared his bed, and Siham set up a schoolhouse on the ground floor of the main house, teaching their children and grandchildren. That left only Bin Laden's most senior wife, Khairiah Sabar, to be brought to Abbottabad.

The only problem was, she was under house arrest in Iran.

POINTING A FINGER

IN 2008, THREE YEARS AFTER he had settled into Abbottabad, Bin Laden decided that the time was right to launch an operation to free his wife Khairiah Sabar from Iranian custody.

In hindsight, this plan was nearly as foolish as the stillborn assault on Pakistan's nuclear weapons. Iran's chief foreign intelligence organization, the Ministry of Intelligence and National Security of the Islamic Republic of Iran (MISIRI), is pervasive, aggressive, and lethal. Taking it on would not be as easy as striking an American soft target. And unlike the Central Intelligence Agency, MISIRI has no rules against paying back violence with violence.

On the face of it, Bin Laden's plan looked simple: kidnap a member of Iranian intelligence, and hold him—the ransom would be the release of several Al Qaeda leaders currently held under house arrest in Tehran. Thrown casually into the exchange lists would be a demand for the release of Khairiah Sabar bin Laden and her children.

The potential for this operation to blow back on Osama should have been obvious, and Ayman Zawahiri might have done something to dissuade his boss—or at the very least, allow the plot to go forward only after a thorough overhaul of Bin Laden's security arrangements. Stung by Osama's recent criticisms, and the failures at al Baya, Amman, and the capture of al-Libi, Zawahiri may have merely been taking the path of least resistance. A better second in command would have looked closer at the risk-to-reward ratio and advised caution. Whatever his ultimate motivations, Ayman Zawahiri did nothing to oppose the Emir, and merely assented to the plan.

The operation went forward, and it would be the beginning of the end for Osama bin Laden.

The only measures of security taken by Al Qaeda seem to have been establishing plausible deniability for the initial kidnapping by using operatives of the Tehrik-e-Taliban (the TTP, Pakistan's domestic Taliban), and then allowing the negotiations to drag out for more than two years. In the end, neither of these ploys would be sufficient, and it is very likely that the operation to free Khairiah Sabar bin Laden was one of the final pieces in the jigsaw puzzle that allowed the United States to pinpoint Osama in Abbottabad.

In no small measure, it was Ayman Zawahiri who led the United States to Osama bin Laden. Zawahiri accomplished this through a complex and persistent series of lapses in security. Some of these slips were subtle, and some of them were so obvious they were laughable; their cumulative effect was undeniable. It is a fact that Ayman Zawahiri betrayed his Muslim Brotherhood coconspirators in the Sadat assassination back in 1981, and that he was involved in the 1989 assassination of Abdullah Azzam, Osama's charismatic mentor. The IED murder of Abdullah Azzam and his two grown sons permitted Zawahiri and his Egyptian cadres to assume control over Osama bin Laden. Once at Al Qaeda's levers of power, Zawahiri was able to influence the "turning outward" of the anti-Soviet resistance into a worldwide anti-Western Jihad. Likewise, the sudden capture of Khalid Sheikh Mohammed in March 2003 immediately benefitted Zawahiri, who used the event to tighten his hold on Al Qaeda operations and to place more of his own men into leadership positions.

In each case, Zawahiri used the death or removal of a rival to better his own material circumstances and authority. Zawahiri was known throughout Al Qaeda as both an ambitious and a ruthless infighter who did not suffer fools or contradiction.

The origin of the final split between Zawahiri and Bin Laden can be traced to late 2004. Documents recovered from Bin Laden's compound in Abbottabad and statements made by Faraj al-Libi while in custody at Guantánamo Bay paint a picture of the tense and deteriorating relationship between Osama and his most callous underling. Following the capture of KSM, Ayman Zawahiri assumed operational control of international operations, but failed repeatedly to employ the chemical weapons Al Qaeda had captured in Iraq. There is also evidence to indicate that Ayman Zawahiri involved Al Qaeda in a 2003 plot to assassinate Pakistan's then leader Pervez Musharraf. This foiled attack led directly the capture of Faraj al-Libi, Bin Laden's director of logistics. Any of these "oversights" might have led to the exposure or capture of Osama bin Laden. Taken in total, these incidents render an unflattering picture of Ayman Zawahiri, who is revealed to be either stunningly incompetent or firmly determined to take out those above him in the chain of command.

Bin Laden did not seem to fully comprehend Zawahiri's treachery but he was aware that operational security had deteriorated within the organization. Bin Laden also came to suspect Zawahiri of financial malfeasance. In October 2004, Osama bin Laden used Ibrahim Khan to carry a letter to Faraj al-Libi, questioning the state of finances of the Al Qaeda organization in Pakistan and Waziristan. It is telling that Osama did not attempt to communicate directly with Ayman Zawahiri in regard to this matter, especially as Zawahiri was living in Shkai, Waziristan, at the time. The letter is referred to in a secret Detainee Assessment Memorandum of al-Libi's Guantánamo interrogations recently published by *The New York Times.* Copies of the original letter were also recovered during the Abbottabad raid. Throughout the period from 2004 until 2011, the matter of finances crops up frequently in Bin Laden's correspondence. It is an interesting coincidence that with the capture of al-Libi, Zawahiri was able to retard Bin Laden's financial inquiry . . . giving rise to speculation that it might have been Zawahiri who tipped off Pakistani authorities about al-Libi's location.

Other files recovered from the Abbottabad compound include a series of letters written about this time from Ayman Zawahiri to Osama, trying to bridge an obvious cooling of affections. Zawahiri found Osama's criticisms to be galling, but he continued to try to carry out Bin Laden's instructions. He had to. Zawahiri, perhaps better than anyone else in the Al Qaeda organization, knew how easy it would be for Bin Laden to be rid of him.

As the Iranian kidnap plans moved forward, Zawahiri chose to move frequently. He had good reason to be wary. The United States had posted a twenty-five-million-dollar reward for his capture. Though much is made of Pashtun hospitality, Zawahiri did not trust his life to the cultural obligations of a tribal people. After some time on the lam in southern Afghanistan, Zawahiri, like his boss, moved to Pakistan. Through connections with the political party Jamaat-e-Islami, Zawahiri, too, came under the protection of the Pakistani intelligence service, the ISI. As long as Zawahiri continued to move under the radar and make no overt moves against his Pakistani hosts, he faced no threat. And notably, as Bin Laden prepared to move forward with the kidnap and ransom plan, Zawahiri made certain of his own personal security, but recommended no change for Bin Laden's.

On November 13, 2008, Hashmatullah Attarzadeh, the commercial attaché to the Iranian consulate in Peshawar, Pakistan, was ambushed as he left his house for work. After blocking his car on a narrow bridge, gunmen in two trailing vehicles opened fire, killing his police bodyguard. Attarzadeh was then dragged from his vehicle and taken to a remote area of South Waziristan. The captured diplomat was held within a few miles of Zawahiri's own hiding place in the Shkai Valley, on the border with Afghanistan.

A month after the abduction, the Iranian government announced that it had identified Attarzadeh's kidnappers as members of Al Qaeda in cooperation with the Pakistani Taliban. Weeks passed, but no organization claimed credit for the kidnapping, and no ransom demands were forthcoming. Iran and Pakistan exchanged notes and summoned diplomats for consultations, but nothing happened. Not surprisingly, Pakistan's investigations went nowhere, and the Iranians could find no one with whom to bargain. It was not until 2009 that Iranian intelligence was able to establish contact with the kidnappers through members of the Taliban-linked Haqqani terrorist network.

After exchanged video footage showed that the diplomat was alive, members of Al Qaeda who were under house arrest in Tehran, Iran, were allowed to communicate by telephone with members of Al Qaeda's *shura,* or operational council, possibly including Ayman Zawahiri himself.

By all accounts, the negotiations were protracted and intricate. At some point, advanced antiaircraft weapons were transferred from Iran into South Waziristan, which resulted in the downing of at least one U.S. drone aircraft between January and March 2009. Iranian weapons trafficking into Afghanistan continues to this day, and may be traced to this initial contact.

Al Qaeda and Iranian intelligence, both deeply suspicious, continued an elaborate minuet. On March 22, 2010, as a gesture of good faith, Iman bin Laden, Osama bin Laden's eighteen-year-old daughter, was allowed to travel to Syria from the Saudi embassy in Tehran, where she had sought refuge after fleeing from house arrest elsewhere in Iran. Then, on March 30, 2010, Hashmatullah Attarzadeh was released from custody in Pakistan and repatriated to Iran.

In exchange, Abu Ghaith, a Kuwaiti-born spokesman for Al Qaeda, was released, along with half a dozen other Al Qaeda members, including Osama's son Saad bin Laden, Saiful Adil, and Khair al Misri, an Egyptian radical and close confidant of Ayman Zawahiri. While it was Abu Ghaith's release that made headlines, the Iranians also quietly released Khairiah Sabar bin Laden and her four children.

Documents recovered from the Abbottabad compound reveal that Osama bin Laden anguished over the possibility that "adversaries" would discover the true purpose of the prisoner exchange and place surveillance on his wife and children as they were released from Iranian custody. Bin Laden communicated directly with Al Qaeda's newly installed chief of operations, Atiyah Abd al-Rahman, and placed him in charge of the prisoner swap. For its part, Al Qaeda had obviously picked its hostage well. Hashmatullah Attarzadeh was a top-ranking Iranian field agent; to get him back Tehran was willing to trade almost a dozen Al Qaeda detainees, in addition to Bin Laden's relatives.

The mid-to-lower members of Al Qaeda were the first to be released. These handovers took place mostly in Waziristan and dragged over the months of March, April, and May 2010. All of these exchanges were in preparation for what both sides saw as the culmination of the deal: the release by Al Qaeda of Hashmatullah Attarzadeh and the repatriation by Iran of Bin Laden's wife Khairiah, her sons Ladin, Hamza, Uthman, Muhamad, and Bin Laden's grown married daughter, Fatima.

In late April 2010, Osama's son Ladin was allowed by the Iranians to depart for Syria. In a personal letter to operational chief Atiyah Abd al-Rahman, Osama worried that his son would telephone other family members to tell of his release, and that these calls would be monitored. Bin Laden then laid out specific and extensive security precautions to be taken at the time his wife Khairiah was released. These included first separating her from their sons Uthman and Muhamad, who were to be delivered to safe houses in Pakistan. His daughter Fatima and her husband were to be separately transferred to a safe house in the Federally Administered Tribal Areas along the Afghan border.

The prime object of the hostage swap, Khairiah, was to be handled by a special set of operatives. Bin Laden involved himself minutely in the details of her transfer. He insisted that she be transported only on days that were overcast, so that she could not be followed by aerial surveillance. Bin Laden also cautioned that every item given to her while she was in Iran, including clothing, luggage, and any item larger than "the size of a sewing needle" were to be taken away, lest they conceal some sort of electronic tracking device. Her release was to be choreographed by no less than three teams of handlers. Bin Laden directed that she be transported from Waziristan to the highway tunnel connecting the Pakistani cities of Kohat and Peshawar. While in the middle of the tunnel, Khairiah was to be shifted into another car driven by a separate set of operatives. Thereafter, these handlers were to drive her to an enclosed shopping mall in the city of Peshawar. There, she was to be handed off to a third set of bodyguards. This team was to make sure it had shaken off all surveillance and then deliver her to a safe house. This elaborate protocol was to be followed only for the person of Khairiah—showing both the importance Bin Laden placed on recovering her, and how wary he was of both the Americans and the Iranians.

Atiyah Abd al-Rahman carried out Bin Laden's instructions to the letter, and Khairiah bin Laden was successfully transferred to Peshawar sometime in June 2010. Bin Laden's elaborate security precautions, it turns out, were wholly justified. The CIA *was* listening in early May when Ladin bin Laden telephoned his family from Syria. Almost from the outset, the Americans were aware of the Iranian hostage swap—and of its real purpose.

The vehicle change in the Kohat tunnel and personnel handoff in the indoor shopping mall was effective in stripping off aerial surveillance. For the next several months, Khairiah's exact whereabouts remained a mystery. It is now known that in September 2010 she appealed directly to Al Qaeda's operational boss, Atiyah Abd al-Rahman, asking to be allowed to join Osama in hiding. Al-Rahman remained cautious and continued to keep her on ice in the Peshawar safe house for another five months. Finally, in February 2011, four months after her request, and fully nine months after her exchange, Khairiah was allowed to join Osama bin Laden and the other wives at the Abbottabad compound.

This final transfer from the Peshawar safe house was overseen by Osama bin Laden's trusted courier Ibrahim Khan. Interestingly, documents recovered from Abbottabad indicate that Ibrahim Khan, after years of loyal service, had submitted a letter asking to be released from his duties. He was scheduled to leave Bin Laden's service in November 2011; but neither Ibrahim Khan nor Osama bin Laden would live to see that day.

It is ironic that after such extensive, thoroughly planned, and successful security arrangements, the arrival of Khairiah bin Laden in Abbottabad would be the beginning of the end for Osama bin Laden. As elegantly compartmentalized as the rest of the transfer had been, the weak spot was Ibrahim Khan. His exposure came through no fault of his own, but rather because someone else in the organization had talked. Under interrogation at Guantánamo Bay, 9/11 mastermind Khalid Sheikh Mohammed had revealed Ibrahim Khan's nom de guerre, Abu al Kuwaiti. With his alias known, Bin Laden's chief bodyguard and courier had come to the attention of the CIA. Bin Laden could not be blamed for this, nor could Ibrahim Khan, as they were unaware that his cover had been blown. The use of

Ibrahim Khan to deliver Khairiah bin Laden to Abbottabad had compromised the entire operation.

But there was one man in Al Qaeda who *did* know that the CIA had pierced the inner workings of Bin Laden's security apparatus. And that person was Bin Laden's trusted number two, Ayman Zawahiri.

It is in the release of Khairiah bin Laden that Ayman Zawahiri's carelessness is most appalling. Despite the obvious motives of the kidnapping, and the fact that the CIA and the Western media had named Abu al Kuwaiti as a known Al Qaeda operative, Zawahiri continued to use Ibrahim Khan as his primary link to Osama's compound in Abbottabad. Zawahiri never warned Bin Laden of this fact, nor did he even suggest that Ibrahim Khan be removed as a member of Bin Laden's close protection unit. This, more than any factor, marks Zawahiri as complicit in the death of Osama bin Laden. The use of a blown courier in such a high-consequence operation is indefensible.

Ayman Zawahiri had several advantages over his boss. Besides having an innate viciousness, Zawahiri could also speak and read English. He was an avid consumer of American news about Al Qaeda. He knew well that Khalid Sheikh Mohammed was in custody in Guantánamo, and that KSM talked. CIA interrogators had pried from Khalid the name of the courier that Osama depended upon for communications with both the outside world and with his protectors in Pakistani intelligence. The CIA now knew that Ibrahim Khan was Bin Laden's chief courier and bodyguard, but they did not yet know where he was.

With the release of Khairiah bin Laden, Zawahiri had to be certain that the CIA was closing in. Khalid Sheikh Mohammed had been transferred from Pakistani custody to Guantánamo, and summaries of his debriefings included Ibrahim Khan's nom de guerre, Abu Ahmed al Kuwaiti. Though Zawahiri knew that Ibrahim Khan was compromised, he did nothing to ease him out of the communication network.

The noose was closing. Faraj al-Libi had been captured in Mardan, a mere few blocks away from the safe house that had hidden Siham bin Laden and her children. To any but the blindest eye, Bin Laden's security apparatus was falling apart. Yet Zawahiri made no effort to reform Bin Laden's bodyguard, or to establish new and more secure means of communications. He just kept using the channels he knew to be compromised. Zawahiri was playing a game, and the prize was the undisputed leadership of Al Qaeda.

It is another inexplicable fact that Osama himself seems to have become blasé, even reckless about his personal security. On January 25, 2011, Pakistani security officials arrested Umar Patek, the mastermind of Jemaah Islamiyah's horrific 2002 Bali bombings. Patek was taken into custody in Abbottabad, a mere mile and a half from Bin Laden's compound. One might ask why Patek traveled five thousand miles to visit an obscure Pakistani garrison town. U.S. intelligence officials, trying to backtrack after the Bin Laden raid, have said they believed that Umar Patek's arrest in Osama bin Laden's home town was a mere "coincidence." Hardly. SEAL Team Six's accelerated targeting of Abbottabad can be traced precisely to this time period. It is obvious that the Americans were now watching closely.

But the story becomes more and more curious. Besides the vapid response of the CIA to the capture of Southeast Asia's most wanted terrorist, two more peculiar circumstances surround Umar Patek's arrest. First, Pakistani intelligence did not make the arrest public for nearly three months—and did so only after leaks and rumors became too persistent to ignore. Even then, Pakistani intelligence officials did not allow Patek to be questioned by Indonesian authorities until mid-May, and did not extradite Patek to Indonesia until August—a full seven months after his arrest.

Seven months might have been considered ample time for Zawahiri to take measures to improve Bin Laden's security. It was almost enough time for Bin Laden to build a new house at another location. Yet Zawahiri said nothing and Osama remained in Abbottabad. Perhaps Osama had again received assurances from his Pakistani hosts. Perhaps he no longer cared. But Al Qaeda's leader was living on borrowed time.

An explicit warning came on May 11, 2010, soon after the hostage transfer that freed Khairiah bin Laden. Secretary of State Hillary Clinton said in an interview that she believed that Osama bin Laden was hiding in Pakistan, and that he was under the protection of the ISI. It is unlikely that Zawahiri, who was known to be a news junkie, would have missed Secretary Clinton's statement, which was widely reported and commented upon in the Pakistani media. Still, Zawahiri did nothing to change Bin Laden's arrangements, or to even suggest any measures to move his family or to tighten security. Quite the opposite.

About this time, Zawahiri made Al Qaeda funds available to purchase Ibrahim Khan a fantastically painted four-wheel-drive truck. Careful to keep his own movements screened, and shuttling between his own ISI-provided safe houses, Zawahiri had Ibrahim make numerous journeys from the compound to meetings in Peshawar and Shkai. The vehicle soon attracted the attention of American intelligence.

By March 2011, the CIA was using a Pakistani national pretending to be a public health official to canvass areas of Bilal Town in Abbottabad. In early April, they had "gathered" Abrar Khan's cell phone number, and on the twenty-sixth of April, offering free hepatitis vaccinations, this CIA asset actually knocked on the front door of the compound. Two days later, SEAL admiral Bill McRaven would brief the White House on Operation Neptune's Spear. Bin Laden's luck was running out.

Was Zawahiri merely negligent, or had he deliberately betrayed Osama bin Laden?

During the Afghan war, Zawahiri had continually urged Osama forward into combat. As Osama's personal physician from 1984 to 2003, Zawahiri examined and treated him frequently. Zawahiri was a trained medical doctor who had studied at one of the finest universities in the Middle East. Yet he failed to diagnose Osama's obvious symptoms of back pain, low blood pressure, and fainting spells. All of these, and a telltale craving for table salt; it was a diagnosis that was obvious, yet Zawahiri never mentioned it to Osama and withheld from him the easy-to-acquire medication that would have kept his disease in check.

Zawahiri tried to get the Russians to kill Bin Laden; they did not.

He hoped that Addison's disease would take him, but it did not.

Now Ayman Zawahiri played his final cards—he acquiesced to a harebrained operation to free Bin Laden's remaining wife from Iranian custody. He allowed this woman to be transported to Abbottabad despite the obvious fact that she was a person too conspicuous for even the Americans to ignore. And he coordinated all of this using a courier that he knew to have been named by Khalid Sheikh Mohammed and Faraj al-Libi in Guantánamo Bay.

Zawahiri repeatedly sent Ibrahim Khan to and from Abbottabad, into and out of the compound. He stood by and did nothing when a prominent Indonesian terrorist was arrested just yards from Bin Laden's compound.

And then, the inevitable happened.

The Americans came calling.

NEPTUNE'S SPEAR

ADMIRAL BILL MCRAVEN STEPPED out of one of the low, Quonset hut–like tents beside hangar five at Forward Operating Base Fenty located at Jalalabad airbase in Afghanistan; he was standing forty miles north of the Pakistani frontier. McRaven had been in the close confines of the Joint Operations Center (JOC) for almost twelve hours, and he needed some air. The admiral, like the other members of the expedition, had been awake for most of the last two days, first on a flight from Norfolk, Virginia—a sixteen-hour marathon with two midair refuelings—and then during the hurried preparations to put together the JOC, from which he would monitor the progress of Neptune's Spear.

As they had done during the *Maersk Alabama* operation, the Twidgets from Det Alpha went to work with a vengeance, unloading pallets of gear from the airplanes, setting up inflatable tents to shelter Web servers and crypto gear, and stringing hundred of yards of cable to connect tons of communications gear and downlinks to plasma-screen monitors and teleconferencing equipment that gave the commander of JSOC the ability to speak with the White House, the Pentagon, and CIA in real time. Det Alpha joked that the admiral could talk to anyone he wanted, except Osama bin Laden—and that was because Osama didn't own a functioning telephone. If he did, Det Alpha could make it ring on his nightstand and reverse the long-distance charges when he answered. These guys were the SEAL Team Six of cyberspace.

Admiral McRaven moved away from the tents and let his eyes adjust to the gathering dark. Already the mountains above the runways were surrendering to night. Two SEAL Six operators dressed in khaki pants and photographers' vests kept pace behind McRaven as he walked. They carried cut-barreled laser-sighted HK-416s, called "choppers." Their weapons could fit under a jacket and fired the same deadly 5.56 mm ammo as their larger cousins, the M-4 assault rifle. Jalalabad was considered a combat zone, and the airbase had been attacked five months earlier when Taliban insurgents dressed as Afghan soldiers slipped onto the airfield and opened fire. The admiral was allowed to take his walk, but the SEALs guarding him kept within a dozen paces.

McRaven went past the hangars that contained the assault group's helicopters. The hangar doors were closed tight and a guard nodded to McRaven as he passed. Officers are not saluted in combat zones and anyway, McRaven wasn't wearing the rank devices that marked him as a three-star admiral. As was his custom, he had on a plain set of Navy battle dress utilities. The guard knew him only because of his height and the two shadows that followed him.

Behind the locked hangar doors were four MH-47 Chinooks and a quartet of top secret stealth helicopters. Two of the "black birds" were generation one Stealth Hawk helicopters—their stablemates were a pair of newer, larger, and more sophisticated Ghost Hawks. The stealth helicopters were just four pieces of a complex high-tech package aimed at the leader of Al Qaeda. Never before in the history of U.S. special operations had so much top secret hardware been put at risk in a combat mission.

McRaven continued his walk between the hangars and down an abandoned taxiway. Jalalabad had once been a Soviet air base. The Russians called it "Location 562," taking the numbers from the airfield's elevation in meters. From Location 562 the Soviets unleashed helicopter-borne fury against the Mujahideen and the Afghan people. More than two million noncombatants perished during the period of Soviet occupation. The departing Russians didn't trouble to pick up after themselves. The Jalalabad airfield was littered with the wrecks of Soviet aircraft, the burned out hulks of Mi-8 "Hip" assault helicopters and the sinister, humpbacked shapes of deadly Mi-24 "Hind" gunships. When the Americans moved into the base, they called it "J-bad." The name seemed to fit.

Stretching his legs, Bill McRaven walked all the way down to where the taxiway met J-bad's Runway 45 Right. The hangars loomed slate black against a moonless sky. The heat was going rapidly out of the air, but the dust gray tarmac still held its warmth. High above, a few clouds rolled through and the night was increasingly brilliant with stars. McRaven looked up. He *owned* some of the stars that he could see, or at least he controlled them.

Four reconnaissance satellites were positioned in geosynchronous orbit over southern Afghanistan. One took pictures, videos really, in the visible spectrum but also in ultraviolet and infrared. Another satellite relayed communications, a third predicted and reported the weather, and the fourth, a massive piece of equipment the size of a Greyhound bus, did everything that the others did, only better. With these orbiting eyes, Bill McRaven could look from outerspace into a man's upturned face.

It was the largest satellite, the formidable KH-12 "Keyhole," that had taken the first high-resolution pictures of the strange, isolated house on the dusty outskirts of Abbottabad. As the evidence mounted that this was the hideout of Osama bin Laden, Keyhole's massive camera photographed a solitary walker who paced a garden behind a twenty-foot wall. Images from the KH-2 measured Bin Laden's shadow.

The wind was blowing down from the mountains, a catabatic wind, as predictable in J-bad as the coming of darkness. McRaven listened to the sound of jet engines taxiing at the far end of the tarmac, a mile and half away. The whine turned to a low rumble as the aircraft went to full power for takeoff.

Hurtling down the runway was a low, flat, dark shape. It first looked like a flying wedge, a deconstructionist impression of an airplane, just wings going off by themselves. McRaven watched as the delta-shaped object lumbered down the runway. When it lifted off he could see the white-hot glow of a pair of afterburners framed by titanium thrust vectors. The exhausts were rectangular, and the fire in them made the aircraft look like two lighted house windows climbing into the sky.

This technological wonder was an RQ-170 "Sentinel" drone. Unlike its famous cousins, Predators and Grey Eagles, the Sentinel was unarmed. It defended itself by being invisible to radar and flying faster than any fighter that might lay eyes on it. Still a closely guarded secret, the RQ-170s were only flown at night. For the next six hours, this unmanned supersonic spy plane would circle the city of Abbottabad and provide real-time video and audio uplinks from the SEALs on target. Their crews called the Sentinel "the Beast of Kandahar." Tonight, in support of Operation Neptune's Spear, an RQ-170 would use the call sign "Beast," and its control van and pilots would answer to the apt handle "Beastmaster." In a moment, the drone had climbed vertically into the darkest part of the sky and vanished.

McRaven walked back to the JOC. Part of the reason he'd taken his walk was to allow the assault element leaders and SEAL Six's commanding officer Scott Kerr to talk to his Team. The two Red Squadron assault element commanders, Frank Leslie and Rich Horn, would also add their own mission-specific briefings. Mel Hoyle, Red Squadron's master chief, would inspect the gear of each operator before they were put into "chill"—an hour-long spell for the operators to relax and compose themselves before launch.

The operation had originally been planned for the previous night, April 30, but clouds over the target pushed the mission back twenty-four hours. The delay was tough on a Team that was ready to go, but it added an extra day for Red Squadron to rehearse and Det Alpha to be sure that everything was perfect—racked, stacked, and ready to fly.

In the final hours before the operation, JSOC planners actually worried that the compound in Abbottabad might be a trap. Osama had often stated that he would fight to the death rather than be captured by the United States, and he went so far as to issue instructions to his bodyguard to shoot him if it looked as though he were about to fall into American hands. Analysts wondered why, after ten years of hiding, Al Qaeda's courier system had become so obvious. Was Ayman Zawahiri burning Osama bin Laden, or was Al Qaeda using their leader as bait to lure American special operations into a clever ambush?

McRaven was surprised when a skeptical JSOC intel analyst first declared that Osama was being set up. Many thought the continued use of Abu Ahmed al Kuwaiti as a courier was merely an operational mistake. But Al Qaeda had gone ten years without mistakes. Was this a ruse? Was Al Qaeda planning to mark the ten-year anniversary of 9/11 by blowing a SEAL Team out of the sky?

All of these last-minute doubts stemmed from the odd-looking, three-sided structure on the roof of the compound's main building. To photo experts, it looked like the firing position for a MANPADS—a man-portable antiaircraft system. A machine gun placed there could sweep the skies above the house. A man with a shoulder-fired missile could destroy any helicopter that got within a mile of the building. It was known that Osama's bodyguard possessed Soviet-made SA-7s. They had been used in Mombasa against an Israeli airliner. Were they now in Abbottabad?

The possibility that SEAL Team Six was being led into an Al Qaeda trap had been discussed with the assault force. The SEALs considered it an acceptable risk. If it was an ambush, Red Squadron would give as good as they got.

As McRaven walked back toward the command center he could hear the operators joking as they suited up. That was another reason why he went for a walk. The guys were different around him because he was an admiral. He knew they needed space to get ready in their own way for the mission.

SEAL Team Six is one of the most storied units in American military history. And rightly so. The operators of Red Squadron are among the most highly decorated men in the United States military. Many were entering into their seventh or eighth consecutive year of combat service. There are no veterans in American history who have endured more combat. The operators of Team Six are heroes, and their operational credentials allow them to speak freely to the men who lead them into battle.

The price of their obedience is truth.

These men are highly intelligent, well educated, and resourceful. Many of them have graduate degrees. They are well read, and they have a thorough understanding of what is and is not happening in world affairs. The operators of SEAL Team Six put their lives at risk daily for a country they love. They may be forgiven if they have precious little tolerance for leaders who put "table manners" ahead of speaking the truth.

This group can only be led by men who share their values and have undergone the same hardships. Especially respected are those SEAL officers who have themselves sweated through Green Team. A SEAL officer puts his career on the line when he enters a Green Team class. Not all SEAL officers make it. To earn a leadership slot at SEAL Six one must compete against the best SEALs in the business. A lieutenant who is attrited from Green Team can expect to be shunted from one dead-end assignment to another until he either resigns his commission or is forced out of the Teams. The members of SEAL Team Six care very little for what they called "ticket punchers," officers who back-door their way into JSOC staff assignments without the risk of going through Green Team. Red Squadron, like the other operational entities at Six, is led into combat only by chief petty officers and officers who are Green Team alumni. These men put the concept of Team and Teammate above all other considerations—within Six and outside it.

Bill McRaven knew as well as anyone that it was an honor to command these men, and it was a test of his own skills as a leader. McRaven had been a shooter once himself. He spent the first fifteen years of his SEAL career as a well-respected operator, first as a platoon commander, then as an element leader. He had helped train the SEAL platoons that had operated in Beirut. In the second fifteen years of his career McRaven advanced to captain, commodore, and then rear Admiral. He commanded Task Force 10 during the early part of the Afghan war, distinguishing himself from all his contemporaries. TF-10 hunted Osama bin Laden and Ayman Zawahiri over the rough mountains of Afghanistan—and also into the tribal areas of Pakistan.

Once he was at the top, Bill McRaven did not always swim to the rescue of every Teammate who got in over their head, but he continued to look out for the SEAL community and did much to help loosen "Big Army's" iron grip on JSOC's command structure. McRaven put SEAL operators into positions of responsibility, and the Army had to get used to the idea of Navy commanders ordering about special operations ground troops hundreds of miles from the ocean in Iraq and Afghanistan.

That wouldn't have happened in the days of "Demo Dick" Marcinko. During the course of Bill McRaven's career, the SEAL Teams went from being considered the "Hell's Angels" of the Navy to being regarded as consummate professionals. He helped make it happen.

But whenever SEALs come into contact with elected officials, it is the fine sense of honor of the SEALs that suffers the embrace. Bill McRaven's outstanding record in Afghanistan brought him to the attention of the White House, and on April 6, 2011, as the noose was closing around Bin Laden, President Barack Obama appointed William McRaven a four-star admiral and appointed him Commander of the United States Special Operations Command. Whether he liked it or not, Bill McRaven was a political player. He had accepted both a White House appointment and a tactical assignment from the commander in chief.

It was Sunday, May 1, and Bill McRaven had been at his new job just over three weeks. As darkness fell, he was a few hours away from launching his first combat operation in the capacity of JSOC commander.

If he was nervous, he didn't show it.

Courage, SEALs learn at BUD/S, is not the absence of fear. The absence of fear in combat is the result of insanity, or an extreme lack of situational awareness. SEALs learn not to ignore fear but to channel it. One of the most popular books at SEAL Team Six is Miyamoto Musashi's *Book of Five Rings,* a 350-year-old manual for the Samurai that touches on strategy and tactics and how a warrior should comport himself. It teaches that a warrior should be calm, use all his senses, and achieve his goals expending the minimum amount of energy. *The Book of Five Rings* is the cornerstone of the Japanese code of Bushido, the philosophy that is "the Way of the Warrior." This code includes concepts of law, respect, obedience, duty, and self-sacrifice, qualities that overlap perfectly with the SEAL Teams' own highly evolved sense of commitment and valor.

One of Musashi's axioms was posted on a bulletin board in an office in Virginia where Neptune's Spear was planned. It said: "Know the smallest things and the biggest things, the shallowest things and the deepest things as if they were a straight road mapped out on the ground. From one thing, know ten thousand things. When you attain the way of strategy there will be nothing you cannot see."

Admiral Bill McRaven knew that his plan was solid.

The CIA made sure that Red Squadron knew everything about the mission that was possible to know.

A forensics lab with state-of-the-art DNA analysis equipment had been set up in one of the hangars—in the event the operation went south, it would be used as a morgue for SEALs killed in action. High above Abbottabad, the Sentinel had started to send back video of the compound. The one hundred technicians and intelligence specialists that supported Red Squadron had done their best to make sure the operation went off and that all of Neptune's equipment functioned as it should.

Bill McRaven was a student of history. He had written a book on special operations and had studied the subject all his adult life. Now it was his turn—not to write about history, but to make it.

Not even Abraham Lincoln could resist the temptation of interfering with the plans of his generals. No sooner had Red Squadron deployed to Afghanistan than the White House began to fiddle with the plan. Fearing an aerial confrontation with the Pakistani air force, the White House first canceled plans for F-18 Hornet fighters from the carrier USS *Carl Vinson* to fly combat air patrol over the helicopters inserting SEAL Team Six into Pakistan.

It is a very small thing for a man in the calm quiet of a map room five thousand miles from the battlefield to cancel air cover for a ground operation. It is quite another experience for the men who have to traverse 120 miles of potentially hostile airspace and do so in a pair of unarmed helicopters.

The cancelation of fighter cover was accepted but there was grumbling. There were sound reasons to scrub the fighter mission. Intruding in Pakistani airspace to interdict the most famous terrorist in the world was probably excusable. It was quite another matter to do so *and* shoot down the fighters of what was, at least on paper, an ally. The Hornets were left on the carrier, and probably for the best.

160th SOAR Ghost Hawk helicopters had been transported to Jalalabad aboard a pair of C-5A Galaxy transports. Reassembled in locked hangars, the mission aircraft included two of the older model Stealth Hawks, and a pair of newer and more powerful Ghost Hawks. In addition to being quieter, the

Ghost Hawks were longer ranged and had a greater payload. The latest Ghost Hawks also had advanced avionics, and carried their own onboard electronic countermeasures. The Ghost Hawks were some of the most highly classified technology that America had ever developed.

The men planning Operation Neptune's Spear were faced with a dilemma. Now that fighter cover was not available they could not in good conscience send this highly classified technology into harm's way. If the Pakistani air force detected an airspace violation they would, at the very least, force the intruders to land. It was more likely that they would shoot first and sort it out later.

For decades, a near state of war has existed between Pakistan and India. Both countries have nuclear weapons and stare at each across a contested frontier that is covered by sophisticated radar and early warning systems. SEAL Team Six would have to skirt this border area to enter Pakistani airspace, cross almost one hundred miles of ground, conduct their operation, and then withdraw back into Afghanistan.

The mission had not changed, but the support package had. If the Pakistanis discovered the helicopters, 160th SOAR pilots would have two choices: surrender and land, or be blown out of the sky. In either case, America's most precious technological secrets would be exposed. Very reluctantly, the decision was made to use the older Stealth Hawk models, though they were smaller, had less range, and could carry fewer operators.

To accommodate the reduced range of the Stealth Hawks, it was necessary to plan a forward air refueling point (FARP) midway between Jalalabad and Bin Laden's compound. No one had to be reminded that an accident at a forward refueling position had doomed the American rescue effort in Iran in 1979. The catastrophic failure of Operation Eagle Claw saw an incumbent president, Jimmy Carter, tossed from office in the 1980 presidential elections.

The Stealth Hawks carried enough fuel to reach Abbottabad, but not enough fuel to return to base. It was decided to fly two CH-47s to a dry riverbed inside Afghanistan to meet the Stealth Hawks when they returned. One of them would carry the fuel bladders and aircrew trained to conduct the refuel operation. It is no small feat to refuel two helicopters with rotors churning on a moonless night in the middle of nowhere. And it required a little luck, too.

Operation Eagle Claw had gone haywire when its refueling spot was stumbled on by a busload of Iranian civilians. In the confusion, a helicopter collided with a C-130 filled with fuel and ammunition. The resulting explosion lit the night sky for miles and forced the rescuers to abandon their plans, three American helicopters, and the bodies of eight dead Americans.

In this operation, two MH-47 helicopters were designated Flashlight 1 and 2. Flashlight 1 was loaded with fuel bladders, and hoses and pumps to gas up the Stealth Hawks when they flew back across the border into Afghanistan. Flashlight 2 would be loaded with twenty SEAL Team Six operators who would secure the forward air refueling position and guard the helicopters from Taliban insurgents. The operators securing the fuel stop were equipped with Stinger antiaircraft missiles in case the Pakistani air force fighters declared hot pursuit and followed the Stealth Hawks back across the border. It would be their lawful right to do so. In the event that an ambush awaited the SEALs at Osama's compound, the operators aboard Flashlight 2 could be used as a quick reaction force to help the SEALs fight their way off the target and back into friendlier territory.

The decision not to risk the Ghost Hawks added layers of complexity to the mission, but was considered absolutely necessary. It would have been foolish to send the Ghost Hawks into combat without cover. Though the fighters were canceled, an EA-6B "Prowler" electronic warfare aircraft would be launched from the USS *Carl Vinson* to jam Pakistan's air defenses as the Stealth Hawks penetrated Pakistani airspace. It was a lot better than nothing.

The Navy's EA-6B Prowlers are complex and highly classified themselves. Prowlers usually fly unarmed. They are not particularly fast or agile, but they have the ability to spoof an enemy's radar, blinding it to airplanes that are present, and even making would-be interceptors see bogies that are not actually there. A lone Prowler would be used to jam Pakistani radar for the 210 minutes that the Stealth Hawks would be in Pakistan. In order to fly this mission, the Prowler would have to be refueled itself, conducting an in-flight rendezvous over the Indian Ocean, at night, with another Prowler fitted with air-to-air refueling gear. On every level, Operation Neptune's Spear depended on the consummate skills of air crews.

At 2100 hours, 9:00 p.m. Afghan time, on the evening of May 1, live video of Bin Laden's compound began to stream into the Joint Operations Center at Jalalabad. The Sentinel's high-resolution cameras rendered the compound in shades of green. The resolution was so precise that one of Bin Laden's bodyguards could be seen checking the lock on the front gate and walking between the buildings carrying a flashlight. Invisible to radar, the Sentinel flew in a circular pattern over Abbottabad. At an altitude of twenty thousand feet, no one on the ground could see or hear it. The Sentinel was a tiny speck in a vast, dark night.

Red Squadron's element commanders joined Admiral McRaven in the operations center and watched the video feed of the compound. Nothing looked different from the hundreds of aerial photographs they had studied. There had been no increase in security, and most important, the overhead imagery revealed that the sliding glass doors of the third floor were open. This would be the SEALs' main entrance.

On the third floor, where Osama had his bedroom, some of the windows facing the front of the compound had been bricked in. The other windows were closed tight as well. The only source of ventilation for the third floor was three sliding glass doors that adjoined a walled-in back patio.

In most other respects the compound was well fortified. Osama and his bodyguards had planned for almost every eventuality to thwart an attack from the ground. The compound was surrounded with a high wall topped with barbed wire. The gates of the compound wall were metal. The doors of the main building were each secured by iron grillwork, and even inside the house similar metal gates were used to cut off one section of the house from another. The stairway through the center of the main house was locked with an iron gate on the first floor. Osama and his bodyguards had considered attack from every angle—except the sky.

Red Squadron's leader is a muscular six-footer with a trace of a Tidewater, Virginia, accent and quick, piercing green eyes. There was almost always a pinch of Copenhagen snuff tucked into Frank Leslie's lower lip. He had been in command of the Red Men for almost two years and was well liked by his shooters. There were two other officers in Red Squadron, and both would play key roles in tonight's mission.

The element commander of Group Two did not present the picture that the American public probably has of a SEAL Team Six operator. He had the lean build of a cross-country runner and was an expert kayaker. He, too, had a trace of a southern drawl, and like his boss seemed to subsist on Copenhagen and black coffee. Rich Horn was fond of saying that all he needed to run an operation was caffeine, nicotine, and kerosene. The kerosene was to be burned by the helicopter that carried him. Nicotine and caffeine he considered health food. The third officer in Red Squadron was a recent graduate of Green Team. He'd seen a lot of Afghanistan as a platoon commander and later a troop leader for SEAL Teams Four and Eight. Although he was relatively new to Six he was no stranger to indoor gunfights.

The lead Stealth Hawk was designated Razor 1 and would be flown by one of the first pilots ever to take a Stealth helicopter into combat. He was experienced and aggressive. Razor 1 would carry ten assaulters, including members of SEAL Team Six's sniper cell, and two demolitionists who would carry plastic explosive cutting charges to blow their way through the terrace doors should they find them locked, or even through the roof itself, if necessary, to gain access to the third floor. Razor 1 would be the ground force honcho until the Command Bird and Scott Kerr arrived with reinforcements. Razor 2, the second Stealth Hawk, would be piloted by a second ten-year veteran of 160th SOAR. Razor 2 would deliver another ten-shooter assault element. It also carried a pair of snipers, veterans of the *Maersk Alabama*, and a designated spotter who would also direct cover fire into the doors and windows of the compound as Razor 1 made its approach and landed on the roof.

The entire operation depended on the snipers' ability to prevent anyone from taking the approaching helicopters under fire. They had to be especially vigilant that no gunmen made it to the roof of any of the buildings, or got a clear shot on Razor 1 as it settled onto the roof of the main building.

The Stealth Hawks were quiet, but they were not silent. It was certain that at some point people inside the compound would notice that a pair of black helicopters was landing on top of them. One determined rifleman could bring down both Stealth Hawks with a single well-placed magazine, and if the men in the compound had time to retrieve their shoulder-fired Strela missiles, they could take down the Stealth Hawks and every other flying thing in sight.

The SEALs were prepared to get through the compound's massive driveway doors, and even the walls of the compound. The breechers packed heavy—each man carried as much as twenty pounds of high explosives. They were prepared to open truck-size holes through cement walls, and precision-cut the doors of the main building and the guesthouses. Every assaulter aboard Razor 1 and 2 knew both his place in the chain of command and what to do if communications were lost with the operations center. They would seize and hold the compound and flush out the man they came after.

After landing on the roof, Razor 1 would clear downward, floor by floor until the main house was secured. Razor 2 would provide sniper cover until Razor 1 assaulters were in the building. They would then land on the guesthouse roof, jump down, and secure the outbuildings. After that, they would blow the gates and rush the main building. It would also be their job to separate the shooters from the noncombatants.

It was not out of the question to anticipate that the terrorists might turn their weapons deliberately or accidentally on the women and children that filled all three structures. The assault would require surgical shooting, split-second timing all in the first thirty seconds—and a not inconsiderable amount of luck.

Following five minutes behind the Stealth Hawks would be two Chinooks carrying the command element and the balance of Red Squadron. Scott Kerr's MH-47 was christened the Command Bird. After Razor 1 came through the roof, the Command Bird would land outside the compound, and Scott Kerr would take charge of a search operation. Another CH-47, armed with three M-134 Gatling guns, would accompany the Command Bird to the compound. The Gun Platform would orbit over the main house and engage any armored vehicles or bodies of troops that attempted to interfere with the operation.

Everyone hoped that no suppressing fire would be needed, that the operation would achieve surprise, and that the raiders would be in and out of the compound before the Pakistanis realized that four American helicopters had come across the border.

A SEAL's hopes very rarely come true.

As many as thirty people were expected to be inside the buildings, including three of Osama's wives and dozens of his children. The instant Razor 1 landed on the roof, the SEALs planned for chaos.

Intelligence had placed Abu Ahmed al Kuwaiti, the courier, Osama bin Laden's twenty-something sons Hazma and Khalid, and four other bodyguards scattered between the main building and the guesthouses. The SEALs were prepared to meet heavy resistance. Aboard the Command Bird, SEAL medical corpsmen were prepared to treat the wounded. Additional communicators were also on hand to make certain that the operation and its results were passed along quickly to the Joint Operations Center.

As Red Squadron rehearsed its assault at Camp Pickett and later in the Nevada desert, the CIA pressed JSOC to include some CIA personnel into the assault force. The SEALs were reluctant to conduct dynamic room-clearing operations with anyone they had not trained or operated with. There was an interagency squabble, and Leon Panetta prevailed. Included in the assault force was a Pakistani-American CIA case officer who would serve as an interpreter. He had never before in his life inserted by fast rope and had to be trained to do so. The interpreter would ride aboard Razor 2 as a passenger, sharing the already overstuffed cabin with Red Squadron's K-9 weapons system, a four-year-old Belgian Malinois named Karo. Karo got his name as a puppy when he somehow found a bottle of the sugary syrup, gnawed off its top, and drank the contents. Both Karo and the interpreter would be set down by Razor 2 outside the compound and would enter after the front gates were blown.

Karo was equipped with his own body armor and a pair of goggles to protect his eyes during the explosive breaching and the firefight that was expected to follow. It was anticipated that sorting combatants from noncombatants would be a complicated process. Karo had the ability to sniff out explosives and would be vital in detecting booby traps or suicide bombs should any be found in the compound.

SEALs on board the Command Bird carried digital cameras so they could photograph each of the residents. After the location was secured, the interpreter would question them and try to determine their relationship to Osama or Al Qaeda. Each SEAL on the mission carried photographs of known Al Qaeda members who were thought to be bodyguards or couriers.

That was the plan.

In Washington, D.C., on the morning of Sunday, May 1, technicians from JSOC led by Deputy Commander Brigadier General Marshall Webb began arriving at the White House. After being signed in, they were shown into the basement situation room, where they established communication with the Joint Operations Center in Afghanistan and the National Military Command Center at the Pentagon. They also set up a video conference link to CIA headquarters across the Potomac in Langley, Virginia. When the connection was made to Afghanistan, General Webb somewhat sheepishly informed Admiral McRaven that the president was spending the morning playing golf. He was not to be expected back until two o'clock, Washington time—just thirty minutes prior to the launch of the Stealth Hawks.

At two o'clock in the afternoon, the president returned from the golf course and had lunch. While he ate, President Obama was informed of the arrival of Vice President Joe Biden, Secretary of Defense Gates, and Secretary of State Clinton. The chairman of the Joint Chiefs of Staff, Admiral Mullen, had been among the first to arrive. They gathered in a conference room and waited for the president to join them.

An experienced SEAL Team operator was sent to CIA headquarters to sit with CIA director Leon Panetta as he watched the video feed from the Sentinel drone circling over Abbottabad. During the operation, this SEAL would have the task of explaining to the director what he was seeing on the overhead feed. Once connected to the White House, Director Panetta would add his commentary to the video links maintained by the unflappable General Webb. This arrangement allowed Leon Panetta to remain at CIA headquarters and provide color commentary to what would later be called a CIA operation.

No one at JSOC batted an eye.

In Afghanistan at 2130 hours local, 9:30 p.m., it was full dark. Flashlight 1 and 2, the Chinooks destined for the refuel site, were towed out to the flight line and started their engines. The Command Bird and the Gun Platform were also readied for flight. The assaulters of Razor 1 and 2 helped 160th SOAR personnel push the Stealth Hawks out of the hangar. The emotions of the flight crews of the Ghost Hawks that were scrubbed from the mission can only be imagined. It was a bittersweet moment to watch the SEALs load aboard the second-string Stealth Hawks and disappear into the night.

At 2200 hours local, 10:00 p.m. in Afghanistan, and 2:00 p.m. Sunday afternoon in Washington, D.C., Razors 1 and 2 lifted off and headed for the Pakistani frontier. The Command Bird, the Gun Platform, and Flashlights 1 and 2 followed. Flying in a line with the Stealth Hawks far in the lead, the six blacked-out helicopters turned toward the border.

Razor 1 flew down a complicated course that took the helicopters between mountains, down steep valleys, and along dry riverbeds, using the cover of the mountains as much as possible to stay under Pakistani radar. Razor 1 communicated using brevity codes to mark its progress. The pilots flew using night-vision devices clipped to their helmets. The lead ship called out waypoints using the names of U.S. cities to mark their progress south. The Stealth Hawks and the trailing Chinooks passed waypoints Charlotte, Atlanta, and Savannah. Locations in Florida meant that they had crossed into Pakistan. Before Razor 1 called out "Jacksonville," Flashlight 1 and 2 broke formation and landed in a wide, dry riverbed three miles from the frontier.

Disembarking from Flashlight 2, fifteen SEAL operators quickly established a perimeter while the helicopters idled. Red Squadron had been joined by an in-country delegation of Bones Men. It was the Bones Men's job to make sure no Taliban fighters attacked the helicopters idling at the forward refueling spot. They would remain on security for the next three hours.

As Razor 1 and Razor 2 approached the Pakistani frontier, the Command Bird and the Gun Platform fell back slightly and then opened the distance between themselves and the Stealth Hawks to five miles. The MH-47 Chinook is the workhorse of special operations forces in Afghanistan. Its powerful engines allow it to operate at high altitudes; it has outstanding range and is an extraordinarily rugged aircraft. But, unlike the Stealth Hawk, a Chinook makes a lot of noise and also presents a big, fat target on radar.

In the operations center, communicators established contact with the EA-6 Prowler. It had also penetrated Pakistani airspace, but from the south, crossing into Pakistan at about the same time Razor 1 and 2 crossed the northern frontier. The Prowler lit off its jammers, concealing itself and the low-flying helicopters from Pakistani air defense.

Electronic warfare is an invisible battle. No one in the operations center or aboard the helicopters could be certain that the Prowler had prevented them from being detected by Pakistani fighters or surface-to-air missile sites. For the next ninety minutes, the Stealth Hawks and the two Chinooks continued toward a rendezvous with destiny.

In Razor 1, snipers and spotters checked their weapons and flipped down their night-vision goggles. Instead of the relatively stable platform of a five-hundred-foot-long Navy destroyer, this time the SEALs would have to shoot from a moving helicopter in near total darkness. To make a shot they would have to put infrared laser beams on target, aim, and fire all while wearing night-vision goggles and hanging out the door of a flying helicopter. Aboard Razor 2, the sniper designated to fire the first shots of engagement repeated the mantra of all SEAL snipers—*Don't let me screw up*.

Aboard Razor 1 and 2 the SEALs were packed on top of each other. In order to keep their arms and legs from falling asleep, men had to periodically shove their teammates. In so doing they pushed people who bumped into other people until the shove came back to the person who started it. The insides of both helicopters were tangles of body armor, weapons, radios, and deadly satchels of high explosives. It occurred to one crew chief that if the C4 went off there wouldn't be anything left to prove they had ever entered Pakistan in the first place.

The Command Bird and the Gun Platform were six miles behind Razor 1 and 2, flying low and using the mountains north of Abbottabad to mask the thumping noise of their rotors. All they could do was hope that the clattering of the Chinooks would not reach the walls of the compound before the Stealth Hawks were able to insert the first assaulters.

At fifty-six minutes past midnight, precisely on time, Razor 1 called out "Palm Beach" over the radio. The pilot cued the intercom and told Frank

Leslie they were three minutes out. The Red Squadron leader disconnected his headphones from the helicopter's intercom and plugged himself back into his personal radio.

In the hot darkness of the Stealth Hawk's cabin he rocked his shoulders against the men piled next to him. He then held up three fingers and the SEALs pulled themselves up onto their feet. Leaning against each other, they crouched and held on as best they could. Members of the sniper cell maneuvered themselves in front of the helicopter's port and starboard doors and made ready their weapons. Some of the assaulters slapped their hands against sleepy limbs; others pulled at the collars of their body armor and felt the trickle of sweat down their backs. Weapons straps were checked, and holsters adjusted. Leaning across the tangle of bodies, shooting partners switched on their buddies back-mounted radios and earphones warbled as transmitters logged on to the secure frequencies that would link the shooters with one another.

Aboard Razor 2 this process was repeated. The assault teams made themselves ready, flipped down their night-vision devices, checked breaching charges, and switched on their night-vision goggles.

Aboard Razor 1 Frank Leslie craned his neck to look out between the pilots through the windshield—he couldn't see the ground or even catch a glimpse of the horizon. Through his night-vision gear all he could see was green static. He had to take the pilot's word that they were getting close.

Frank saw the pilot lift his left hand off the helicopter's collective and make a peace sign. They were two minutes out. Aboard Razor 1 and 2 crewmembers threw latches and pulled back the port and starboard doors.

The hot, muggy night swirled into the cabin. Wind through the open doors fluttered their uniforms against their arms and legs. The SEALs could smell the scent of farmland and pine as Razor 1 came out of the hills and descended to an altitude of twenty feet. Fields and orchards flashed under them—they were now heading straight for the compound.

As the doors came back on Razor 2, Mel Hoyle positioned himself on the starboard side behind the pilot. His spotter crouched beside him, his headset connected by the helicopter's intercom to the pilots on the flight deck. In the Nevada desert they had practiced yawing the helicopter sideways so that the snipers could get a clear shot out of the open doors of the helicopter. That was what they planned tonight.

Thirty seconds.

Razor 2 settled at an altitude of fifty feet, trailing Razor 1 and slightly to the left. Ahead was the square shape of the main house and the high, triangular wall that screened the compound from the dirt road in front and the farm fields spreading behind.

One hundred yards from the main house, Razor 1 climbed to thirty feet; the nose of the helo lifted and settled toward the roof of the main building.

The pilots were shocked to find that the boxlike structure on the roof was twice as high as expected—instead of being three feet tall, it was almost five. The pilots had counted on setting down directly on the roof but in the pitch dark they didn't dare. The wall looked too high. The pilot steadied the pitching helicopter seven feet above the roof and managed to hold it there.

Framed in the open hatch, Frank Leslie hesitated for a second. His night-vision goggles showed the roof, but he knew from experience that distance was a hard thing to gauge electronically. He cocked his head so that his eyes could look around the bottom of his NODs. He knew the helicopter had been put into a hover, and he knew they were some distance from the roof, obviously above the three-sided box. There was no time to discuss the situation with the flight deck.

He jumped, and his SEALs followed him, throwing themselves into a lime-colored void.

They landed on the roof with a series of heavy thumps. Under the weight of their gear, several of the assaulters landed hard. They crawled to the edge of the roof and dropped down onto the third-floor patio.

While Razor 1 was hovering over the main building, Mel Hoyle and Razor 2 were passing slowly down the perimeter of the compound at an altitude of about thirty feet. Razor 2 went into a hover at the apex of the compound's triangle-shaped perimeter. Just inside the angle, the south-facing doors and windows of the guest quarters were the only way in or out. Razor 2 was on perch, and the doors were covered. It was Mel's job to make sure no one from the guesthouse came or went. As he had done aboard the *Bainbridge* Mel would spot for the primary shooter, but he was armed and ready to lay down suppressing fire to keep the compound clear.

Aboard Razor 2, Mel and the primary marksman were positioned tight behind the starboard portion of the flight deck. Cradling a long-barreled M-4 rifle, the shooter was sitting cross-legged next to the open door. Mel was leaning over him like an umpire. He was in a position to talk to both the pilot and direct fire.

Through the open starboard hatch the assaulters aboard Razor 2 could see that Razor 1 was now in a hover over the roof. The brief was for Razor 2 to wait fifteen or twenty seconds before landing themselves on the roof of the guesthouse. Twenty seconds in combat can be an eternity.

As Razor 2 moved down the walls, the scent of a barnyard wafted up into the cabin. Mel could see a trio of cattle moving across the wide enclosed area to his left. Around the cattle he saw small shapes darting about. He raised his rifle to his eye and sighted in: they were chickens. Pushed about by the helicopter's down blast, the birds flapped around the spooked cattle. There were dozens, scores of chickens running about. Some were stampeded under the legs of a pair of milk cows, now headed as far away from the helicopter as possible. The sight was comical, but no one laughed.

Directly below Razor 2, lights came on in the guesthouse. A shadow moved in front of one window and then another, and then a door opened. Two people crowded the doorway; one carried an AK-47 assault rifle. Osama's courier, Ibrahim Khan, had just stepped out of a lighted room into a moonless night and he was blind. Razor 1 was behind him, on top of the main building, cut off from his view by the guesthouse and another wall. Either he could not see, or did not look, above him. If he had, he would have seen the Stealth Hawk, and he might have caught a glimpse of the two riflescopes that now pointed in his direction. The shooter lifted his rifle, aiming high.

Mel heard the words "Bust him" crackle in his headset. It was his own voice; the words had materialized from between his ears to the tip of his tongue. He wasn't aware of even thinking about speech—his attention was down range on the target. It was a firefight now and he switched his rifle from fire to auto.

Razor 2 yawed slightly to port. As Ibrahim Khan came into view, the sniper seated next to Mel fired twice. Mel leveled two three-round bursts at the man with the rifle. The silencers chuffed. Every one of their bullets hit the target. The bullets passed through the glass in the doorway, and Ibrahim Khan was blown off his feet. His AK-47 spun in a half circle up and out of his hands. He had not even managed to fire a shot, or set foot outside the building.

THIRTY-EIGHT MINUTES

THE SOUND MADE BY Stealth Hawk helicopters is difficult to describe: Some claim that they don't so much hear it as "feel" it. It is an aircraft that renders a sensation before it makes a noise. An approaching Stealth Hawk makes a low sound but it is neither resonant nor deep. It begins at the threshold of hearing as a fizzing, a hissing, and then proceeds to a steady hum like a fan blowing in a distant room. Even when waiting for one—knowing that it will come, and knowing where it will land—your ears deceive you. It is not silent but it is also not loud enough for a person to connect the noise with an aircraft that can hover and fly. Hovering, they make the noise of a small waterfall, a blank, white noise. It is a sound that doesn't carry very well.

Impressive and frightening, Stealth Hawks carry a crew of three and can hold as many as twenty men in the cabin. They and their big brothers the Ghost Hawks are only flown by 160th SOAR, and only operate at night. The rear fins angle sharply, and the tail rotors are shrouded. The acutely angled cockpit windshields and the steeply pitched fuselage sides make it look sinister, like a thing that is alive, not something that was made by men.

A series of black triangles are set around the frames of all the windscreens and the cabin doors. These zigzags scatter radar waves as they hit the glass. The Stealth Hawks are painted the color of the sky they fly in—some are black, some are gray, and a few are a mottling of both. Up close, the Stealth Hawk looks like a long, slightly humpbacked shark.

That night, two of them flew out of the mountains and then low across the fields outside Abbottabad. Razor 1 was "on the deck," lower than fifty feet and Razor 2 trailed in echelon to the left, maybe twenty feet higher. They made their run into the target at 130 miles an hour. That low to the ground, and flying that fast, they would be on top of the compound mere seconds after the noise of their engines could be heard.

Osama's third-floor bedroom was down a short hall from the stairs. The room in which he slept with Amal and his second wife, Siham, opened to a third-floor patio screened by a seven-foot cement wall. The terrace's wall provided complete privacy. It meant no one could see in, but no one could see out either. A person on this terrace or in a room next to it could only hear "up"—the only direction that sound could come. That helped to block the noise of the approaching Stealth Hawks. Osama did not hear the helicopters until they were right on top of him.

At five minutes to one, he was in bed, and he was asleep. The lights were off. At 1:00 a.m., his bedroom started to fill with a buzzing sound. The night had been calm and the sliding glass doors that led to the terrace had been left ajar to let in some air. As Razor 1 hovered, the down blast of its rotors poured a hurricane into the narrow space of the terrace, hurling a pair of plastic chairs against the windows. A violent gust of air hammered the sliding glass doors and they shook in their tracks and bowed in against the pressure. The curtains next to the open doors flailed into the room, pulling the curtain rods out of the wall as they fell.

Osama threw back the blanket from his bed. He tried to put his feet on the floor and he could feel the house shake. He had ninety seconds to live.

Siham leapt from her bed and ran toward the terrace doors. She saw the curtains and she saw the plastic chairs and then she saw the shapes of men. They were jumping from the roof onto the terrace, landing with thuds that shook the floor. She could not see their faces. They were like solidified chunks of night.

It took less than six seconds for the assaulters of Razor 1 to jump from the hovering helicopter, land on the roof, and crawl over to the back. There, they jumped again, seven or eight feet down onto the terrace. Siham saw them come through the glass doors, and she saw them come toward her in the hallway, weapons raised.

Siham must have expected to be torn to pieces by a hail of gunfire, but the men did not shoot. Instead, a searing white strobe light flashed into her eyes. It erased her vision, turned it white, and then to a pulsating red-pink and she stumbled backward.

She was grabbed by her arm and pushed to the floor. Only twenty seconds had passed since she'd heard the noise of a waterfall and thrown herself out of bed. The men made no noise. Siham curled onto the tiles and the other men went past—two straight down the hallway one behind the other, their weapons at the ready.

Then two things happened very quickly.

A door in the third-floor hallway opened. Osama stuck his head out, saw the Americans, and slammed the door loudly.

One of the operators hit his inter-squad radio and called out, "Geronimo, Geronimo, Geronimo," indicating that he had "eyes on."

Some of the assaulters ran toward Osama's door as the stairwell lights suddenly lit up, switched on from the second floor. Khalid bin Laden ran up the stairs to the landing. When he saw the men remaining at the top of the stairs, a green laser swept from the wall toward his chest, and as his momentum carried him forward, two suppressed shots were fired. Khalid was struck in the chest just below his throat. He twisted forward, landing on his right side with his arm tucked under his head. A pair of spent cartridges tinkled down the cement stairs past his corpse.

In the hallway above, the first assaulter reached the door where Bin Laden had been glimpsed. He waited two seconds to feel that another operator had joined him, then kicked the door open and went inside. He was followed closely by his shooting partner.

The blinding lights on their weapons swept down a short hallway, and then into the open space of the bedchamber. The lights and lasers swept into the room, illuminating the figures of a man and a woman. The woman was shouting but seemed to be moving in slow motion. So, too, the man behind her—he was moving toward the bed, just reaching it, diving across it—but all of this seemed to be unfolding in a slide show: *click, click, click*. The lights on the SEALs' weapons clearly illuminated an AKSU machine pistol leaning against the left side of the bed. The SEALs both saw it, both measured its length and breadth and determined that the man was turning, extending his hand and reaching toward it. The man with the beard shoved the woman toward the men and moved behind her. He was a threat; the woman was nothing. He was one. She was zero. The SEALs lifted their weapons and tracked the man.

When a room is entered, SEALs go into a state like satori—a wide-awake Zen consciousness that allows them to perceive and react with a minimal space between for thought. It puts them instantly in the here and now—connected not only to the situation, but tapping into the thoughts and intentions of the enemies. Time dilates. All of a SEAL's senses are magnified; the smallest sound, the slightest smells, the textures of the floor and walls, all are burned into his consciousness. Movements made by the enemy seem to take minutes instead of seconds—while the movements made by the shooters seem to glide on a plane removed from exertion. To move, a SEAL needs only to think. To place a bullet he needs only to concentrate.

Every member of SEAL Team Six has engaged in hundreds, even thousands of close-in gun battles. The two shooters who entered Osama's bedroom had spent so many hundreds of hours in combat that they had seen almost every sort of behavior that could be exhibited by a fleeing, fighting, or surrendering human.

There are SEALs that report that in a firefight they seem to remember the entire event as though it were filmed by a camera placed above and behind them. Something like slow motion that zooms into every move of the enemy, and allows the operators to even see themselves as though they, too, were objects moving about a stage. First person meets third person.

Amal was screaming. She'd heard the voices in the hallway, and a multi-syllable word said over and over. "Geronimo" was even now crackling from headsets all over the compound. She had been shoved toward the end of the mattress, kneeling half on and half off, steadying herself on the end of the bed. To her left, two SEALs aimed past her and their lights converged.

She shouted in Arabic, *"No, no, don't do this."*

Osama was standing by the back wall. He dived across the king-size bed to get at the AKSU rifle he kept by the headboard. The room smelled like old clothing, like a guest bedroom in a grandmother's house, a place sort of frozen in time.

Pinned in the lights, Amal lifted her hands to her eyes. She said, "It's not him," in Arabic, and then something else that the operators could not hear.

Four suppressed shots were fired, two rounds and two rounds. Both SEALs discharged their weapons in the same second and the reports all seemed pushed together into a single phrase.

The first round sailed past Osama's face and thudded into the mattress. Osama shoved Amal as he clawed across the bed. A second bullet, aimed at Osama's head, grazed Amal in the calf.

SEALs do not shoot to wound: they are trained to shoot to kill. Amal was hit because Osama placed her between himself and the men who entered his bedroom. As his wife crouched forward, wounded, Osama's hand reached for his AKSU. He never made it. Two U.S. Navy M855 5.56mm Predator bullets slammed into him. One struck him next to his breastbone, blowing apart his aorta. The last bullet went through his skull, killing him instantly.

Across the compound Razor 2 was still on its "perch" hovering over the guesthouse. Razor 2 was lowering to land on the guesthouse roof when the call of "Geronimo, Geronimo, Geronimo" came over their radios. Razor 2 would land and then the breachers would blow a hole through the second compound wall that separated the guesthouse from the main house. The assaulters would climb through the hole, rush in, and start clearing the outbuildings, all in twenty seconds.

Some thought it might have been better to simply fast rope onto the guesthouse roof, but Razor 2 carried two combatants who weren't much good at fast roping. One of them was the canine Karo, Red Squadron's K-9 badass. The other was the CIA interpreter who was a novice fast roper at best. The team didn't think that he was ready to try a hundred-foot fast rope, at night, with bullets flying. If he broke his leg or fell to his death, there would be no one to question the noncombatants.

As Mel and the sniper covered the compound, Razor 2 lowered itself toward the guesthouse roof. When the tires bounced, the assaulters all tumbled out. Karo and the "Terp" (the interpreter) were manhandled off the roof. Razor 2 lifted back up fifty feet and perched on a hover, Mel and his shooter back to covering the entire compound—looking for "squirters," anyone trying to flee from the buildings.

"Geronimo Geronimo Geronimo, third deck," came over their headsets again. Led by Rich Horn, four shooters of Razor 2 split off for the main house. They had no idea what Razor 1 had gotten into. As cool as it sounds when cops say it, SEALs do not call out "shots fired." All Razor 2 knew was that their boss was in the main building and things were going to get hot.

The other operators from Razor 2 had plenty to do. The guesthouse was a low, flat-roofed shoe box of a building. Three families shared two bathrooms and each living space had a small kitchenette. There was a warren of adjoining spaces, and one shooter had already come out of the building. If there were more hostiles in the guesthouse the SEALs would have to take them out surgically.

A three-year-old boy had toddled out of one of the open doors and was crying, pointing up at the helicopter. There were women and children in the building, so "clearing it out" could not involve just throwing in a hand grenade. It meant that each room would have to be entered. The SEALs would have to determine bad guys from nonplayers during active gunfights. Shooting to separate hostage from hostage-taker and terrorist from human shield is called "close quarters combat." There are no practitioners in the U.S. military who come close to Six in this regard. They are unexcelled at precision combat marksmanship and the process of flowing through targets.

As they swept in to secure the rooms, the SEALs stepped over the body of Ibrahim Khan. He had achieved his life goal of martyrdom and had gone down fighting. Had he aimed up, instead of into the compound, he could have shot down Razor 2 and killed every man onboard.

But that wasn't to be. Not tonight.

Each of the rooms was entered. There were three children and a woman inside. The noncombatants were secured and the sweep continued until all the rooms were cleared. The process took less than thirty seconds and no shots were fired.

Rich Horn now led his assault group toward the main house, splitting off small groups to search and clear two small buildings in the backyard.

Razor 2 returned to its hover position over the south apex. It would remain on perch for the rest of the SEALs' time on target. The sniper and spotter on Razor 2 were the SEALs high ground, covering the entire compound as the team consolidated on the main house.

Rich could hear the pounding rotors of the Chinooks as they lumbered out of the mountains and converged on the compound. At this point the chickens came out and started to walk around. Perhaps they expected to be fed. It was later determined that there were more than a hundred chickens—and that was a count of the ones who had flapped their way over the walls. The cows and a pair of buffalo were also lowing; the target was beginning to seem like Noah's Ark.

Rich and his team reached the back door of the main house and kicked it open. As they entered, a door to the right-hand bedroom jerked open. Ibrahim Khan, Osama's chief bodyguard, took a half step out of the room. In his hand was an AK-47 rifle. Ibrahim seemed paralyzed as weapon lights and aiming lasers swept over him. As he lifted his rifle, two shots struck him in the chest, passed through his body, and killed the person standing behind him. It was his wife, Bushra.

The remaining rooms on the ground floor were entered and cleared. In the bedroom opposite, the SEALs found Osama's two daughters, and in the remaining ground-floor apartments, Bin Laden's first wife, Khairiah, and ten children—Bin Laden children and grandchildren.

Reporting that the ground floor was secure, Rich ordered his guys to tear the place apart and find the Strela missiles intel said might be there to guard Osama. It was imperative that they be found. No helicopter within two miles would be safe unless the missiles were captured—and the two Chinooks were their ride home. The Stealth Hawks couldn't carry them all.

The SEALs had been in the compound for less than five minutes when the Command Bird landed and Scott Kerr led his assault element to the compound's front gate, slapped on a breaching charge and blew it open. A thunderclap rolled over the city of Abbottabad. If they didn't know the SEALs were in before, they did now. The explosion could be heard for miles.

Across the city, fingers flew over keyboards and keypads, tweeting and e-mailing about the explosion and the helicopters now circling the compound. No one had tweeted until the Chinooks came on station. The Stealth Hawks had lived up to their billing.

Scott came into the compound followed closely by a communicator—one of the Det Alpha satcom maestros. He went past the blown gate, with its sharp smell of cordite and cut steel, and into the smell of the barnyard, the animals and the chickens.

Razor 1 now held the third floor. Rich Horn's assault element was placing a second charge to blow its way through the locked gate that blocked the first-floor stairway.

A voice came out of the darkness: "Who are you?"

"The skipper," Scott's communicator answered.

It was one of Razor 2's breachers who asked. He was preparing a firing device and a piece of NONEL instantaneous fuse.

"Better find some cover, Skipper. We're going hot."

Scott and his guys crouched behind a cement wall.

"Fire in the hole."

WHUMP. There was a blinding flash, and then came the deafness felt by the SEALs closest to the explosion. Without being told, Razor 2 boiled up the stairs and onto the second floor. Within seconds, they had linked up with the assaulters of Razor 1 who had begun to search the rooms on the second floor, spreading in all directions, checking in rooms and behind closet doors.

SEALs do not wear helmet cams—if they were to be issued, it is likely that they would become the most frequently malfunctioning equipment in the U.S. military. SEALs are many things, and they are not politically naïve. They know very well politicians would love nothing more than to ponder over video recordings of the split-second life-and-death decisions they make in combat. Days and weeks after the danger, their split-second life-and-death decisions would be picked apart by armchair commandos in Washington.

Had cameras been worn into the main house, it would have looked like the lobby of an elementary school. There were whiteboards and desks and books.

"Fire in the hole."

Another explosion, this one high and sharp. A steel-cutting charge had blown open the metal grate that secured the ground floor from the floors above. Pieces of the gate banged off the marble floors and fragments found ground-floor windows to fly through. The smoke cleared, and Scott started up the stairs.

"We're coming up! Hey, goddamn it, we're coming up!"

"Panama!" was shouted by the men upstairs. It was the challenge and response—the way to tell friend from foe.

"Red," came back the answer. Tonight's challenge and response.

Scott Kerr came up the stairs to the third-floor landing, and saw a body.

"Whose is it?"

"We're working on it, Skipper. It's either Hamza or Khalid."

A voice called from upstairs. "Here, Skipper. In here."

"Six is moving. Be advised, Six actual is moving."

No accidental shootings tonight.

Scott entered the third-floor hallway. A SEAL stood guard over Siham, her face streaked with tears. The third-floor lights had been turned on, and she was surrounded by huge men with guns. She had no idea if she would live or die. Osama had told her that the Americans would murder her on sight. Scott Kerr looked at her face. He knew who she was.

"Number two," said Frank.

"Yeah. We're gonna keep her up here until we go. No point in spreading the news too far." Frank wasn't a squadron commander for nothing. Keeping the captures separated by location also prevented them from fabricating stories about atrocities. Even though the SEALs took precautions, several of the noncombatants would tell stories that Osama was captured alive and then murdered. The Pakistani press would spread this story, even though it was told by people who were not in the main house or on the third floor at the time of the assault.

Scott went into Bin Laden's bedroom. Amal was leaning against a wall, her wounded leg thrust out in front of her. She, too, was sobbing.

Kerr did not recognize Amal's face. But she was in pajamas, she was in Osama's bedroom, and she was the right age for number four. He walked over to the bed.

Osama had been pulled off the mattress and laid face up. His photo was taken and the data chip was handed to the communicator. He put it into a reader attached to his satellite radio.

Kerr looked into the face of the man who had brought down the World Trade Center and started two wars that had lasted a decade. The Predator round had blown out the back of his head. Bin Laden was dead, but not one person on the Team thought this meant an end to Al Qaeda or to terror. Not by a goddamn long shot.

"It's him," said Frank Leslie.

"It is." Kerr stood. "Get a DNA sample." As soon as Kerr saw Bin Laden's body, he communicated the news to Admiral McRaven in the Joint Operations Center. The SEALs' intersquad radios were not monitored by higher command. It was up to Scott Kerr to communicate with the admiral back in Jalalabad, and it was Bill McRaven's job to communicate with Washington.

Scott Kerr thought back to the day at JSOC headquarters when he was told about Neptune's Spear. Until ten seconds ago he never really believed . . . He thought it was all going to be . . . He didn't know what, but he didn't think that four months later he would be standing in Pakistan, looking down at the corpse of Osama bin Laden.

Kerr turned to the Red Squadron leader. "What happened?"

"Easy day. We got onto the roof. No one heard us approach. In five seconds we were on the terrace. We were in the hallway in thirty. One was coming at us up the stairs. He got tagged, and the door opened. Crankshaft stuck his head out, saw us, and slammed the door. We kicked it in, and were on him."

"What happened to number four?"

"She was on the end of the bed, both feet on the mattress, sort of squatting and holding up the covers. He jumped across the bed behind her. We shot. One miss. One went through her leg and two went into him as he was diving across the mattress."

"What was he doing on the bed?"

"He was going for this." The Red Squadron leader held up a short AK-74. It was the AKSU that Osama always posed with. The gun was as famous as he was. Scott Kerr looked over the weapon. It had been fitted with a special forty-round extended magazine. Kerr jacked back the receiver and a shell tinged onto the floor. It was loaded with armor-piercing ammunition.

"We got a Marakov 9 mil pistol, too. Behind the bed."

Scott handed the AK back to Frank. "This is for Red Squadron."

"Hoo yaa, Skipper."

Frank was a squadron leader, an operator, but he, too, had a drop of the politician in him. "Maybe the admiral would like the pistol, sir. Compliments of the Red Men."

Kerr smiled. *Hell,* he thought, *I'd like to keep it myself.*

While the communicator went to the terrace and set up the satcom, Kerr had a minute or two to look around the room. It was fairly neat, and someone had placed two cheap pictures on the wall—decorative art, abstracts sort of. Kerr was also aware of the stuffiness of the room. To him it smelled like boxes of clothing kept in a musty garage.

He soon had a satellite and established voice communication. Kerr got on the satcom and contacted the JOC. He was talking on encrypted voice, one of the least secure methods of communication, and he used the brevity codes that had been established for the operation. He knew that his words would be heard not only by his boss, Admiral McRaven, but in Washington as well.

Scott started with what he considered most important: "Apache okay." No SEALs dead, wounded, or missing. He continued, "Tomahawk negative at this time." They had not found the Strela missiles—if they had ever been here at all.

"Comanche, Chippewa, Echo. KIA." Bin Laden's courier, Ibrahim Khan, and Abrar Khan, enemy, killed in action.

"Chappo, Echo. KIA." Chappo was the war chief Geronimo's son—and the code name given to Khalid bin Laden. The message meant that Khalid was dead.

"Cochise, Echo. Mike at this time." Bin Laden's second son, Hamza, had been given the code name Cochise. He had been thought to be in the compound. If he was, they hadn't found him. If he had run away, then he was more invisible than a Stealth Hawk. The SEALs had established an airtight perimeter. Hamza was Echo, Mike. Enemy and missing.

Kerr got to what they were waiting for. He said slowly, "Geronimo, Echo. KIA." Osama bin Laden was dead.

At CIA headquarters the director squinted through his glasses at the typed sheet that had been transmitted to him when the mission launched. It was the list of brevity codes. He'd listened to Scott Kerr's voice as he went through his list, following along with a pencil a bit like a bingo player. Finally, he heard a word that really meant something. Geronimo.

Panetta was connected to the White house via General Webb's laptop. He had been chirping in via a small video window of his own, adding what comments he could. All he had to go on was the feed from the Sentinel drone. It had showed only the outside of the building. It was an agonizing fifteen minutes before Scott Kerr confirmed that Osama was in the building and had been killed.

Panetta was delighted to pipe in, "Geronimo, E, enemy. Killed in action."

The president said, "We got him."

Later, pictures from the White House situation room would show several famous faces watching the target feed in rapt attention. Secretary Clinton would be shown with a hand over her mouth—looking horrified. Others would look stoic.

The photograph does not show President Obama, Secretary Clinton, and Vice President Biden at the moment they learned Osama bin Laden's fate. The picture was taken minutes later, when it looked like catastrophe had finally caught up with SEAL Team Six.

On the video feed a helicopter had just crashed.

Razor 1 was finally able to settle and land on the roof of the house. During the assault, it remained there, rotors turning, doors open. It was then ordered to lift off and land outside the compound so that the operators could be reembarked.

In Earth's orbit, four satellites were watching. Twenty thousand feet above Abbottabad, the Sentinel flew in a lazy circle, its cameras turned on the objective—it was streaming video to the Joint Operations Center in Jalalabad, and that video was being relayed in real time to Leon Panetta at CIA headquarters and the White House situation room.

At an altitude of three hundred feet, the Chinook helicopter designated as the Gun Platform was making slow quarter-mile turns around the compound, watching for troops or vehicles coming to the garrison stationed at the Kakul Military Academy less than a mile from Bin Laden's front door.

Razor 2 was still on perch, hovering at fifty feet above the apex of the compound's southern perimeter.

Departing from the roof of the main building, Razor 1 headed for a landing spot along the road one hundred yards west of the Command Bird. In the pitch-black darkness, the Stealth Hawk crossed over the narrow walled driveway bisecting the compound. Slowly, the helicopter started to drop. Losing altitude, Razor 1 canted sideways. It began to rotate clockwise, until its tail was pointed east and it was flying backward. An important component of the flight deck controls had failed. Called a "green unit," this removable system controlled flight inputs and communications, and managed navigational problems. In spec ops it is often said that, "One is none, two is one." The green unit in the Stealth Hawks was considered important enough to have a backup system. Razor 1 could fly perfectly well with just one functioning green unit, but it could not fly with both of them off-line. And both of them went out at the same time—a million-to-one shot. Almost gracefully the doomed Razor Hawk sank tail-first into the large, walled enclosure east of the main house.

The snipers and air crew aboard Razor 2 watched in horror as dust started to tornado up from the sprawling animal pen. The Stealth Hawk settled so gradually that a cow and two buffalos had time to amble out of the way. Then the helo's landing gear thumped into the ground and the machine bucked upward and started to spin in a wrenching, high-speed circle. These were Razor 1's out-of-control death throes. When it hit the ground a second time it was with such violence that the helicopter broke into two pieces.

For ten seconds the rotors flailed in the dirt and the fuselage flopped around like a fish thrown on a dock. Finally, mercifully, the rotors broke off, the engines flamed out and the pieces stopped. All of this started so moderately and ended so violently that it astounded everyone. Washington had no idea what had just happened. All the Joint Operations Center knew was that a helicopter, a Stealth Hawk, had just crashed.

Two operators had bagged Osama's body and were taking it down out of the ground floor of the main house when they heard the sound of a high-pitched buzz . . . almost a shriek. Scott Kerr ran out of the main house and looked up. He had not seen the crash. Because of the high walls and the several tasks the SEALs were carrying out, very few of the assaulters knew what had happened, either.

"Razor 1 is down!"

On the ground, it had to be thought that the helicopter had been shot down. Operators and corpsmen rushed to the wreckage. The flight deck, one of the most reinforced parts of the helicopter, had survived almost intact. A SEAL corpsman found the flight crew shaken up and in shock, but all right.

The SEALs had been on target approximately twenty minutes. They had gathered an impressive haul of actionable intelligence from Bin Laden's home. It filled a dozen garbage bags and more. Now they had to get out—on one less helicopter than they had come in on.

All of Kerr's training came into play. *The plan must survive the blunders of men.* He loaded Bin Laden's body onto the Command Bird. "Gather up the intel, bag it up, everything, and we are out of here in ten minutes. Wheels up, ten minutes!"

Kerr looked at the wreckage. It was too destroyed to fly and too intact to leave. The Stealth Hawk had to be destroyed. The pilots were still shaken up, but they helped to smash the avionics and other flight controls. The most highly classified pieces of equipment, including the two failed green units, were put onto the Command Bird. They'd be taken back to base and examined to find out what had gone wrong.

As this was happening, all of the noncombatants were questioned and photographed. This part of an operation is called "the sort." Rich Horn called for the interpreter.

"Group them up with their moms. Get everyone's name, and get their pictures. Keep them all here, in the ground floor bedroom," he shouted. "No one in, no one out. Keep a count."

DNA samples were taken from the three dead terrorists, and Amal's wounds were dressed and she was given a tetanus shot. Kerr directed that the exfil begin. The trash bags containing the intel went aboard the Command Bird. During the operation, hundreds of pictures had been taken of the rooms, the bloodstains, the beds, the cupboards, the clothing, the weapons, the ammunition—pictures of everything except the missiles. They could not be found.

SEALs would carry away five hundred data systems, hard drives, computers, laptops, monitors, notebooks written in Arabic and English, papers, financial records, and wire diagrams of a new Al Qaeda that Osama was planning—one that did not include Doctor Ayman Zawahiri.

Osama had watched the news, too. He had considered now that Egypt had its revolution, Zawahiri's principal qualification for being in the ranks of Al Qaeda's leadership was gone. Bin Laden did not want attacks carried out against Egypt, and documents show that Zawahiri was planning a spectacular bombing in Tahrir Square. Ironically, intel analysts reading through Bin Laden's papers would discover that Osama was planning a full break with Zawahiri. That move came too late to prevent Zawahiri from moving against him.

Even Al Qaeda has its politics.

Demolition charges were set in the wreckage of Razor 1. Explosives were set on all the sensitive parts of the aircraft, especially the engines. Blocks of C4 were wired up with long strings of orange det cord that stretched across the barnyard to a detonator. As the SEALs got a head count and reloaded into the helicopter, Scott Kerr, the interpreter, and his bodyguard were the last Americans to leave the compound. They told the noncombatants to stay where they were, tucked safely behind the guesthouse wall. They obeyed.

In the street, Kerr told the head breacher to set a three-minute delay. The charges were set and the last four men walked into the Command Bird now turning its rotors in the field across the dirt road from the compound. They walked up the helicopter's tail ramp and Scott gave a thumbs-up. The engines roared and the big Chinook shook itself and started to climb into the sky.

Scott Kerr stood on the tail ramp and looked down at the compound. He felt the helicopter's deck throb through his boots and the smell of jet exhaust and JP-5 wiped away the smells of the house. He lifted his vision goggles—now he saw it the way Bin Laden had seen it. There were a few lights on. Kerr could see the bone-colored building in an odd-shaped triangle, the "embassy" Bin Laden had built for himself—two acres of sovereign Al Qaeda territory where he thought he was beyond the reach of the nation upon which he had declared war.

Osama had been wrong to think Abbottabad was a safe place.

Scott Kerr watched as the self-destruct charges ripped through what was left of Razor 1. The explosion thudded through the night, setting off car alarms, waking up babies, and rattling windows in Abbottabad. A fiery mushroom cloud lifted over the wreckage and flaming pieces came down around the compound.

In Abbottabad, a dozen people sat at keyboards and tweeted exactly what Scott Kerr was thinking: *Maybe Abbottabad wasn't really a safe place after all.*

Operation Neptune's Spear, SEAL Team Six's greatest triumph, had started with a whisper and ended with a night-shattering bang.

WHAT CAME AFTER

FIFTY-FIVE MINUTES PAST MIDNIGHT on the morning of May 2, 2011, Lt. Colonel Naseem Anwar led a detachment from the guard force of the Pakistani Military Academy through the school's front gate, toward the entrance of Bilal Town, the ramshackle suburb two miles northeast of Abbottabad. There had been reports of a low-flying helicopter, and the duty officer at the academy had called to say that several small explosions had been reported near the perimeter of the academy. Thinking that a Pakistani aircraft may have conducted a forced landing, Colonel Anwar turned southwest on the Kakul Road.

As his small convoy approached the intersection of Awami Road, Naseem Anwar pulled to the shoulder, put his window down, and listened as best he could in the moonless dark. For a moment, the colonel thought he could hear the sound of rotors—a low buzzing noise, almost like a hiss. If it *was* a helicopter, it was flying low and moving off to the north. After a few moments, a set of headlights pulled into the intersection behind him, and another officer stepped into the road.

Colonel Anwar's search party was joined by the commander of the Inter Services Intelligence detachment assigned to the military academy; a man Colonel Anwar knew only as "Jwad." He and several of his men had also heard the noise, and, like their military colleagues, they had been driving the roads, looking to catch a glimpse of the mystery aircraft. The two officers discussed splitting up to widen their search when the sky above Bilal Town was torn open by a blast of orange-yellow light. An ear-splitting boom rumbled through the buildings and vacant lots, then echoed back from the distant hills. The officers jumped back into their cars and drove south toward a mushrooming fire in the sky. Both Colonel Anwar and Jwad were convinced that there had been a crash—and now there was a fire, too.

This account is based on both eyewitness testimony and a report written by Pakistani Brigadier General Shukat Qadir. General Qadir has had a distinguished career in the Pakistani army, where he served at company, field, and command levels as an infantry officer, an instructor at the Command and Staff College as well as a professor of strategy at the National Defense University. Since his retirement, Shukat Qadir has written broadly on terrorism and counterterrorism, and is a respected journalist both within Pakistan and the international community. His deep connections within the Pakistani armed forces and intelligence organizations allowed him to conduct an independent investigation into the circumstances leading up to and following the raid conducted by American forces on May 2, 2011.

In the days and weeks following the raid, General Qadir was able to interview ISI officers, military first responders, and civilian eyewitnesses. His report contains information that can be cross-referenced with the recollections of U.S. military personnel as well as with the intelligence officials who planned and carried out both pre-mission activities in the raid itself. As far as can be ascertained, General Qadir has written the most reliable account of what happened on the ground in Pakistan before and immediately following Operation Neptune's Spear. His report states that he was allowed access to Bin Laden's home after the raid and that he has also read the classified version of Pakistan's official investigation. Qadir's account of the mission varies significantly from both the official U.S. and Pakistani accounts of what happened.

Within seconds after hearing the explosion, Colonel Anwar led his first responders toward what was obviously a crash scene. As he drove, Anwar phoned his deputy, Major Nassan, and told him to deploy the academy's Quick Reaction Force and to follow him south into Bilal Town. It was a few seconds past one a.m., and a fire was roiling into the sky just four hundred meters to the south, flickering over the housetops.

Tires skittering on the dusty roads, three left turns brought Jwad and Anwar to a pillar of black smoke rising behind a high compound wall. Neither of the men had any idea what they were about to discover.

The metal gate to the compound stood open, and already a dozen neighbors were gathering in the street in front of the house. Colonel Anwar led his men though the gate and into the complex. They could hear the sirens and bells of an approaching fire brigade, but the scattered wreckage in the livestock pen had now nearly burned itself out. Anwar's men were able to use shovels to put out the few small fires that remained. As flashlights played through the smoking wreckage, Colonel Anwar could see no identifiable human remains.

There were bits and pieces of aircraft piled about, but none of it was recognizable. Outside the south wall of the livestock pens, Jwad and Anwar both pointed their flashlights at a gray, oblong bit of wreckage. The tail rotor of the crashed helicopter had been thrown by the explosion up and over the wall. It was largely intact, but the wreckage now only deepened the mystery. The wreckage looked like no tail rotor either of the officers had ever seen. The vertical stabilizers were raked forward like the fins of a shark, and the rotor blades were shrouded and ducted. The small sections of fuselage that survived the explosion seemed to be made not of aluminum, but of strands of carbon fiber.

Both officers called their respective chains of command to inform them that a foreign helicopter had apparently crashed in Pakistani territory. They were told to lock down the crash scene and to cordon off the area. Jwad was now in personal contact with General Ahmad Shuja Pasha, the director general of the ISI, who told him to continue to update him directly.

It was now two a.m. The ambulance crews had sorted through the wreckage and found no bodies. Colonel Anwar turned toward the three-story home next to the crash site. Strangely, there were no lights on in the home, or the annex just to the south; both were dark.

The officers first went into the annex. Through a set of broken windows, they could see the body of a man. Their flashlight beams revealed that he had been shot in the head and chest. Colonel Anwar pushed his way through the door into a bedroom on the left. Crowded into it were three children and Myriam Khan, Ibrahim Khan's wife. In Pashto, Colonel Anwar asked the woman to state her name; she replied only that she was from the province of Swat.

Anwar called for paramedics, and both officers realized for the first time that the house had been the object of some sort of military operation. Detailing some of his men to watch over the woman and her children, Colonels Anwar and Jwad walked into the main house. Its door, too, was open.

Calling out, Colonel Anwar and Jwad entered the house through the rear porch. Flashlight beams sweeping, they walked into the downstairs hallway. In a bedroom on the right-hand side of the hallway, sprawled slightly back from the door, were the bodies of a man in his mid-thirties, and a woman of the same age. The dead would later be identified as Abrar Khan and his wife, Bushra. Both had been shot through the chest.

The officers heard sobbing from the bedroom across the hall. When they entered, their flashlights fell on three women and ten children huddled together. They were plainly terrified but none was injured. Continuing into the house, Colonel Anwar and Jwad shined their torches into each of the several rooms on the ground floor. Furniture was turned over, cupboards were open, and their contents were spread out on the floor.

Moving around the back of the house, they came to a central stairway. At the foot of the stairs was an iron grill—its lock had been blown off, and the gate hung open on bent hinges. Just beyond this barrier, on the second-floor landing, was another body, this one of a young man of about twenty. A pool of blood spread under him and dripped down onto the step below. Jwad noted that there were no footprints in the pool of blood and that this man, too, had been shot in the head. Both bullets had entered his skull above the level of his eyes, and it looked to the intelligence agent as though the dead man had been shot from above. Tensely, the two officers moved upstairs.

There was no one on the second floor, but its rooms had also been roughly searched. Closets and cupboards had been left open and clothing and broken pieces of furniture littered the floors. The officers checked each of the empty rooms, looking under mattresses and beds, and finally moved on to the third floor.

In the right-hand bedroom off the main stairwell, a flashlight settled on a pool of blood. In it was another woman, with a bullet hole in her calf. Her leg had been bandaged, and a tourniquet placed above the wound, but she had bled heavily. Jwad shouted down the stairs at the ambulance attendants to bring up a stretcher. Colonel Anwar may be forgiven for not immediately identifying the people in the house. None spoke Urdu, the principal language of Pakistan, and all were in a state of shock.

As paramedics took away the bleeding woman, it was decided that the remaining family members would be taken to a safe house. As they were gathered together, the oldest woman, Khairiah Sabar, asked Colonel Anwar if she might get some of her personal effects and clothing. Colonel Anwar assented to this request. Khairiah then asked that the second woman be permitted to get her clothing as well. Jwad carefully noted the rooms to which each woman went to gather their clothing. From their movements, Jwad determined that the older woman lived on the first floor, and the younger woman on the second. As Siham moved up the stairway to the second floor, she knelt by the body on the stairs to pray. She looked at Colonel Aswan and said, indicating the body, "Khalid bin Laden."

Colonel Anwar was astonished. The woman did not speak Pashto or Urdu, only Arabic. The colonel asked her in a kind of pidgin Arabic augmented with hand gestures, "Who are you?"

She answered, "Umm Khalid." I'm the mother of Khalid.

It was by now three o'clock in the morning, and this, according to Pakistani investigators, was the first moment that local officials learned that they had converged on the hideout of the world's most wanted terrorist, Osama bin Laden.

Colonel Anwar continued his questioning, again filling in the gaps with hand gestures. Siham indicated that her son Khalid and Osama bin Laden had been killed by American commandos, and that Osama's body had been taken away by helicopter.

Jwad immediately telephoned the director general of the ISI, General Pasha, to inform him of what he had learned. It may be wondered what General Pasha was feeling as his subordinate told him that it appeared that the United States had located Osama bin Laden, killed him, and taken his body away from a safe house in Abbottabad. Many have speculated that Osama bin Laden could not have safely spent a decade in Pakistan without the knowledge of the ISI. Whether General Pasha was personally aware of the operation to hide Osama remains a matter of speculation.

While Colonels Anwar and Jwad were searching the house, at about two in the morning local time, the chairman of the U.S. Joint Chiefs of Staff, Admiral Mike Mullen, placed a personal phone call to the chief of the Pakistani Army Staff, General Ashfaq Kayani. Admiral Mullen knew General Kayani well as his opposite number in Pakistan's armed forces hierarchy and a frequent visitor to Washington. In what must have been a tense phone call, Admiral Mullen informed the general that the United States was responsible for the Abbottabad raid. Admiral Mullen knew certainly that all hell was about to break loose for his Pakistani counterpart.

What had been Pakistan's darkest secret was about to splash over the world's headlines. And it would be weeks before the government of Pakistan made any statement about the raid at all.

General Qadir's investigation was undertaken in a time of great uncertainty in Pakistan. At no inconsiderable risk to himself, General Qadir spent almost four months interviewing eyewitnesses in order to untangle a web of contradictions and to paint a clear picture of what happened on the night of the raid, and also what had happened in the weeks leading up to the assault—including clandestine operations conducted by the CIA to identify the compound and its occupants.

Both the White House and the government of Pakistan stuck to the story that one of the American helicopters had crashed on approach to the target. General Qadir was able to locate and debrief an eyewitness to the raid, Muhammad Bashir, who lives directly across from the Abbottabad compound. Bashir stated to General Qadir, and on live Pakistani television, that he had witnessed the American helicopters approach the target and that he had seen the lead aircraft land on the roof of the main building and deposit troops. Speaking to a Pakistani journalist on May 4, Mr. Bashir reiterated that ten to twelve Americans jumped from a helicopter, which had landed on the roof of the main building. These men had then jumped from the roof onto a third-floor terrace and gained access to the house. Bashir was equally adamant that the crash had occurred while the helicopters were *leaving* and not on insertion. General Qadir was introduced to several other civilian witnesses who also confirmed that they had seen troops deposited on the roof of Bin Laden's residence, and that the helicopter crash had occurred during the middle and not the beginning of the raid. This corroborates eyewitness testimony from Special Operations personnel who conducted the mission.

The "crashed on insertion story" is still put forward by White House spokesmen, though it flies in the face of logic and tactical sense. Evidence from inside the house also supports a top-down assault, rather than the "ground floor up" version offered by the White House. General Qadir was given a guided tour of the Bin Laden residence and was able to determine that Khalid bin Laden was killed on the second-floor landing, and that the bullets that had struck him had likely been fired from above. His observations are consistent with an assault that began on the third floor and moved downward. In his statement, General Qadir expressed puzzlement that media outlets were scrupulously ignoring eyewitness testimony.

Qadir also stated that by five minutes past one in the morning, Pakistani F-16s had been scrambled to shoot down the departing American helicopters. General Qadir claims the targeting radar on board these fighters detected the American helicopters—but that the aircraft had been ordered first to assume station over the Pakistani nuclear facility at Kahuta. By the time the fighters had been vectored toward the helicopters, the Americans were safely in Afghan airspace. It is very likely that had the Pakistani F-16s been sent directly to Abbottabad, one or more of the American helicopters would have been shot down.

The official Pakistani position was that Osama bin Laden had been living in Abbottabad without the knowledge or permission of the government of Pakistan. Caught red-handed, the Pakistani military and intelligence services could now only attempt to plead incompetence rather than complicity. Regardless of *why* Osama bin Laden was living eight hundred meters from the front gate of Pakistan's main military academy, the security services were careful in processing what they now called "a crime scene." DNA tests carried out on blood found in the home and on samples taken from the body of Khalid bin Laden proved without a doubt that it was Osama bin Laden who was killed on the morning of May 2.

General Qadir also spoke to members of the ISI who investigated CIA activities prior to the raid, and his written statement provides the clearest account yet of the pre-mission activities of CIA assets on the ground in Pakistan prior to Operation Neptune's Spear.

Qadir shares the opinion that Osama bin Laden was set up by lapses of security within the Al Qaeda organization. He has concluded that the Americans were able to pinpoint the compound after Al Qaeda swapped prisoners with the Iranian intelligence services between March and May 2010. General Qadir makes a strong case that CIA ground assets were able to close their searches first on Abbottabad generally, and the compound specifically, after the arrival of Khairiah Sabar in March 2011.

To confirm Osama bin Laden's location, the CIA employed a paid asset named Shakeel Afridi. A Pakistani national and medical doctor, Afridi had once held a public health position in the Khyber Agency. When he was fired from that agency, he became ripe for CIA recruitment. Beginning in about March 2011, Afridi was told to run a hepatitis screening program in the outlying neighborhoods of Abbottabad. Doctor Afridi's American controller, known only as Peter36, instructed him to go door to door, offering to take blood samples to determine who might be in need of treatment. Although the doctor did diagnose and treat cases of hepatitis as they were encountered, the program was a ruse to collect DNA from the residents.

That Afridi was initially told to conduct house-to-house searches in Nawan Sher and Bilal Town reveals that at least until April, the CIA did not have the compound specifically targeted. It is known that a lone American intelligence officer, disguised as a local, did a "drive by" on the compound location in the middle of March 2011. This was the only time Americans had "boots on the ground" in the target vicinity before the operation.

All of the pre-mission targeting and reconnaissance was conducted using ground-based Pakistani assets and satellite and aircraft surveillance. By the end of April, the CIA had targeted the Abbottabad compound specifically. Although the doctor might not have known the original purpose of the screening operation, he quickly determined that he was involved in the search for a high-value individual.

Near the end of April, Peter36 instructed Afridi to knock directly on the doors of the Bin Laden residence and offer hepatitis screening. The doctor reportedly asked for and received $10,000 cash to complete this last portion of the operation.

On April 26, Afridi rang the bell and spoke to Ibrahim Khan, who identified himself as Tariq. Ibrahim told the doctor that they had all been tested previously and there was no need to take blood samples. When Afridi reported this to Peter36, he was provided with a cell phone number, also believed to be Ibrahim's. The doctor was instructed to have his female assistant call the number on the evening of April 26, and again ask for the residents to participate in the hepatitis screening. Afridi's female assistant was told to speak in Urdu, with some English thrown in.

The assistant spoke initially to Ibrahim, and the phone was then handed to Khairiah bin Laden, who communicated in English and Arabic. Afridi had been instructed to tape-record the conversation. Afridi provided Peter36 with a hard copy of this recording, and kept one for himself, which was captured with him by the ISI a week later. According to Qadir, the English portion of the conversation was garbled, and neither Afridi nor his assistant could make out what it was Khairiah was attempting to say in English. Qadir suspects the woman may have been disoriented, or possibly under the influence of sleeping medication as none of the words she tried to put together made sense. This tape is presently in possession of both the ISI and the Central Intelligence Agency.

After the phone call, Peter36 told Afridi to continue the screening program, though he determined by Peter36's reaction that they had found the people they were looking for. Afridi did as he was told, but began preparations to flee Abbottabad.

The CIA has admitted that Afridi's hepatitis screening program began sometime in March 2011, with the doctor being given a large area to canvass. This time period coincides with Khairiah Sabar bin Laden's arrival at the compound—again indicating that the CIA was aware of the Al Qaeda/Iranian prisoner swap that had occurred earlier in the year. When Operation Neptune's Spear was launched, the CIA and the SEALs could be fairly sure that a high-value individual was located in the compound. Taken in context, the pieces of the intelligence puzzle were fitting together nicely.

Ibrahim Khan's widow, Myriam, confirmed to ISI interrogators that

Doctor Afridi and his assistant called her husband's telephone on the evening of April 26. Again, monumental lapses in security, acts of either omission or commission, were committed by Al Qaeda higher-ups. The CIA was able to "gather" Ibrahim's cell phone because it had been associated with the transfer of Khairiah Sabar bin Laden to Abbottabad. Once the high-profile hostage exchange had gone through, Ayman Zawahiri should have insisted, at a minimum, that Bin Laden be moved and that his couriers be replaced. These oversights were the reason the United States was able to locate and strike Osama bin Laden's residence.

At 11:30 p.m. on Sunday, May 1, President Obama appeared on television to make a short statement. He said that "a small team of Americans" had found the author of 9/11 in a compound in Pakistan. "After a firefight, they killed Osama bin Laden and took custody of his body." The president said, "No Americans were harmed. They took care to avoid civilian casualties."

Several versions of the mission began to make the rounds in Washington. Vice President Joe Biden, who'd watched the raid in the White House situation room, gave a speech three days after the operation: "Folks, I'd be remiss also if I didn't say an extra word about the incredible events, extraordinary events, of this past Sunday. As Vice President of the United States, as an American, I was in absolute awe of the capacity and dedication of the entire team, both the intelligence community, the CIA, the SEALs. It just was extraordinary."

Joe Biden told the world that it was a SEAL Team operation.

But worse was to come. A "45-minute firefight" story was bandied about, and then revealed to be an exaggeration. The White House floundered, and a series of conflicting statements managed to impart the impression that Osama was nowhere near a weapon. The press had a field day. The story evolved that Bin Laden had been killed at the end of an extended gunfight where the SEALs had fought their way up three flights of stairs, found Osama in his bedroom, and had shot him in cold blood.

Facts were in short supply even to those at the top. In an interview given to PBS, Leon Panetta admitted, "I can tell you that there was a time period of almost twenty to twenty-five minutes where we really didn't know just exactly what was going on."

In the absence of a briefing from the White House, rumors morphed into uglier and uglier tales.

The facts are these: During the entire operation, SEAL Team Six fired only twelve bullets. These shots killed Osama bin Laden, his son, and two bodyguards. All of these men were armed or in close proximity to weapons.

The wife of Abrar Khan was killed accidentally. She was standing behind her husband as he exchanged gunfire with the SEALs on the ground floor of the main building. The operators who entered Bin Laden's bedroom did not wait for him to arm himself; they shot first. Amal was grazed by a bullet when the SEALs fired at her husband, who was at that instant concealed behind her nightgown and reaching for an automatic weapon. Bin Laden died with a hand stretched toward a rifle and pistol in plain sight next to his headboard.

After the mission, Bin Laden's body was loaded aboard one of the MH-47s and flown back to Forward Operational Base Fenty at Jalalabad. It was photographed and fingerprinted, and another DNA sample was taken. The body was then transferred aboard a V-22 Osprey and flown to the carrier USS *Carl Vinson* in the Indian Ocean.

The DNA samples confirmed Osama bin Laden's identity and blood work aboard the carrier revealed a very low level of plasma cortisol, supporting a diagnosis of Addison's disease. In accordance with Islamic tradition, Osama was washed, wrapped in clean cloth, and buried at sea as the carrier steamed south from the coast of Pakistan.

Just days after the success of Operation Neptune's Spear, the CIA started to meet with authors. The agency knew that JSOC would not cooperate with journalists or historians—and that would allow the CIA a chance to "inform the narrative" of the raid at Abbottabad. There was a legend to be made, and all that was necessary was to pour out the facts into the waiting notebooks of eager journalists.

But which story was the right one? The 45-minute firefight? The "Kill Mission" to Abbottabad? The story was becoming muddled with corrections, and it looked like the tail was starting to wag the dog. The White House cracked down, and in the second week of May, the word went out: no more leaks. Anyone who talked would be fired. The CIA's Office of Public Affairs (OPA) had already begun to meet with several authors. Writers and screenwriters who had been invited to headquarters for talks on background suddenly found themselves frozen out. Calls to OPA officers went unanswered. E-mails were ignored. The winks and whispers were replaced with glacial silence. Now the story was that there was no story.

As far as JSOC was concerned, that was just fine.

They wanted no part of any publicity whatsoever. The SEAL Teams were astounded when they'd returned to the United States to find that they had been outed. More confusing was why the White House had said anything at all. The SEALs had recovered hundreds of pounds of priceless intelligence, a mother lode of information that could have put Al Qaeda away for good. If the operation had been kept entirely secret, it would have posed a perplexing mystery to the Pakistanis and an unfathomable nightmare for Al Qaeda.

The mission could have been announced later—preferably *after* the SEALs had neutralized the rest of Al Qaeda's leadership. SEAL Team Six had risked their lives to obtain the computers and hard drives stored at Al Qaeda's nexus. Television braggarts made almost all of this intelligence meaningless by confirming that the SEALs had taken it. What's worse, they placed the families of the SEALs at risk by naming the unit and its location. Television news trucks went so far as to cruise neighborhoods in Virginia Beach, searching for a SEAL family to show the world.

The hunters of Abbottabad became the hunted.

Even before Operation Neptune's Spear, relations between the CIA and Pakistani intelligence had been strained. In most allied countries, the host nation's intel outfits are called "Liaison Services," and are courteously informed of CIA operations. They share intelligence and, in most cases, work together. In the years leading up to the Abbottabad raid, U.S. frustration with Islamabad mounted as numerous incidents of Pakistani collusion with Taliban and Al Qaeda fighters were noted by Washington. Still, the Pakistanis kept up a front, saying one thing to Washington, and doing another thing on the ground in Afghanistan. Within minutes after the last helicopter rumbled across the border back into Afghanistan, the Pakistanis knew their game was up. Their government was convulsed first with bewilderment, then embarrassment, and then rage. But there were no Americans to strike back at—Peter36 had already left the country.

The CIA's "Pakistani assets," who had surveyed Bin Laden's compound, were soon rolled up by Pakistani counterintelligence. Doctor Afridi and the landlord who rented him office space were arrested, beaten, and tossed in prison. So was a military officer alleged to have CIA ties and six policemen suspected to have diverted traffic the night of the assault. Snatching defeat from the jaws of victory, the CIA's "boots on the ground" were so poorly compartmentalized that it took less than thirty-six hours for the Pakistanis to arrest everyone who had anything remotely to do with the operation.

A little more than a year later, on May 23, 2012, Doctor Afridi was sentenced to thirty-three years of hard labor for a variety of charges, including treason. Prosecuted by a Khyber Agency Tribal Court, Afridi was not present in the courtroom, and was not given an opportunity to either examine the evidence against him or defend himself. Several other lower-level CIA assets remain in ISI custody and their fate is unknown. To date, not a single arrest in Pakistan has been made in connection with the harboring of Osama bin Laden.

Determined somehow to return a blow against the Americans, the Pakistanis held an auction for the chunk of Razor 1 that had been left behind. The Chinese won, paid cash, and were allowed to disassemble, photograph, and take material samples of the tail rotor and the scraps that were heaved up around the compound. Out of spite, the Pakistanis allowed the Iranians and the North Koreans to come and have a look as well.

Two weeks after the raid, Senator John Kerry traveled to Islamabad, hat in hand, to ask that the parts be returned. He came home with the wreckage.

U.S.–Pakistan relations were put into a permanent state of strain by the Bin Laden raid. They were made more tense after a border incident on November 28, 2011, where U.S. forces fired upon a Pakistani border post, killing more than twenty-four Pakistani soldiers. Though downplayed by the Western media, the incident brought Pakistan and the United States to the brink of war, and resulted with Pakistan placing surface-to-air missiles on the border with Afghanistan.

Following the incident, the Pakistani government closed down the southern distribution network, a ground logistics path that runs from Karachi toward Quetta and Kabul. This network previously supplied up to 85 percent of the food, ammunition, and fuel used by NATO forces in Afghanistan. At present, international troops operating in Afghanistan must rely on vehicles routed through the former Soviet Republics of Georgia and Azerbaijan.

For his performance as CIA director, and "leader" of Operation Neptune's Spear, President Obama nominated Leon Panetta to succeed Robert Gates as secretary of defense. He was confirmed on June 22, 2011.

A story appeared in the *New Yorker* magazine on August 8, 2011, and appeared to corroborate an ugly tale of murder. The article reiterated the "ground up assault" theory, claiming that a helicopter crashed while trying to land at the compound. Implausibly, this narrative then had a second helicopter land on the wrong side of a twenty-foot concrete where it inserted troops. These men then had to breach their way into the compound, blast through the back doors of the main building, and then fight their way up three flights of stairs—all of this while Osama Bin Laden waited patiently in his third-floor bedroom. It looked like Bin Laden had been killed by a gang as brutal and ruthless as he was. The *New Yorker* article gained "credibility" as several knowledgeable administration officials were quoted about the operation. The author eventually admitted that he had not spoken to any of the members of the assault team.

No matter what the real story was, Leon Panetta was in high cotton. As he prepared to move over to the Pentagon, he gave a CIA tour to a gaggle of twenty-five freshman congressmen. The topic of the Bin Laden movie actually came up, and one of the congressmen asked Panetta who he wanted to have play him in the movie. Panetta answered right away—"Al Pacino," he said.

Before Leon Panetta left the CIA, he'd quietly given OPA the go-ahead to bring back the writers. But not just any writers. Those frozen few journalists and historians who had hoped the agency would call them back now read that the CIA was in the movie business.

Vanity Fair reported that Oscar-winner Kathryn Bigelow would direct the CIA's version of the Abbottabad raid for Sony Pictures. As Ms. Bigelow lunched in the CIA's food court, she unlikely spotted a table of plain-clothed SEALs . . . but they saw her.

Invisible as ever, two SEALs overheard one of OPA's deputies promising Ms. Bigelow an introduction to the CIA operator who had accompanied the SEALs into the compound. Even the OPA types had no idea who was sitting at the other table. They aren't called Jedis for nothing.

When the movie story hit the cable-news outlets, there was a kerfuffle. Sony Pictures had held an in-studio fund-raiser for the president back in April—the first time a film studio had ever done so.

The optics, as they say, didn't look good.

The chairman of the House Homeland Security Committee, Republican Peter King, called for an investigation into possible disclosure of classified material, citing news that director Kathryn Bigelow and her screenwriter had been given high-level Pentagon access.

White House press secretary Jay Carney fielded some tough questions, and went to the extent of reading a prepared statement:

> When people, including you in this room, are working on articles, books, documentaries, or movies that involve the president, ask to

speak to administration officials, we do our best to accommodate them to make sure that facts are correct. That is hardly a novel approach to the media. I would hope that as we face the continued threat from terrorism, the House Committee on Homeland Security would have more important topics to discuss than a movie.

But the story about the story refused to go away. A year later, in 2012, Freedom of Information Act requests and a congressional investigation revealed that administration officials had leaked classified information to screenwriter Mark Boal and director Kathryn Bigelow in an attempt to influence the script of a movie to be released before the November election. E-mails released by the Department of Defense indicated that Boal and Bigelow's requests for information were fast-tracked, while all others were denied access. Meeting transcripts and e-mails provided by FOIA requests show that the filmmakers met with top administration officials, including secretary of defense for intelligence Michael Vickers, John O. Brennan, chief counterterrorism advisor to President Obama, and Denis McDonough, who serves as President Obama's deputy national security advisor. A July 14 meeting transcript also indicates that the DOD provided Boal and Bigelow, exclusively, and in violation of federal restrictions on revealing the name of any covert special operations officer, with the identity of a "planner, SEAL Team Six Operator and Commander."

The transcripts also reveal that Obama White House officials realized they were treading on thin ice as they wrote to Boal: "The only thing we ask is that you not reveal his name in any way as a consultant because . . . he shouldn't be talking out of school." Vickers went on to say during another Pentagon meeting: "This at least, this gives him one step removed and he knows what he can and can't say, but this way at least he can be as open as he can with you and it ought to meet your needs."

Boal later responds, "You delivered."

Was the administration even-handed with access to sources? It would appear not. DOD assistant secretary for public affairs Douglas Wilson had sent an e-mail to his colleagues back in June, telling them to limit media access for everyone except Boal and Bigelow. ". . . We need to be careful here so we don't open the media floodgates on this. I'm going to check with WH to update them on status, and will report back."

An e-mail to an official at the Office of the Secretary of Defense suggests that the request from Bigelow and Boal to meet with Under Secretary of Defense for Intelligence Michael Vickers came *via the White House press office.* A day later, a White House official wrote Department of Defense communications staffers, saying: "Okay to set up the second session with Vickers. I am getting additional guidance from WH."

Judicial Watch President Tim Fitton launched the Freedom of Information Act lawsuit that brought the Moviegate e-mails to light. He found the administration's naked hypocrisy infuriating:

> These documents, which took nine months and a federal lawsuit to disgorge from the Obama administration, show that politically connected filmmakers were given extraordinary and secret access to Bin Laden raid information, including the identity of a SEAL Team Six leader. It is both ironic and hypocritical that the Obama administration stonewalled Judicial Watch's pursuit of the Bin Laden death photos, citing national security concerns, yet seemed willing to share intimate details regarding the raid to help Hollywood filmmakers release a movie "perfectly timed to give a home-stretch boost" to the Obama campaign.

On June 14, 2011, while the White House was hand-feeding its chosen filmmakers, I filed an official complaint with the Office of the Inspector General of the CIA, complaining that Mark Boal and Kathryn Bigelow had been given preferential treatment over other journalists and historians researching the raid. As of this writing, my complaint has been ignored by the Office of the Inspector General, and follow-up requests for information have been stonewalled.

To date, the administration's attempts to convert Special Operations successes into political capital have included not only the attempts to turn Operation Neptune's Spear into an action movie, but also the accelerated release of documents taken in the raid, a prime-time special recounting the operation from inside the situation room, and a May 2012 "victory lap," revealing the use of a Saudi double agent to thwart the use of an enhanced body bomb targeting U.S. airliners. These actions have engendered much bitterness within both the Special Operations and intelligence communities, and led to retired chairman of the Joint Chiefs Admiral Mike Mullen to issue a statement decrying the politicization of the Special Operations forces.

On June 30, 2011, Attorney General Eric Holder announced that the Justice Department would conduct a full investigation, not into leaks from Neptune's

Spear but into the deaths of two Al Qaeda terrorists who had been held in CIA custody. Holder was out for blood. He appointed special prosecutor John Durham, and explained that the review would "examine primarily whether any unauthorized interrogation techniques were used by CIA interrogators and if so, whether such techniques could constitute violations of the torture statute or any other applicable statute."

In 2010, Obama administration prosecutors went after the SEALs; now they were going after the CIA. The attorney general was not initiating a new attack, just picking up where he'd left off. The CIA had already terminated two career employees who had interrogated Khalid Sheikh Mohammed and identified Osama's courier. The CIA was still devouring its own.

On a sunny afternoon in May 2011, Admiral Bill McRaven met President Obama on a runway in Fort Campbell, Kentucky. The base is the home of the famed 101st Airborne Division and the Army's Special Operations Air Regiment, the pilots who flew the mission. SEAL Team Six had been flown in from Virginia and assembled in the conference rooms adjoining a hangar, far from the press. The Death Star, their base in Virginia, was deemed too sensitive for a presidential visit; this was, after all, a photo opportunity.

After the president made a speech to the 101st Division, Admiral McRaven and the commander in chief went into the locked hangar for a close-up look at a Ghost Hawk helicopter. The president met some of the members of Det Alpha and the staff of the Joint Operations Center. He was given a briefing by Frank Leslie, who ran through the operation on a scale model of the compound that had been used to train the assaulters. The president was allowed to pet Karo, Red Squadron's K9, though the secret service asked that the dog remain muzzled.

The president was given a three-by-five-foot American flag signed by the SEALs and 160th SOAR pilots who conducted the raid. An inscription read: "From Joint Task Force Operation Neptune's Spear, 01 May 2011: For God and country. Geronimo."

President Obama promised to put their gift in a place that was "somewhere private and meaningful."

Red Squadron had earlier presented Admiral McRaven with a 9mm Marakov pistol taken from Osama's bedside. Inches from Bin Laden's fingers, the Red Men also recovered Osama's prized *Suchka* machine pistol. That weapon now hangs on two nails driven into a wall in Red Squadron's team room at the Death Star. Next to it are the pictures of a dozen Red

Squadron operators who have been killed in action since the team went on line in 1981.

In the hangar that afternoon, the president seemed in no hurry. He posed for pictures and bestowed the Presidential Unit Citation on the 160th Special Operations Air Regiment and SEAL Team Six. Obama made a couple of jokes and everybody laughed.

The president made sure to shake the hands of each of the operators. As he was introduced to the men of Razor 1, the president asked, "So which one of you guys took out Osama?"

There was a respectful pause, and Frank Leslie said, "We all did it, sir. It was all of us."

HOW THIS BOOK WAS WRITTEN

The primary sources for this history were the men of SEAL Team Six who told me what they saw, what they thought, and what they felt. The preparations and rehearsals for Neptune's Spear spread over several months; in the weeks and months leading up to Neptune's Spear, it was my privilege to help troops and platoons train for sub-missions, and run parallel HVT (high-value target) missions. Neptune's Spear was a highly classified operation that hid its training evolutions in the "plain sight" of other SEAL Team exercises. Even in rehearsals, the Invisible Empire remains invisible. During a complex mission, no one SEAL can see all of an operation, or witness directly what happened in every corner of the target. Von Clausewitz calls this "the Fog of Battle." Sometimes individual operators did not know what was happening on the other end of the compound. Sometimes they did. The story I have written seeks to draw together these fragments into a cogent narrative. I often had to "de-conflict" the statements of individual operators in order to gain a full picture of who saw what, where they saw it, and when it happened. To a great extent, it is the SEALs themselves who wrote this book. I have based my narrative on their stories, and, whenever possible, I have used their own words.

My research took me far afield. Since the operation, some of the mission commanders have become public figures—I have made use of their correct names. In every other case I have done my best to protect the identities of both operators and analysts, while at the same time drawing accurate pictures of them as people.

Like any endeavor regarding intelligence or counterterrorism there is a "white" side—open for business and overt; a gray side, a shadow state somewhere between being public and not being there at all; and then there is the dark side. The dark side is the realm of black programs, covert organizations, and hidden agendas. In the world of black programs, organizations don't exist, people don't have names, and things go bump in the night. I have thanks to give in all three shades, white, black, and gray, and I hope the reader will forgive me if I occasionally get a little vague.

About halfway through, I began to realize that the farther I got from the Beltway the more accurate the information I got. In Washington, politicians who traipsed through the nightly news congratulating themselves on "gutsy decisions" were suddenly struck dumb when I came calling. It was as though having cheered for and congratulated themselves, and after outing the SEALs, they tried to make up for their indiscretions by biting their tongues. I learned long ago to never be disappointed by people. Especially politicians.

This book details the events of the night of May 1, 2011, and has been based on the first-person accounts of members of SEAL Team Six.

For reasons of operational security, it has been necessary to obscure, rather than clarify, certain aspects of the mission at Abbottabad. The success or failure of future SEAL missions requires that some of the facts of the operation against Osama bin Laden remain secret. While this may be a passing annoyance to historians, it is necessary to protect men and women in the here and now. The fight against Al Qaeda is not over. The lives of America's war fighters depend on keeping what they do, and how they do it, a mystery to an enemy who has sworn to kill them and bring terror to our own doorsteps.

Winston Churchill once said that the truth was so important that it had to be surrounded by a bodyguard of lies. Almost sixty years after World War II secrets are still emerging about the special operations carried out by the forebears of SEAL Team Six, the Office of Strategic Services, the Jedberg Teams, Navy Combat Demolition Units, and the Underwater Demolition Teams. Likely it will be another half century before all is revealed about Operation Neptune's Spear. Until the Joint Special Operations Command writes its own story, history must content itself with the few precious details that have come to light. This book has been written with the best information available. It will be left to some future historian to write the final story of Neptune's Spear. It will also be the life's work of another scholar to detail the inner machinations of Al Qaeda and the deadly rivalry between Ayman Zawahiri and Osama bin Laden.

The best biographical material on Osama bin Laden may be found in Lawrence Wright's magnum opus, *The Looming Tower;* it is the best and most reliable single source for details of his life and the 9/11 conspiracy. Other key foundations of the present history include *The Bin Ladens* by Steve Coll, *Holy*

War, Inc. by Peter Bergen, *Mastermind: The Many Faces of the 9/11 Architect, Khalid Shaikh Mohammed* by Richard Miniter, *Osama: The Making of a Terrorist* by Jonathan Randal, *Bin Laden: The Man Who Declared War on America* by Yossef Bodansky, and *Inside Al Qaeda Global Network of Terror* by Rohan Gunaratna. A complete bibliography of reference books can be found on my Web site: www.chuckpfarrer.com. The work of these scholars, historians, and investigative journalists allowed me to accurately sketch the life and travels of Osama bin Laden. If the present history succeeds, it is because this work stands on the shoulders of giants.

In the preparation of the paperback edition of this book, additional information has come into the public domain; specifically, a number of captured documents taken by members of SEAL Team Six during the raid on the Abbottabad compound. These documents included Al Qaeda internal memoranda, policy papers, attack plans, and letters written to and by Osama bin Laden. These documents were translated by the Combating Terrorism Center at the United States Military Academy at West Point, and were crucial in placing into context known facts about Osama bin Laden and his actions in the final weeks and months leading up to Operation Neptune's Spear.

Also critical to the new chapters in this book is an independent report written by retired Pakistani Brigadier General Shukat Qadir. His analysis, insight, and objective reporting made it possible to connect the dots in the complex history of both Operation Neptune's Spear and Osama bin Laden's secretive Pakistani sojourn. General Qadir is a patriot, and an honest man who represents what is best about the people and the nation of Pakistan.

Lastly, I would again like to express my thanks to the men and women of the U.S. Intelligence and Special Operations communities who courageously shared their recollections about Operation Neptune's Spear. I am proud to say that these brave Americans who made history also contributed to its writing.

ACKNOWLEDGMENTS

On the civilian side, I have to thank my literary agent, Julia Lord, who stayed with this project and found a home for it amid the honking and clattering of competing projects. Thanks also to my editor at St. Martin's, Michael Flamini, who gave me a very long leash even if he couldn't give me much time. Thanks and love to my mother and father and my wife, Louise, who cared for me, patched me up between trips, and kept the lights on. Louise applied her considerable talents as an editor and writing coach to make sure that this book was the best it could be. She spent many a late night correcting drafts and rewrites as well as turning the galley proofs around in record time. As Dante said, *Il Miglior Fabbro.* Thanks and love to my son, Paddy, who waited patiently and was brave while his dad was away. And thanks again to my own father, who researched open source material and helped sift fact from fiction. Many thanks to Murray Neal of Dragon Skin, who put together my "armored vehicle." I'm delighted that I didn't have to put his body armor to the test. Thanks a million to the professionals at the Makko Group, especially Dylan Saunders, who made sure that I was well turned out for my travels in harm's way. Thanks to Pinnacle Armor and the Makko Group, I am the envy of operators in three war zones.

A special thank-you to my oldest friend, Lisa Paul, herself a veteran of many a tough bivouac and a cool head under fire. Thanks also to my friends Doug Stanton, Pack, and Becca Fancher, and thanks always and again to the Doctors Brice, Charlie and Judy—a pair of psychiatrists and poets who are among the smartest and most loving people I know. Thanks to Emily and Anna Iannucci, who provided me with a safe house in a place no one would have found me. Friends are the riches of the world. Lance Moody and my comrade Panu Vesterinen are long-suffering friends as well as patriots, gentlemen, and scholars—their ship's come in, and I congratulate them heartily. Thanks to Lee Wanaar and Rick Kosinsky—two fighters that never quit: you know what you did to make this book possible. Thanks to Dave and Erika DeTar, Otto Bebe and Terry Starr—we'll eventually have that beer.

Other friends, in the gray world, also provided vital help. Sincere thanks to my teammate Jon Ciderquist for services rendered. Jon has been on the frontlines in the war on terror for the last fifteen years—and his contributions to the security of this nation could fill another book. Thanks to Steven Kitchen, and every operator from call sign Warlord: the Domingoes, the Eddies, Lance, Ren, Dave, Mike, Cap'n Cook, and *los tipos suaves.* In Washington, I owe thanks to KE and LE; KE is a friend and teammate of thirty years standing, and LE is one of the most stalwart wives in the history of Naval Special Warfare. It was my privilege to work for KE at SEAL Six, and then at the legendary National Red Team. KE was one of the most outstanding and heroic commanders to ever have served at Six, and is proudly entering his fourth decade of service to his country.

And now to thank the people who hardly exist; those on the dark side. Behind the scenes, book projects can often turn on the cooperation of a single person. In the Teams we say "One is none; two is one." That goes for people as well as parachutes and helicopters. It's always a good idea to have a backup plan—or two of them. There were many points at which this book almost didn't happen. I regret to say, there were several people who did their best to make sure *SEAL Target Geronimo* was never written. I consider those who made their feelings known, and spoke to me directly, to be honorable men. We have differed only on whether the valor and achievements of our comrades should be made public. The events that took place in Abbottabad are the embodiment of the fighting spirit and professionalism of the United States Navy, and the facts of that operation are a vital part of our nation's history. I am honored to tell the story. There were a small number of persons who worked behind the scenes to derail this history, and substitute one of their own making. Those efforts continue to this day. For some, the object of this rewrite was political, for others, the facts of Neptune's Spear were squabbled over as commercial property to be exploited as rapidly as possible. The light of day shines on fact as well as fiction.

I have been blessed with friends and teammates who fought for me even as I faltered and it looked like this book would never happen. It is a brave person who risks his own neck to save a guy whose head looks to be already in the noose.

A special thanks to Ian Conway. Ian is a teammate and comrade in arms who has served with me around the world, and in close-combat in the deadly corridors of Washington. He's a tougher man than I am.

Finally, most important, humble thanks to my comrade and friend Bill Kerns, who started his military career, as did I, at the Staunton Military Academy. Bill went on to become a storied officer in the Green Berets, and later, a philanthropist of the first order. His kindness to me during an illness kept a roof over my head. This good deed, done without the slightest desire to be compensated or acknowledged, is one of the hallmarks of the special operations community. The operators of USSOCOM, SPECWARCOM, and JSOC—both active and retired—are the embodiment of the altruism, selflessness, and quiet valor that make America exceptional.

It is to them that this book is dedicated; they are truly a band of brothers.

GLOSSARY

160th SOAR 160th Special Operations Aviation Regiment, formerly Task Force 160. The Army's elite special forces helicopter squadron. Also known as Night Stalkers, this unit specializes in deep insertion and extraction of special operations forces in both land and maritime operations.

5.56. The caliber of an M-16 rifle, in millimeters. NATO ammunition for the M-16 and M-4 carbine.

5326. Naval education code (NEC) for a "combat swimmer," the Naval Personnel Bureau's designation for an enlisted SEAL operator.

7.62. The caliber of an M-60 machinegun, in millimeters. NATO ammunition for the M-60, G-3, and M-14 rifles. These weapons fire the NATO standard 7.62 × 51 cartridge. Russian-made weapons, like the AK-47, fire the same caliber bullet, using a shorter cartridge, 7.62 × 39. Russian ammunition is referred to as "7.62 intermediate."

AAA. Antiaircraft artillery.

Al Qaeda. Arabic for "the Base." A global terrorist Sunni Islamist group founded by Osama bin Laden.

antiterrorism. Defensive measures used to reduce the vulnerability of personnel and facilities to terrorist acts. Such measures include guard patrols, vehicle barricades, and hardening targets, as well as the immediate actions taken by military and security forces following a terrorist attack. Also called "AT."

AO. Area of operations. Bailiwick.

API. Armor piercing, Incendiary. Ammunition designed to pass through armored vehicles and start fires inside.

assault element. A SEAL unit varying in size from four to twenty-five operators. Elements are tailored to fit specific mission requirements.

AWACS (E-3 Sentry). The AWACS E-3 is an airborne warning and control aircraft that provides all-weather surveillance, command, control, and communications. The E-3 Sentry is a modified Boeing 707/320 commercial air frame with a rotating radar dome.

Black Hawk. The MH-60 helicopter, the workhorse of special operations. Its Navy equivalent is the SH-60, called the Seahawk.

boat crew. A variably sized SEAL element, literally the number of SEAL inserted by one boat or helicopter. Usually no smaller than four operators, a boat crew can be as large as twenty operators.

booger eater. Generic term for bad guys.

BUD/S. Basic Underwater Demolition, SEAL training. SEAL basic training. A twenty-six-week-long ordeal conducted at the Naval Amphibious Base in Coronado, California. All SEAL operators attend this course. BUD/S is the only school in the U.S. military where officers and enlisted men attend the same school and take the same course work.

Budweiser. The badge awarded to qualified Naval Special Warfare Operators. Called a "trident" by the Navy, it is the emblem and insignia of the SEAL Teams. The device features a pistol, anchor, trident, as well as a screaming eagle that is vaguely reminiscent of the logo on a can of Budweiser beer. In the Naval service, enlisted warfare badges are silver and the officers' gold. The Budweiser is the only gold Navy warfare device worn by both officers and enlisted alike.

C4. Composition 4. Plastic explosive.

cadre. The hard-core operational and training elements of a terrorist organization. Also, the training cell within a SEAL Team.

cake eater. A Naval officer. Any commissioned officer.

CCT. Combat control teams. Air Force Special Operations Forces specializing in air traffic control and communications.

Chinook. MH-47. Twin-rotor, long-range, heavy lift special operations helicopter. Capable of high-altitude operations, the MH-47 is the workhorse of special operations forces in Afghanistan.

cleared hot. Granted permission to open fire. Cleared for action.

click. Kilometer. One click equals one kilometer in range or distance.

counterterrorism. Offensive measures taken to deter, prevent, and respond to terrorism. These active measures include assaulting hostage barricade sites, retaking of hijacked vehicles, vessels, or aircraft, and direct action against terrorist personnel, support, and infrastructure. Also called "CT."

CQC. Close quarters combat. The precision shooting used by SEALs to clear ship spaces and rooms. CQC is the epitome of surgical shooting. SEALs frequently practice dynamic target shooting where terrorist targets are mixed with real people playing hostages.

CRRC. Combat rubber raiding craft.

CTF. Commander, task force.

Delta. Special Forces Operational Detachment, Delta, aka Delta Force. It is frequently joked by SEALs that the high-profile Delta Force is SEAL Team's best cover. *See also* Hardee Boys.

ding. To hit with a bullet. To kill.

direct action. Combat actions undertaken against enemy targets.

FARP. Forward air refueling position.

fast rope. A spongy, hawserlike rope used to deploy troops rapidly from helicopters. Also called a "zip line," fast ropes are manufactured in thirty-, sixty-, and one-hundred-and-twenty-foot lengths.

FLIR. Forward-looking infrared.

FOB. Forward operating base.

frog hog. A female SEAL groupie.

full mission profile. A SEAL mission cycle, complete from planning, rehearsal, deployment, insertion, infiltration, actions at the objective, exfiltration, extraction, recovery, and debriefing.

Goon Squad. The slow and the stupid. In BUD/S, the slowest 20 percent of any run or evolution. Instructors single out these class members for extra physical instruction.

GPS. Global positioning system. Navigational aide utilizing a series of military satellites to exactly pinpoint any location on earth.

Green Bean. Green Beret.

green room. The compartment on an aircraft carrier where personnel are held before being released onto the flight deck.

Green Team. Training and selection program for SEAL Team Six operators. This grueling one-year selection course is known to be even tougher than the Navy's notorious BUD/S program.

green tip. Also called Predator rounds. Special antipersonnel bullets designed for the M-4 assault rifle these bullets are particularly effective in close combat operations. Made from special composite materials, the bullet is designed to do maximum damage to soft or hard tissue but remain in the original victim.

Grey Fox. Unofficial name of JSOC's intelligence-gathering units.

group. A variously sized SEAL unit consisting of multiple SEAL Teams, troops, or platoons. *See also* platoon, troop, and assault element.

haj. An enemy combatant. Short for "haji," the honorific for a Muslim who has performed the pilgrimage to Mecca. Also a contraction of Mujahideen, a holy warrior.

Hardee Boys. Delta Force.

helmet fire. To panic. Also, to be absentminded or to make a mistake.

HUMINT. Human intelligence. The time-honored skills of "people-oriented" intelligence gathering. Also refers to all manners of intelligence tradecraft to include agent handling, asset recruitment, and placement and the running of information-gathering networks.

HVI. High-value individual. Used to designate persons in terrorist or insurgent leadership.

HVT. High-value target.

indige. Indigenous. Of or belonging to a certain locale. A local indigenous person, or local vessel (indigenous craft). *See also* haj.

IR. Infrared. Invisible light frequencies below red, used as passive night vision, in night vision goggles and active, as an infrared spotlight.

IR strobe. A blinking signal light using infrared light.

IRGC. Iranian Revolutionary Guard Corps.

ISI. Inter Services Intelligence. Pakistan's intelligence service.

ITAG. Intelligence and Terrorism Analysis Group. Parent unit of the National Red Team, a group of former SEAL Team Six operators and intelligence professionals who tested security procedures by staging simulated terrorist attacks against targets within the United States.

Jedi. A member of the Naval Special Warfare Development Group or the Army's Special Forces Operational Detachment-Delta.

JOC. Joint Operations Center.

JP-5. Jet Propulsion (Grade) 5. Jet fuel.

JSOC. Joint Special Operations Command.

JTF. Joint Task Force.

Kaffiyeh. An Arab headdress.

Kalashnikov. Any of a variety of Russian-made assault rifles designed by Mikhail Timofeyevich Kalashnikov. Kalashnikov weapons include the AK-47, AK-74, AKSU, and RPD machine guns, as well as the Druganov sniper's rifle.

K-Bar. SEAL Team fighting knife.

Little Creek. Naval Amphibious Base located in Norfolk, Virginia. Home of the East Coast SEAL Teams.

M-4. Carbine version of the M-16.

MANPADS. Man-portable antiaircraft defense system. Man-portable antiaircraft weapons. Refers to both Strela and Stinger heat-seeking missiles and rocket-propelled grenades fired at aircraft.

MISIRI Ministry of Intelligence and National Security of the Islamic Republic of Iran.

MNF. Multinational force.

Mustang. A commissioned officer with prior enlisted service.

Naval Special Warfare. Navy SEAL Teams, SEAL Delivery Teams, and Special Boat Units.

Naval Special Warfare Development Group. In 1990 SEAL Team Six was redesignated as the Naval Special Warfare Development Group.

no joy. Radio speak for "I do not see the target."

NOD. Night observation device. When worn by an operator, they are referred to as "nods."

non qual. A nonoperator. A person outside the SEAL community.

NRO. National Reconnaissance Office.

NSA. National Security Agency.

Operator number. Alpha-numeric given to SEAL operators to identify them within an operational unit.

organic. In military argot, equipment or personnel assigned and controlled by a specific unit. The fast-attack vehicles were organic to SEAL Team Eight.

personnel interdiction. An operation designed to neutralize or capture an individual.

Phalange. A Lebanese Christian militia. Originally formed in 1936 as a Maronite paramilitary youth organization by Pierre Jumayyil. Militant and violent, the Phalange bears responsibility for the 1983 massacres at Sabra and Shatila.

platoon. Traditional SEAL operational unit, comprised of two officers and twelve enlisted men.

PLO. Palestinian Liberation Organization.

pocket litter. The content of the target's pockets to include a wallet, money, and scraps of paper.

poodle shooter. M-4 rifle. So called because it is small and light.

Qur'an. Koran. Literally "The recitation." The Muslim holy book, revelations made to Muhammad by the Angel Gabriel.

R and S. Reconnaissance and surveillance mission.

Red Team. A group or unit assembled to test counterterrorist and antiterrorist measures or procedures. The use of enemy tactics techniques and procedures. The National Red Team was a group of former SEAL Team Six

Operators and intelligence professionals who tested security procedures by staging simulated terrorist attacks against targets within the United States.

ring out. To quit. From the three-rings-and-you're-out quitting method at BUD/S.

ROE. Rules of engagement. Orders dictating the circumstances and limitations under which U.S. forces may initiate combat.

RPG. Rocket-propelled grenade. Russian-made recoilless antiarmor weapon. RPGs have a variety of warheads to include antiarmor, antipersonnel, antiaircraft, and thermobaric warheads.

SA-7 (NATO code-named Strela). A shoulder-fired, heat-seeking guided missile used as an antiaircraft weapon.

SBU. Special boat unit.

SDV. SEAL delivery vehicle. A wet minisub used to deliver SEALs into target areas and also to attack enemy ships and facilities.

SDV Team. SEAL Delivery Vehicle Team. SEAL unit specializing in maritime sabotage and operation of SEAL submersibles.

SEAL Team. SEAL Teams are comprised of a number of platoons or detachments, as well as support personnel. Usually captained by a commander (O-5), platoons and detachments are mostly commanded by lieutenants or lieutenant commanders. Although SEAL Teams are geographically specialized, all Teams are trained to operate in all environments. Geographical areas of focus are as follows: SEAL Team One, Southeast Asia; SEAL Team Two, Northern Europe; SEAL Team Three, Middle East; SEAL Team Four, South America; SEAL Team Five, Korea; SEAL Team Six, worldwide; SEAL Team Seven, worldwide; and SEAL Team Eight, Africa.

SF. Special Forces. Refers to the Army's Green Berets.

shift fire. Coordinated movement of SEAL Team fire. Instantaneous engagement of a second target. Also used to indicate a shift in focus or a change of tasking.

Shiite. Also known as Shias. Shiites comprise the second largest Islamic sect in Lebanon. The word "Shia" comes from *Shiat Ali,* or "party of Ali." Shiite Muslims believe that Ali, Muhammad's cousin and son-in-law, should have succeeded the Prophet.

SIGINT. Signals intelligence. The gathering and analysis of an enemy's communications, written, as well as electronically transmitted.

sleeve. A slick sleeve, i.e., a person without a Navy rating. A useless idiot. A non-SEAL Team member, regardless of rank.

snake eater. Any member of the special operations community.

sneak attack. Underwater maritime sabotage operation, usually conducted at night with rebreathing Scuba.

SOF. Special Operations Forces, to include Army, Navy, Air Force, and Marine Corps Units.

soft duck. Insertion of a CRRC by helicopter.

SOP. Standard operating procedure.

squadron. A combat unit consisting of an assembly of SEAL troops.

SQT. SEAL Qualification Training. Post-BUD/S training to prepare candidate SEAL Team members for deployments.

SR. Special reconnaissance. Deep-penetration reconnaissance operations, carried out by both clandestine and covert means.

Stinger. U.S.-made man-portable antiaircraft missile.

Strela. An SA-7 surface-to-air missile.

Suchka. Russian namc for machine pistol version of the AK-74. Also called the AKSU, it was used by *Spetsnaz* forces in Afghanistan.

Sunni. The largest Muslim sect. Those who believe that Muhammad's successor should have been chosen by the community came to be known as Sunnis.

tadpole. BUD/S student. An inexperienced operator.

Taliban. Meaning "students" in Arabic, a violent fundamental Islamist militia that has ruled parts of Afghanistan since 1996.

tango. Terrorist. A bad guy.

target lock. Loss of situational awareness resulting from overconcentration on the target. The state of being too goal-oriented.

TF-10. Task Force 10. Special Forces including JSOC elements in Afghanistan.

TF-20. Task Force 20. Special Forces including JSOC elements in Iraq.

TOC. Tactical operations center.

troop. A SEAL combat element consisting of two or more SEAL platoons.

UDT. Underwater Demolition Team. The original frogmen, specializing in maritime sabotage, reconnaissance, and recovering NASA space capsules.

UNODIR. Navy acronym meaning "unless otherwise directed."

VBSS. Vessel board, search or seizure. Also called an "underway," this is the operation where SEALs board and seize a ship on the high seas.

wadi. Arabic. A canyon or watercourse.

SELECTED BIBLIOGRAPHY

Al Banna, Hasan, and N. M. Shaheed. *Memoirs of Hasan al Banna Shaheed.* Karachi: International Islamic Publishers, 1982.

Al Qaeda in Its Own Words. Edited by Gilles Kepel and Jean-Pierre Milelli. Translated by Pascale Ghazaleh. Cambridge, MA: Belknap Press of Harvard University Press, 2008.

Alexander, Yonah, and Michael S. Swetnam. *Usama bin Laden's al-Qaida: Profile of a Terrorist Network.* Ardsley, NY: Transnational Publishers, 2001.

Atwan, Abdel Bari. *The Secret History of al Qaeda.* Berkeley: University of California Press, 2006.

Bansemer, John D. *Intelligence Reform: A Question of Balance.* Maxwell AFB, AL: Air University Press, 2006.

Bergen, Peter L. *Holy War, Inc.: Inside the Secret World of Osama bin Laden.* New York: Free Press, 2001.

———. *The Osama bin Laden I Know: An Oral History of al Qaeda's Leader.* New York: Free Press, 2006.

Bin Laden, Najwa, Omar bin Laden, and Jean P. Sasson. *Growing up Bin Laden: Osama's Wife and Son Take Us Inside Their Secret World.* New York: St. Martin's Press, 2009.

Bodansky, Yossef. *Bin Laden: The Man Who Declared War on America.* Roseville, CA: Prima, 2001.

Cirincione, Joseph. *WMD in Iraq: Evidence and Implications.* Washington, DC: Carnegie Endowment for International Peace, 2004.

Coll, Steve. *Ghost Wars: The Secret History of the CIA, Afghanistan, and bin Laden, from the Soviet Invasion to September 10, 2001.* New York: Penguin Press, 2004.

Cronin, Audrey K. "Terrorist Motivations for Chemical and Biological Weapons Use: Placing the Threat in Context." Ft. Belvoir: Defense Technical Information Center, 2003.

Duck, Kenneth E. *Islamic Revolutionary Guard Corps (IRGC): An Iranian Instrument of Power.* Maxwell AFB, AL: Air War College, 2009.

Forrest, Christopher. *Coercive Engagement: A Security Analysis of Iranian Support to Iraqi Shia Militias.* Ft. Belvoir: Defense Technical Information Center, 2009.

Fury, Dalton. *Kill Bin Laden: A Delta Force Commander's Account of the Hunt for the World's Most Wanted Man.* New York: St. Martin's Press, 2008.

Geraghty, Timothy J. *Peacekeepers at War: Beirut 1983—The Marine Commander Tells His Story.* Washington, DC: Potomac Books, 2009.

Global Risk Governance: Concept and Practice Using the IRGC Framework. Edited by Ortwin Ronn and Katherine D. Walker. Dordrecht, The Netherlands: Springer, 2008.

Globalization and WMD Proliferation: Terrorism, Transnational Networks, and International Security. Edited by James A. Russell and James J. Wirtz. Hoboken: Taylor & Francis, 2007.

Gunaratna, Rohan. *Inside Al Qaeda: Global Network of Terror.* New York: Berkley Books, 2003.

Hammel, Eric. *The Root: The Marines in Beirut, August 1982–February 1984.* San Diego: Harcourt Brace Jovanovich, 1985.

Henzel, Christopher. "The Origins of al Qaeda's Ideology: Implications for US Strategy." In *Parameters,* Vol. 35 (Spring 2005).

The History of Terrorism: From Antiquity to al Qaeda. Edited by Gérard Chaliand and Arnaud Blin. Berkeley: University of California Press, 2007.

Jervis, Robert. *Why Intelligence Fails: Lessons from the Iranian Revolution and the Iraq War.* Ithaca: Cornell University Press, 2010.

Judicial Watch Press Room, "Judicial Watch Obtains DOD and CIA Records Detailing Meetings with bin Laden Raid Filmmakers," *Judicial Watch,* May 30, 2012. http://www.judicialwatch.org/press-room/press-releases/13421/.

Mansfield, Laura. *His Own Words: Translation of the Writings of Dr. Ayman al Zawahiri.* Old Tappan, NJ: TLG Publications, 2006.

Maudud, Syed Abul A'La. *The Meaning of the Qur'an*, 9th ed. Lahore: Islamic Publications, 1999.

Moghaddam, Fathali M., and Anthony J. Marsella. *Understanding Terrorism: Psychosocial Roots, Consequences, and Interventions.* Washington, DC: American Psychological Association, 2003.

Moghadam, Assaf. *The Globalization of Martyrdom: Al Qaeda, Salafi Jihad, and the Diffusion of Suicide Attacks.* Baltimore: Johns Hopkins University Press, 2008.

National Commission on Terrorist Attacks. *The 9/11 Commission Report: Final Report of the National Commission on Terrorist Attacks upon the United States.* New York: Norton, 2004.

Only for the Love of Allah, by Night and by Day: Readings on Charity and Kindness in Islam, 2nd ed. Plainfield, IN: ISNA Development Foundation, 2002.

The Osama bin Laden Files: Letters and Documents Discovered by SEAL Team Six During Their Raid on Bin Laden's Compound. New York: Sky Horse Publishing, 2012.

Princeton Readings in Islamist Thought: Texts and Contexts from al-Banna to Bin Laden. Edited by Roxanne Leslie Euben and Muhammad Qasim Zaman. Princeton: Princeton University Press, 2009.

Qutb, Sayyid. *In the Shade of the Qur'an.* Translated by M. A. Salahi and A. Shawi: S. Markfield, Leicester, UK, and Nairobi, Kenya: The Islamic Foundation, 2005.

Riedel, Bruce. *The Search for al Qaeda: Its Leadership, Ideology, and Future.* Washington, DC: Brookings Institution Press, 2008.

Taylor, Scott, and Brian Nolan. *Tested Mettle: Canada's Peacekeepers at War.* Ottawa: Esprit de Corps Books, 1998.

Wright, Lawrence. *The Looming Tower: Al Qaeda and the Road to 9/11.* New York: Knopf, 2006.

Zawahiri, Ayman. *Al-Sharq al-Awsat Serializes Book by al-Qa'ida's Ayman al-Zawahiri.* Rosslyn, VA: FBIS, 2001.

Zawahiri, Ayman, and Osama bin Laden. *The Al Qaeda Reader.* Edited and translated by Raymond Ibrahim. New York: Doubleday, 2007.

SELECTED HISTORICAL AND OPERATIONAL REFERENCES

Adams, Michael S. *Forming Standing Joint Special Operations Task Force Headquarters.* Carlisle Barracks, PA: U.S. Army War College, 2003.

Friedman, Thomas L. *From Beirut to Jerusalem.* New York: Farrar, Straus & Giroux, 1989.

Kapusta, Philip. *Interview with LCDR Philip Kapusta.* Ft. Leavenworth, KS: Combat Studies Institute, 2006.

Moeller, Jason P. *Soldiers without Uniforms: CIA Paramilitary Operations in Afghanistan.* Springfield: Missouri State University, 2007.

Neville, Leigh. *Special Operations Forces in Afghanistan.* Oxford: Osprey, 2008.

Shelton, Henry H., with Ronald Levinson, and Malcolm McConnell. *Without Hesitation: The Odyssey of an American Warrior.* New York: St. Martin's Press, 2010.

WEAPONS OF MASS DESTRUCTION

BBC News, "'Sarin bomb' reopens Iraq WMD debate," May 17, 2004 http://news.bbc.co.uk/z/hi/middle_east/3722855.stml.

New York Times, "US Finds Shell With Nerve Gas In Iraq," May 17, 2004 www.nytimes.com/2004/05/17/internatinal/middleeast/17CND-SARI.html.

Fox News, "Tests Confirm Sarin in Iraqi Artillery Shell," May 19, 2004 http://www.foxmews.com/story/0.2933,120268,00.html.

Department of Defense, Public Health Laboratory Services, Vol 2, No 6: *Two U.S. Soldiers Exposed to Sarin Nerve Agent in Iraq*, June 2004. http://www.geis.fhp.osd.mil/GEIS/SurveillanceActivities/Laboratory/PHLSJun04Newsletter.pdf.

Iraq Survey Group Final Report: Iraq's Chemical Warfare Program Annex F Detailed Preliminary Assessment of Chemical Weapons Findings, Chemical Munitions—Other Finds, Mar 10, 2008 http://www.globalsecurity.org/wmd/library/report/2004/isg-final-report/isg-finalreport_vol3_cw-anx-f.htm.

Washington Post: "Iraqi Chemical Stash Uncovered Post-Invasion Cache Could Have Been For Use in Weapons," by Ellen Knickmeyer, August 14, 2005 http://www.washingtonpost.com/wp-dyn/content/article/2005/08/13/AR2005081300530.html.

Blix, Hans. *Disarming Iraq.* New York: Bloomsbury, 2005.

Clarke, Richard. *Against All Enemies: Inside America's War on Terror.* New York: Free Press, 2004.

Ali, Javed. "Chemical Weapons in the Iran Iraq War: A Case Study in Non Compliance." In *The Nonproliferation Review Spring, 2001.* Accessed June 13, 2012 http://cns.miis.edu/npr/pdfs/81ali.pdf.

Sada, Georges, with Jim Nelson Black. *Saddam's Secrets.* Dallas: Thomas Nelson, 2006

The United Nations Monitoring, Verification and Inspection Commission: "Iraq's chemical weapons program," Technical Report, S/2006/342, May 2006.

The United Nations Monitoring, Verification and Inspection Commission: "Iraq's biological warfare program: Technical Report No. S/2005/545 August 2005 http://www.un.org/Depts/unmovic/new/documents/technical_documents/s-2005-545-bw.pdf.

The United Nations Monitoring, Verification and Inspection Commission: "Assessment of Iraq's remotely piloted and unmanned aerial vehicle programs, S/2004/693 August 2004. Accessed http://www.un.org/Depts/unmovic/new/documents/technical_documents/s-2004-693-handling_of_cbw_munitions.pdf.

Selos, Christian. "Lessons from Iraq on Bio Weapons." In *Nature 398,* 187–188 March 18, 1999. Accessed www.nature.com/nature/journal/v398/n6724/full/398187a0.html.

The United Nations Monitoring, Verification and Inspection Commission, "Overview of the chemical munitions recently found in Iraq," S/2006/701 August 2006 Accessed June 13, 2012 http://www.un.org/Depts/unmovic/new/documents/technical_documents/s-2006-701-munitions.pdf.

The United Nations Monitoring, Verification and Inspection Commission, "Analysis of chemical munitions recovered in Iraq by coalition forces since 2003," S/2006/701 August 2006. Accessed http://www.un.org/Depts/unmovic/new/documents/technical_documents/s-2006-701-munitions.pdf.

World Net Daily, "Saddam's Secret Weapons Exports: Iraqi dictator's bombs used in war against south Sudanese Christians," by Anthony C. LoBaido, January 28, 2001. Accessed June 12, 2012 http://www.wnd.com/news/article.asp?ARTICLE_ID=21497.

BBC World News, "Poison cake kills Iraqi children," by Jim Muir, February 9, 2008. Accessed June 12, 2012 http://news.bbc.co.uk/2/hi/middle_east/7237086.stm.

Fox News, Permanent Select Committee on Intelligence, US House of Representatives. "The National Ground Intelligence Center, 'Key Points' of CLASSIFIED report, Chemical Weapons Recovered in Iraq," by John D. Negroponte, June 21, 2006. Accessed June 12, 2012 http://www.foxnews.com/projects/pdf/Iraq_WMD_Declassified.pdf.

Nuclear Weapon Archive.org: *India's Nuclear Weapons Program: Smiling Buddha: 1974* http://nuclearweaponarchive.org/India/IndiaSmiling.htm.

Guardian (UK), "Brothers in arms—Israel's secret pact with Pretoria," by Chris McGreal, February 6, 2006. Accessed June 12, 2012 http://www.guardian.co.uk/world/2006/feb/07/southafrica.israel.

George Washington University, "National Security Affairs Archive, NSC memo: South Atlantic Nuclear Test October 22, 1979." Accessed June 12, 2012 http://www.gwu.edu/~nsarchiv/NSAEBB/NSAEBB190/01.pdf.

CDI Russia Weekly #251_ *Up in Arms over Iraqi Arms,* April 3, 2003. http://www.cdi.org/russia/251-9.cfm See also *Time* magazine: http://www.time.com/time/covers/0,16641,19870601,00.html; Federation of American

Scientists, "Iraq's Nuclear Reactors, Osiraq/Tammuz. http://www.fas.org/nuke/guide/iraq/facility/osiraq.htm.

Institute for Science and International Security (ISIS), "Development of the Al-Tuwaitha Site," April 26, 1999. Accessed June 12, 2012 http://www.isis-online.org/publications/iraq/tuwaitha.html.

Federation of American Scientists; al-Josiah / Al Kindi General Establishment Jaber bin Hay an General Establishment. Accessed June 12, 2012 http://www.fas.org/nuke/guide/iraq/facility/al_jesira.htm.

Hamza, Khidhir, with Jeff Stein. *Saddam's Bombmaker.* New York: Scribner, 2001.

The United Nations Monitoring, Verification and Inspection Commission: Chapter II: The Organizational Structure of Iraq's Proscribed Weapons Programmes (2006). Accessed June 12, 2012 http://www.un.org/Depts/unmovic/new/documents/compendium/Chapter_II.pdf.

Earley, Pate. Comrade J. New York: Putnam, 2008.

Telegraph (UK), "UN inspectors uncover proof of Saddam's nuclear bomb plans," by Con Coughlin, 19 Jan 2003. Accessed June 13, 2012 http://www.telegraph.co.uk/worldnews/northamerica/usa/1419364/UN-inspectors-uncover-proof-of-Saddams-Nuclear-bomb-plans-html.

USAF Institute for National Security Studies, "Out of (South) Africa: Pretoria's Nuclear Weapons Experience," by Lieutenant Colonel Roy E. Horton, August 1999. http://www.fas.org/nuke/guide/rsa/nuke/ocp27.htm.

New York Times, "U.S. Web Archive Is Said to Reveal a Nuclear Primer" by William J. Broad, November 3, 2006. Accessed June 13, 2012 www.nytimes.com/2006/11/03/world/middleeast/03documents.html?pagewanted-all.

Intelligence Summit: Public Address, Russian Spetsnaz moved Iraq WMD. Former Deputy Undersecretary of Defense John A. Shaw, Arlington, VA, February 19, 2006.

New York Times, "A Nation at War: Web Says Two Ex-Generals Visited Iraq Before the War," by Sabrina Tavernise, April 4. 2003. Accessed June 13, 2012 www.nytimes.com/2003/04/04/world/a-nation-at-war-russia-web-says-two-ex-general-visited-iraq-before-the-war.html?n-Top%2fReference%2fTimes%20Topics%2subjects%2FT%2Terrorism.

Gazeta.Ru "We didn't fly to Baghdad to drink coffee," by Alexander Kornilov, April 2, 2003. Accessed June 13, 2012 http://www.gazeta.ru/2003/04/02/Wedidntflyto.shtml.

Eighth Gate: "Israeli raid on Syria fuels speculation over Damascus' WMD capability," September 22, 2007. Accessed June 13, 2012 http://www.andrewtabler.com/2007/09/israeli-raid.on-syria-fuels-speculation.html.

New York Times, "Photos Show Cleansing of Suspect Syrian Site," by William J. Broad and Mark Mazzetti, October 26, 2007. Accessed June 13, 2012 www.nytimes.com/2007/10/26/world/middleeast/26syria.html.

DECLASSIFIED INTELLIGENCE DOCUMENTS

Declassified Intelligence item SOCCOM-2012-0000003; Special Site Exploitation, (SSE), personal letter authored by Osama bin Laden and addressed to Atiyah Abd al-Rahman on August 27, 2010. Recovered by members of SEAL Team Six during the raid on Abbottabad, May 2, 2011.

Declassified Intelligence item SOCCOM-2012-0000004; Special Site Exploitation, (SSE), personal letter authored by the American Al Qaeda spokesman Adam Gadan, written late January 2011. Recovered by members of SEAL Team Six during the raid on Abbottabad, May 2, 2011.

Declassified Intelligence item SOCCOM-2012-0000005-HT; Special Site Exploitation, (SSE), personal letter authored by Osama bin Laden (signed "Zamarai") to the leader of the Somali militant group Harakat al Shabab, dated August 7, 2010. Recovered by members of SEAL Team Six during the raid on Abbottabad, May 2, 2011.

Declassified Intelligence item SOCCOM-2012-0000006-HT; Special Site Exploitation, (SSE), personal letter likely written by Ayman Zawahiri, addressed to "Azamari," one of Bin Laden's several noms de guerre. Recovered by members of SEAL Team Six during the raid on Abbottabad, May 2, 2011.

Declassified Intelligence item SOCCOM-2012-0000010; Special Site Exploitation, (SSE), personal letter authored by "Abu Adbdalla," Osama bin Laden, to Shayk Mahmud (Atiyah Abd al-Rahman), dated April 26, 2011. Recovered by members of SEAL Team Six during the raid on Abbottabad, May 2, 2011.

Declassified intelligence item: SOCCOM-2012-0000015-HT. Special Site Exploitation, (SSE), personal letter authored by Osama bin Laden to Shayk Mahmud (Atiyah Abd al-Rahman) dated October 21, 2010. Recovered by members of SEAL Team Six during the raid on Abbottabad, May 2, 2011.

INDEX

INDEX

Chuck Pfarrer is a former assault element commander of SEAL Team Six. He has written op-eds for *The New York Times* and the Knight Ridder syndicate, and appeared as an author and counterterrorism expert on C-SPAN2, NPR, Alhurra, IPR, Voice of America, Fox News, and *America Tonight*. Pfarrer serves presently as an associate editor of *The Counter Terrorist,* the American Journal of Counterterrorism. Pfarrer is the author of the bestseller *Warrior Soul: The Memoir of a Navy SEAL*. His Hollywood credits include writing and producing work for *Navy Seals, Darkman, Hard Target, The Jackal, Virus,* and *Red Planet*. He lives in Michigan.